D1163670

IMAGES OF TRANSFORMATION
IN TRADITIONAL
HISPANIC POETRY

Images of Transformation
in Traditional Hispanic Poetry

by

PAULA OLINGER

Gettysburg College

Juan de la Cuesta
Newark, Delaware

I wish to thank Luis Yglesias, Samuel G.
Armistead, and Gettysburg College for their
help and support.

To my mother, Mae
my grandmother, Effie
and my daughter, Axa

CONTENTS

INTRODUCTION

THE TEXTS of numerous folk songs that were popular among the peoples of the Iberian peninsula during the Middle Ages have survived to the present and have become the object of study of scholars who, like me, are fascinated by their timeless charm and ineffable beauty.

While contemporary critics have succeeded in shedding light on many aspects of this poetry, many other aspects pertinaciously defy strict definition and analysis. Should it be called *lírica española* or *hispánica*? Should it be considered traditional, since some scholars perceive it as folk poetry, or should it be labeled popular, since others regard it as a blend of folk and cultured poetry? Almost everyone agrees that it originated as song, though we call it poetry now since only the texts have survived. Yet we do not know which poems really belong to this amorphous body of song texts. Some of these poems are quite clearly courtly reworkings of traditional songs, in that they embody figures of speech that seem totally alien to folk song, but which, all the same, conform to a traditional structural mold.

Those who have studied the structure of the traditional lyric have concluded that it has no easily definable form. The most that can be said is that these poems are generally short, with short verses, and often consist of an *estribillo* (refrain) and a gloss—but not always. Many of the surviving poems are nothing more than an *estribillo*, and many others have highly conceptual glosses attached to what seem to be popular *estribillos*. The songs of the traditional *cancionero* (yet another term applied to the collective whole) seem to be organized from within by a mysterious and undefinable spirit. They are extremely difficult to imitate in any conscious way, since their simplicity eludes the workings of reason. They are paradoxical.

It is impossible to establish chronological limits for this poetry. Some of these songs are believed to date from the first millenium of the Christian era, but their beginnings remain lost in the silence of prehistory. It is certain, though, that the vast majority were originally written down during the late Middle Ages and the Renaissance by court poets, musicians, and scholars.

The songs usually included in modern anthologies of this poetry come from a wide variety of peninsular sub-cultures, some being Mozarabic, others Galician, others Catalonian, others Castilian. Scholars have speculated about whether or not these sub-traditions share a common root, whether they are branches of the same tree, but a majority consensus would hold that they do.

In recent years much pathfinding scholarship has been carried out concerning both the philology and the literary criticism of the early Hispanic lyric.

A number of extensive and literarily perceptive anthologies have been compiled by Margit Frenk Alatorre, José María Alín, Dámaso Alonso and José Manuel Blecua, Vicente Beltrán, and J. G. Cummins.[1] Each of these excellent collections is accompanied by an important introductory study.

Several book-length studies, as well as numerous articles, have appeared within the last fifteen years. Margit Frenk Alatorre has given us a host of fundamentally important articles, brought together now in an indispensable book, *Estudios sobre lírica antigua*. She has also explored the prehistory and origins of the Hispanic and Pan-Romance traditional lyric in her authoritative book on the Mozarabic *kharjas*.[2] Eugenio Asensio's splendid monograph, now in its second edition, has opened a variety of perspectives on the early Hispanic lyric.[3] José Romeu Figueras' monumental edition of the *Cancionero musical de palacio* is also indispensable to our knowledge of the Medieval lyric.[4] Antonio Sánchez Romeralo's sensitive computer-aided stylistic study of the *villancico* is likewise a crucial contribution.[5] Stephen Reckert has written a perceptive appreciation of the primitive lyric in his *Lyra mínima*[6] and, with Helder Macedo, has contributed a splendid book on the Galician *cantigas de amigo*.[7] Bruce Wardropper's incisive analysis of repetition in these Galician songs constitutes a substantial advance in their appreciation as literature.[8] Dionisia Empaytaz has surveyed early Hispanic dawn songs in two very useful books.[9] Specific topics and motifs recurrent in the Hispanic lyric have also received increasing attention: Egla Morales Blouin, Alan Deyermond, and Margaret Van Antwerp.[10]

There remains, however, the mystery of just what makes this poetry so appealing. Why does it live on? Why has it fascinated Spanish poets, both learned and illiterate, throughout the centuries? One can feel in it the presence of "duende," that ineffable something best captured by Lorca's sensitivity to traditional verse. "Duende" has much to do with the archetypes Jung has written of so extensively— the numinous essences that dwell in the darkness of the psyche and manifest themselves to us through symbols. Jung believes there is a relationship between one's personal happiness and one's contact with those rarefied archetypal essences. Thus it is important to the individual to be aware of symbols, since symbols are the bridge to the archetypes that rule one's inner harmony.

Whether consciously acknowledged or not, these archetypal symbols constitute the vital essence, the very life-blood of the traditional lyric. An individual creates a song which, when heard, strikes so deep a chord within the hearer that he, too, remembers it, repeats it, and a folk-song is born. No one cares who composed it, when, where, or why. All that matters is that the song has power over a person's inner being. It is public domain. It is numinous.

The meaning of the traditional lyric lies embedded in its symbols. Under the umbrella-term "symbol," I include more than noun-words that call to mind some visual images, like "rose," for instance. Symbol I take to be any formulaic phrase, stylistic element, situation, concept, word, name, place, time, or whatever, in a traditional song that signals something more than its semantic content. Now in a very real sense, every word and indeed every *thing* is potentially, at least, a symbol. It is the perceiver who ultimately determines what is symbolic and what is not. The perceiver likewise determines what the symbol means. In other words, nothing very definite can be said about it. At best an individual perceiver can talk about the symbols as they speak to his or her consciousness. And that is what I do in the following study.

What qualifies this endeavor as a work of scholarship is not so much *what* it asserts in the process of interpretation, but rather the method. And the method itself cannot be defined analytically, since the method, like the poetry, is organic. The only way to communicate it is to present a model for interpreting the traditional lyric—a model which could as well be applied to any other culture's body of folk-song. For there exists within any tradition a network of interrelationships among its symbols which cluster loosely around major archetypal numens. Out of each poem of the traditional lyric radiate countless tiny filaments in this vast network, connecting it to other poems, which in turn, further its connection with the total body of traditional poems. Reading one poem is like striking a bell and hearing a harmonic of over- and under-tones which enrich the beauty of the original tone struck.

Even while approaching the traditional lyric in this way, that is, following its inner network of symbolic meanings, there are many different levels from which to view it. I have sought to consider the symbol network in terms that might explain the popular appeal and the timelessness of this poetry. I see it as communicating a message to the human mind about the nature of life, about consciousness, about existence, about the dynamic of the universe—love. Love is the energy that passes between apparent opposites, that keeps things in motion, that unifies. And love is the principal theme of the traditional lyric.

Now, in a sense, the poetry discussed in this study is merely a fossilized remnant of a living tradition, which, like everything that lives, changes. The tradition is not dead, certainly, for some of these lyrics are still being sung even today, though almost always in some variant form.[11] But the tradition as it was at the time these poems were collected no longer exists. The archeological remains that we must work with are specimens only, which were preserved at the discretion of individuals with their own experiences, their own preferences, their own criteria. We cannot know what oral songs they did not deem worthy to preserve in written form. But extrapolating from modern Hispanic folk song, and trusting in the diversity of collectors and recorders, we can accept it as a fair representation of the songs to which people danced and sang. And love seems to be the one theme that has attracted the attention of both the people who chose to perpetuate these songs through oral repetition, and the scholars and artists who found them worthy of being written down in chronicle, song-book, play, dictionary, novel, or of imitating in their learned verse. An hour of listening to a popular music station in the United States today should be ample proof that the basic concern of mankind does not differ much from age to age or culture to culture.

Even the symbols themselves differ surprisingly little. There are still trees, and wind, and hair, and hands, and eyes, and waves by the seashore, flowers and thorns, that echo deep within the modern consciousness as they apparently did within the consciousness of Medieval and Renaissance man and woman. There are new symbols, of course, while others have lost their numinous impact. Certain symbols grow out of particular historical and geographical contexts. The *morena* in the traditional lyric, for example, is entirely *sui generis*. She may be related to the dark-skinned beloved of the *Song of Songs*, or dark ladies in other traditions, but her symbolic treasure lies buried in Spain, in its history, its life-style, its religion. In the broadest of terms, she symbolizes victory in suffering. She is tragic paradox. And she is sister to, or perhaps in the popular consciousness, identical with great religious figures of salvation-through-paradox: the virgin-mother, the outcast-redeemer. Yet even as this *morena* symbol springs forth from a particular soil, she nevertheless transcends her time and place, and touches an archetype within universal man. She is stained. She is innocence lost. She is fragmented and yearns for wholeness.

The folk song of any people reflects their cosmic vision. It is ironic that the official religion of the Spanish people centers around a masculine trinity—Father, Son, and Holy Ghost. Yet the popular expression of the cosmic or natural order is centered around a feminine trinity—mother, *morena*, and virgin. Woman represents transformation, change wrought, not through masculine will, but through passive acceptance of the natural order. This is not poetry by, for, and about women. It is poetry by, for, and about the transformation of consciousness. And it belongs to everyone.

The symbols discussed in this study are loosely arranged in four categories, to which the names of the four elements have been assigned. Wind and water correspond neatly to the two major clusters of symbols. Fire and earth are used as terms to speak of more varied symbol clusters that seem to gravitate around the poles of a masculine-feminine, or transformer-transformed dichotomy. But no symbol pertains to any specific category exclusively. The symbol does not embody any one meaning, but rather a vast potential for meaning. It can be masculine in one place, feminine in another, and still make perfect sense to the psyche of the perceiver.

Because of the logic-defying structure of the traditional lyric, its knotted mass of interconnections, there is no one starting place. Every poem will lead eventually to every other. So let us begin—*in medias res.*

---

1 M. F. Alatorre, *Lírica española de tipo popular* (Madrid: Cátedra, 1977). J. M. Alín, *El cancionero español de tipo tradicional* (Madrid: Taurus, 1968). D. Alonso and J. M. Blecua, *Antología de la poesía española. Poesía de tipo tradicional* (Madrid: Gredos, 1969). V. Beltrán, *La canción tradicional* (Tarragona: Tarraco, 1976). J. G. Cummins, *The Spanish Traditional Lyric* (N. Y.: Pergamon, 1977).

2 M. F. Alatorre, *Las jarchas mozárabes y los comienzos de la lírica románica* (El Colegio de México, 1975).

3 E. Asensio, *Poética y realidad en el cancionero peninsular de la edad media,* 2nd. ed. (Madrid: Gredos, 1970).

4 J. Romeu Figueras, *La Música en la Corte de los Reyes Católicos: Cancionero musical de Palacio,* 2 vols., (Barcelona, 1965).

5 A. Sánchez Romeralo, *El villancico* (Madrid: Gredos, 1969).

6 S. Reckert, *Lyra Minima: Structure and Symbol in Iberian Traditional Verse* (London, 1970).

7 S. Reckert and H. Macedo, *Do cancioneiro de amigo,* 2nd ed. (Lisbon: Assírio e Alvim, 1980?).

8 B. Wardropper, "On the Supposed Repetitiousness of the *Cantigas d'amigo,*" *RHM* 38 (1974-75), 1-6. Wardropper has two other excellent articles related to the traditional lyric: "'La más bella niña'," *Studies in Philology,* 63 (1966), 661-76; and "The Color Problem in Spanish Traditional Poetry," *MLN* 75 (1960), 415-21.

9 D. Empaytaz, *Antología de albas, alboradas* (Madrid, 1976), and D. Empaytaz de Croome, *Albor: Medieval and Renaissance Dawn-Songs in the Iberian Peninsula* (University Microfilms International, 1980).

10 E. Morales Blouin, *El ciervo y la fuente* (Madrid, 1981). A. Deyermond, "Pero Meogo's Stags and Fountains: Symbol and Anecdote in the Traditional Lyric," *Romance Philology,* 33 (1979), 265-83. M. Van Antwerp, "*Razón de Amor* and the Popular Tradition," *RPh* 32 (1978-79), 1-17.

11 Margit Frenk has brought to light an example of this survival of the traditional lyric to the present in her recent article, "Permanencia folklórica del villancico glosado," *NRFH* 29 (1980), 404-11.

❧ 1 ❧

Air

HE TRADITIONAL lyrics of the *cancionero* are cryptic and suggestive, connoting rather than denoting. Many of these poems would appear to be surrealistic fragments when isolated from the tradition, for they shun the logic of discursive reason. Yet taken from within the tradition, their meaning becomes patent. Perhaps the tradition can be best understood as a common repository of poetic elements which recur in the very poems which pertain to it. These elements may be syntactical units, images, symbols, individual words or stock phrases. Some are more versatile than others, and could be found in any poem of the tradition. Some elements tend to cluster around a particular situation, and when this occurs, any one element of the cluster may be used by the poet to evoke other elements not explicitly mentioned. This permits an enormous economy of expression.

Upon first reading a traditional Spanish lyric poem, one may end up as mystified by the experience as the young *vaquera* in the first poem we shall study is mystified by the unusual sensation in her heel. What both reader and *vaquera* lack in order to clarify the mystery is experience.

Our study of the following poem will illustrate this phenomenon, while demonstrating the symbolic use of air, a symbol only implicitly present in the poem, and yet critical to its understanding.

#1   No sé qué me bulle   I don't know what is stirring
en el calcañar   in my heel,
que no puedo andar.   so that I can't walk.

Yéndome y viniendo   Going back and forth to my cows
a las mis vacas,   I don't know what is stirring
no sé qué me bulle   among my skirts,

entre las faldas
que no puedo andar.
No sé qué me bulle
en el calcañar.

so that I can't walk.
I don't know what is stirring
in my heel.

The speaker of the poem is a *vaquera*, who indirectly reveals her identity by alluding to her clothing ("faldas") and activity ("yéndome y viniendo/a las mis vacas.") She focuses her attention in the poem on an unusual, unidentifiable, sensation which impedes her walking. The strangeness of the sensation emerges through the incongruous image which attempts to describe it: whatever it is *boils* (or stirs) in her *heel*.

The three lines of the opening *estribillo* state the essence of her problem, yet this *estribillo*, which introduces both poem and problem, is vague. Were we limited to the *estribillo* alone as our text (the case with scores of traditional lyrics) we would have no way of knowing the sex or occupation of the poetic voice, and yet the nature of the problem would still be discernible to the adept reader of traditional lyrics. Three aspects of the *estribillo* give the mystery away: the very mystification of the speaker; the verb "bullir": and the limiting effect which the sensation produces. These three aspects all relate, within the tradition, to love.

The poem opens with a negation. More traditional lyric poems begin with the word "no" than with any other word, usually as part of a negative command. Here there is no command, and no dialogue, for there is but one character present in the poem: the speaker. She is musing in solitude—a fact of considerable importance in understanding the poem's irony, which will be discussed further on. Her opening, "no sé qué," then, is sincere, for there is no one present whom she might wish to deceive: she is genuinely mystified. Furthermore, we see in the *estribillo* that she feels somehow victimized by the sensation. Because of the action "bullir," done *to* her (indirect object "me," line 1) she is confused ("no sé") and limited ("no puedo").

The expression "no sé qué" became a commonplace in learned Renaissance lyric poetry in Spain, primarily because of its repeated use in Petrarchan poetry. This little phrase most frequently attempts to capture the ineffable, to describe the indescribable qualities associated with love. The following, which appears in a collection of lyrics by Iñiguez de Medrano in 1608, is undoubtedly hybrid, i.e., it contains a mixture of learned and traditional elements.

#2 Amor es un no sé qué
    y nace no sé de dónde
    y mata no sé por dónde
    y hiere no sé con qué.

Love is I know not what
which comes from I know not
   where
and kills I know not how
and wounds with I know not
   what.

In this poem the "no sé qué" element becomes a sophisticated device upon which the clever artistry of the poem hangs—a far cry, to be sure, from its use in our poem.

The vagueness and uncertainty which the phrase "no sé qué" expresses could not be more characteristic of the tradition. *Something* stirs in her heel, something which exists, but which defies description. In similar fashion, another young girl worries over the tardiness of her lover, which she can only blame on his having been delayed by *something* in the country:

#3 Aquel pastoricico, madre,	That shepherd-boy, mother,
que no viene,	who doesn't come,
algo tiene en el campo	has something out in the fields
que le duele.	which pains him.

Another well-known lyric wherein we find the same use of "algo" speaks of the mystery of sexuality:

#4 Aquel árbol que vuelve la foxa,	The tree that turns its leaves
algo se le antoxa.	yearns for something.

In this example, however, we find that the ignorance of the poetic voice is feigned, for in the gloss (which will be quoted and discussed later) we discover that the speaker realizes that this "algo" is the urge to blossom and bear fruit. Still and all, that urge itself remains a mystery which defies a verbal delimitation more precise than "algo."

In each case (and many more could be adduced) the unknown factor produces an effect (prevents walking, detains the lover, stirs the leaves) by which it may be dimly understood (in "Aquel pastoricico" very dimly, for the conclusions the waiting girl reaches are based more on her need to protect her pride than on logical deduction).

In the following poem the unknown becomes manifest precisely through its effect:

#5 A la villa voy,	To town I go,
de la villa vengo;	from town I come;
que si no son amores	if it isn't love,
no sé qué me tengo.	I don't know what I've got.

"If it isn't love" is both rhetorical and emphatic. It most certainly *is* love which stirs this restless motion, as the enamored poetic voice assures us. Unlike the *vaquera* of our first poem, the speaker here recognizes her problem because she is experienced. Our *vaquera*, then, is surely a youthful novice at love and its sensations.

In poem #5, restless motion is taken to be a manifestation of love. This restlessness takes two explicit forms in our poem: in the coming and going of line 4; and in the action of boiling. (It is further

contained implicitly in the word "faldas" which we shall get to later.)
A more graphic verb than *bullir*[1] to describe restlessness would be
difficult to imagine. When heat is applied to liquid, it becomes
agitated and bubbles, and a vapor is produced which, if not released,
causes pressure to build. All this is taking place inside the heel of our
young *vaquera*! What she feels then is a ticklish agitation slowly
building in her heel, which stimulates her restless walking to and fro.

While the verb *bullir* is rare in the traditional lyric, we find a
derivative adjective in another poem:

#6	Bullicioso era el arroyuelo	Wild (boiling, bubbly) was the
	y salpicóme;	creek
	no haya miedo, madre,	and it splashed me;
	que por él torne.	don't worry, my mother,
		about me returning to it.

Here a girl has been splashed by a noisy frothy brook. She reassures
her mother that she will not go back to it. Clearly the "arroyuelo"
symbolizes a young man, and most likely a young man whom she
finds most attractive (notice the endearing diminutive). He is a lively,
passionate young fellow (perhaps boiling with love for her) and he
"splashed" her. Just how serious the splash was is left to the imagination, but it was clearly intended to infect her with the splasher's own
passion, for that is exactly what the girl insists to her mother did not
happen. She claims, at least, that she will not return to him, though
her mode of expression reveals fascination and delight.

In this poem we find that not only the adjective "bullicioso"[2]
implies restless, passionate love, but also the noun itself, "arroyuelo."
In countless traditional lyrics different bodies of water—fountain,
stream, river, ocean—serve as the highly symbolic setting for amorous encounters. (We shall discuss this in Chapter II.) Here the
condensation is great. The location becomes symbolically identical
with the lover himself, whose agitated feelings break their bounds
and "splash" upon the beloved.

Just as a stream indicates an amorous encounter, and a turbulent
one even more, so trees indicate another favorite spot for a meeting
of lovers, and when the trees that sway are next to a river, as *álamos*
usually are, there can be no doubt as to what is meant:

#7	De los álamos vengo, madre,	I come from the poplars, mother,
	de ver cómo los menea el aire.	from seeing them sway in the wind.
	De los álamos de Sevilla,	From the poplars of Seville,
	de ver a mi linda amiga.	from seeing my pretty love.
	De ver cómo los menea el aire,	From seeing them sway in the wind,
	de los álamos vengo, madre.	from the poplars I come, mother.

Here the verb is *menear*[3]—again, things get stirred up when love is involved. But now we meet the air, the agent of restlessness, as a direct and unmistakable symbol of love.

Let's return to Hurtado de Mendoza's poem:

#4 Aquel árbol que vuelve la foxa
    algo se le antoxa.

The tree that rustles her leaves
yearns for something.

Aquel árbol del bel mirar
face de maniera flores quiere dar:
    algo se le antoxa.

The tree that looks so fair,
it seems she wants to flower,
she yearns for something.

Aquel árbol del bel veyer
face de maniera quiere florecer:
    algo se le antoxa.

The tree that looks so fine,
it seems she wants to blossom,
she yearns for something.

Face de maniera flores quiere dar:
ya se demuestra; salidlas mirar:
    algo se le antoxa.

It seems she wants to flower;
behold, her flowers come forth,
she yearns for something.

Face de maniera quiere florecer:
ya se demuestra; salidlas a ver:
    algo se le antoxa.

It seems she wants to blossom;
behold, her blossoms appear,
she yearns for something.

Ya se demuestra; salidlas mirar.
Vengan las damas la fructa cortar:
    algo se le antoxa.

Behold, her flowers come forth.
Come, ladies, to cut her fruit,
she yearns for something.

Ya se demuestra; salidlas a ver.
Vengan las damas la fruta coxer:
    algo se le antoxa.

Behold, her blossoms appear;
Come, ladies, to pick her fruit,
she yearns for something

The tree (perhaps an allegorical tree of love) rustles its leaves—an action which the poetic voice interprets as a sign of its yearning ("algo se le antoxa"). Just as in the poem of the bubbling brook the scene of love becomes identified with the lover, so in this poem, the tree, under which so many lovers meet in the traditional lyric, becomes identified with the young girl—both are beautiful and both are destined in time (the time of this poem collapses into a circular, timeless present) to bud, flower, and bear fruit. Hence it is a virgin girl whose rustling leaves signal her awakening sexual yearning. In this poem, as in the one we are studying, the presence of the air is implicit, for what else makes a tree's leaves rustle? The air is the breath of nascent sexuality.

In yet another poem, a young girl confides to her mother that her blood becomes agitated when she sees her lover:

#8 Cuando le veo
    el amor, madre,
    toda se arrevuelve
    la mi sangre.

When I see
my love, mother,
my blood gets
all a-stir.

And finally we find, in a Galician poem, built around a learned play of contrasts, another lover plagued by this boiling sensation.

#9 Noutes d'inverno   Winter nights,
    quamanhas sondes!   how long you are
    mouro-me de frio,   for I die of cold
    perco-me d'amores.   and boil with love.

Here the boiling of love is a torment, since it must be suffered in the cold solitude of winter nights.

By now it is obvious what the verb *bullir* connotes in our poem, but even more unusual seems the location of this agitation. Why her heel? Two explanations seem likely, and one, for which no supporting evidence can be found within the lyric tradition, will be offered at the end of our discussion of this poem. But the other is suggested by a number of traditional poems wherein we find a young girl barefoot, and invariably she is beside or headed for a body of water. Water symbolism relates to sexual encounters. The *niña's* barefootedness, in each case, seems to serve primarily to reinforce and expand that association with water:

#10 Yo vi a Joana estar lavando   I saw Juana washing,
     en el río y sin çapatas,   barefoot by the river,
     y díxele sospirando: and I said to her with a sigh:
     di, Joana, ¿por qué me matas?   Say, Juana, why are you killing
                                         me?

The focus in this poem is, of course, on the speaker, not Juana, and consequently, what we learn about her barefootedness is his reaction to it—it drives him wild.

#11 Descalça vai para a fonte   Barefoot towards the spring goes
     Leonor pela verdura;   Leonor amidst the green;
     vai fermosa e não segura.   lovely she goes and insecure.

Here the focus is on Leonor, barefoot in the grass, headed toward the spring, and therefore probably toward a meeting with her lover. She is both "descalça"[4] and "não segura,"[5] two parallel states of being that reflect each other in this poem, first because they are both negative (not wearing shoes and not secure, or certain) and because of their respective positions at the beginning and end of the poem. Her barefootedness makes her appear vulnerable, which must be what the would-be lover in the other poem found so attractive. Simultaneously, because the description is apparently objective, the "não segura" could just as well indicate what she feels. She is most likely a virgin, naturally ambivalent about her imminent transformation: she is ready ("descalça"), but not quite ("não segura").

In a poem by Gil Vicente, we find the following scenario: the lover comes for his *doncella*[6] at dawn (a customary hour for the meeting of lovers in the traditional lyric) according to a pre-arranged plan to run off together. He tells her:

#12	Si estáis descalza	If you're barefoot,
	nam curéis de vos calzar,	don't bother to put on shoes,
	que muchas agoas	for many rivers you have
	tenéis de pasar.	to cross.

Again the double barefoot-water motif, and again the speaker is a man. He advises her to forsake protective defenses, for he sees in the absence of his beloved's shoes her readiness to wet her feet in the waters of sexual love.

The very act of walking is frequently related to sexual activity. When the walking involves a to-and-fro motion, the symbolism is evident (remember "A la villa voy / de la villa vengo"). The verb *andar*[7] often serves as a quasi-euphemism for the sexual act, as we see in the following poem, in which a young girl laments that her mill no longer "walks," i.e., grinds.

#13	Solía que andaba	It used to be that
	el mi molinó,	my mill ground.
	solía que andaba,	It always used to grind,
	y ahora no.	but now it won't.

In order to understand the sexual symbolism of this poem, it must be understood that the verb *moler* is a common euphemism for the sexual act in modern and ancient folk song. In this poem *andar* replaces *moler* as the verb of action.

As we shall see shortly, the wind in the traditional lyric most frequently symbolizes the masculine sexual impulse. In the following poem *andar* describes the activity of a wind that the speaker finds irresistibly seductive.

#14	¡O, qué ventecíño	Oh, what a fine breeze
	anda en aquel valle!	blows in that valley.
	Déxame, carillejo,	Let me, dear one,
	yr a buscalle.	go to seek it out.

Given the association between sexual activity and feet, or their movement, the presence of *calcañar*[8] in our poem is less surprising than it first appeared. However, by following the trail of feet in the traditional lyric, we also discovered a certain unexpected symbolism attached to the verb *andar*. How will this affect, then, our understanding of the third line of the *estribillo*—"que no puedo andar"? Our original reading of the line, i.e. the agitation in her heel prevents her from walking, remains valid, especially given the number of poems in which passion interferes with the lover's activity:

#15	Quiero dormir y no puedo,	I want to sleep and cannot
	qu'el amor me quita el sueño.	for love has stolen my rest.

#16 Que no puede navegar   The sailor cannot sail
    el marinero,   for the winds of love
    que los aires del amor   have turned him round.
    se le han vuelto.

While this is surely the better reading, still there exists the faintest of
hints that an equally plausible reading might be "I can't enjoy sexual
involvement yet." A protest, in short, against the biological urges
which begin to well up in her, stimulated by the contact of her heel
with the earth as she travels back and forth, tending her cattle.

As we begin our study of the gloss of the poem, let us look again
at this restless motion, the consequence of a surfeit of sexual energy
which young lovers in the traditional lyric all seem to possess. In the
following poem, as in "A la villa voy/de la villa vengo," the young
girl's restless movement is a dead give-away. Notice again the verb
andar.

#17 Zagala, no me agradáis,   Lass, you're disturbing me.
    váis y venís a la aldea,   You come and go to town,
    andáis triste y no sois fea: you look sad and you aren't ugly;
    dome a Dios si vos no amáis.   I'll be blessed if you're not in love.

In the following poem, the first verse of which is identical to the
fourth in our poem, we find a new aspect of this back and forth
motion. Not only does it represent the restlessness of passion, but
also the give-and-take, the ups-and-downs, the joys and sorrows of
love.

#18 Yéndome y viniendo   Going back and forth,
    me fuí namorando,   I came to fall in love,
    una vez riendo   sometimes laughing
    y otra vez llorando.   and the next time crying.

For other lovers, the ebb and flow of the ocean is a reminder of
love, but since those characters in the traditional lyric most closely
associated with the ocean are women who are either seeing their
lovers off to sea, or who are anxiously, and often despairingly,
awaiting their lovers' return, the coming and going of the waves can
only mean the perpetual flow of sorrow, as we see in this poignant
song:

#19 Van y vienen las olas, madre,   The waves, mother, come and go
    a las orillas del mar: by the edge of the sea;
    mi pena con las que vienen,   my sorrow with those that come,
    mi bien con las que se van.   my joy with those that leave.

Despite the sorrow love brings, we all seem to crave it. And in
this charming poem we are given some advice by one who has left his
love, probably to cross the sea:

#20 Quien amores ten   If you have a love,
    afinque los ben,   hold on to it well,

que nan he veinto
que va y ven.

for there is no wind
but that comes and goes.

Quien amores ten
allá en Castel,
e ten seu amor
en dama donzel,
afinque los ben
e non parta della,
que nan e veinto
que va y ven.

If you have love
over in Castile,
and this love you have placed
in a maiden young,
hold on to it well,
and don't leave her alone,
for there is no wind
but that comes and goes.

Here we see that "a wind that goes and comes" is the beloved, stolen from him by another. The lovely contrasts established in the poem ("ten"—"nan he"; "afinque"—"va y ven") suggest that he not only has lost his never-enjoyed beloved, but that he now has nothing, not even the flighty wind. This poem is unique among the traditional lyrics in its identification of woman and wind.

Returning now to our poem, we find that this coming and going of the first line of the gloss firmly orients the reader toward the real meaning of the sensation in our *vaquera's* foot. Her awareness of the true nature of the problem begins to awaken along with our own. She now associates the agitation with the movement required by her job, for after describing her labor she repeats the first line of the poem. Awareness of the sensation springs from the back-and-forth motion.

In the light of this new awareness, the entire *estribillo* is repeated in the middle of the gloss with one extremely important difference: the second verse of the *estribillo*, "en el calcañar," is replaced by "entre las faldas." Obviously, "entre las faldas" includes a much more extensive area of her anatomy than just her heel.

We have reached the center, in every respect. With the word "faldas,"[9] full consciousness of the meaning of the mysterious sensation dawns in the minds of both reader and protagonist. Let us examine the process of recognition in the reader, by searching out other instances where we find this word more explicitly used.

In the following poem we encounter a flirtatious, joyful game taking place between the wind and a girl, who speaks:

#21 Un mal ventecillo
loquillo con mis faldas:
¡tirá allá, mal viento!
¿que me las alzas?

A bad little wind
wild in my skirts:
let go there, bad wind!
You want to lift them?

The endearing diminutives applied to the wind and the coquettish tone of her protest make it certain that not just the wind plays with her skirts.

The next poem is a humorous aside spoken by a lover who is in the presence of his "amiga" but who is not enjoying the good fortune of his counterpart in the last poem:

#22 Agora viniese un viento   I wish a wind would come up now
     que me echase acullá dentro.   and blow me over in there.

     Agora viniese un viento   I wish a wind as strong as I could
     tan bueno como querría   want
     que me echase acullá dentro   would come up
     en faldas de mi amiga.   and blow me over in there,
     Y me hiciese tan contento   into the skirts of my girl.
     que me echase acullá dentro.   And it would make me so happy
                                                 to be blown over in there.

Here the lover's wish is to ride the wind into the skirts of his beloved.
In another the young girl views her skirt (this time her *saya*—an inner
skirt in the city, an outer skirt in the country) as an accomplice or
witness to her encounter with her lover, and admonishes it to keep
silent:

#23 Azotaba la niña la saya: The girl was beating her petticoat:
     "Saya mía, no digas nada."   "My petticoat dear, don't you
                                                    breathe a word."

   From these examples it is evident that the "faldas" of our poem
point to sexuality. The *vaquera*, I have suggested, also becomes aware of
the relationship between the feeling in her heel and her own budding
sexuality, for after recognizing the more general area of the agitation
she experiences, she quickly represses her awareness, and again, at
poem's end, confines the sensation to her heel. The movement from
heel to skirts to heel parallels in words the movement from innocence
to awareness and back. But of course, innocence lost can never be fully
regained, and hence when she repeats "en el calcañar" in the final verse
of the poem, those words can no longer signify what they did when we
first met them at the end of the *estribillo*. They are now laden with
irony. Given this movement towards repression, our alternative
reading of "que no puedo andar" gains credibility, i.e., that *no puedo*
really means *no quiero*. We perceive her effort to repress the nascent
consciousness of her own sexuality, but recognize the ultimate futility
of such an effort.

   The literature compiled during the last century by psychologists
and social scientists who have studied the language of universal
symbolism reveals some interesting data which lend support to our
reading of the poem. Jung tells us, for instance, that the foot, as the
point of our anatomy in closest contact with the earth, is often
regarded as being the seat of man's generative powers. And a tickling,
quaking or trembling sensation in any part of the body indicates a
build-up of libidinal energy. The act of treading, in many cultures, is
viewed as a generative action—a fact reflected in dance ritual.

   But the heel is significant in world symbolism for another reason.
Whenever man's imagination creates a situation in which he flies, the
wings which he sprouts for the purpose are always located on his
heels! This suggests another way to view the stirring in our *vaquera's*

heel. The poem traces a psychological process, a movement from innocence of sexuality to awareness and then to repression of the awareness (albeit temporarily). She is ready, almost, to move into a new world, a new state of consciousness. The movement from one state of consciousness to another is viewed as vertical movement through the air, and is often symbolized by flight. It seems possible to view the stirring in our *vaquera's* heel as a restless inner activity of birth, like the chick in the egg, or a seed sprouting in the earth. What she feels in her heel, then, are the wings, about to sprout, which will transport her through the air into a new reality.

The various poetic elements, the building blocks of the traditional lyric, tend to form "clusters" around a particular theme or motif. Air symbolism cropped up in our attempt to unravel the mystery of the *vaquera's* song in which no direct allusion to air occurs, in three different ways. We found it linked to the "restlessness" cluster which symbolizes libidinal energy, particularly in connection with trees: swaying branches, rustling leaves. It was shown to be central to the "faldas" cluster, as the masculine sexual impulse blows up into a woman's skirts. And finally, it is connected to the "flight" motif, only obliquely suggested, as the medium through which one must travel in order to move from one state of consciousness to another.

We are now ready to embark on a closer study of air symbolism, as we trace its association with other motif clusters. Because of the overlap which occurs among the various associative clusters (one poetic element may be common to any number of clusters) it will be possible to begin our investigation with any of the poems in which air occurs as symbol, and follow its trail from one cluster to another.

Let us begin with a poem which illustrates the relationship between air and the color of a girl's skin. This is the *morena*[10] motif, one of the most common and characteristic motifs of the Spanish traditional lyric. But once again the central motif of the poem is implied by association, rather than expressly stated.

#24	Las mis penas, madre,	These my sorrows, mother,
	d'amores son.	they are of love.
	Salid, mi señora,	Step forth, my lady,
	de so'l naranjale,	from under the orange tree,
	que sois tan hermosa	so beautiful you are,
	quemarvos ha ell aire,	the wind must burn you:
	d'amores son.	they are of love.

At first glance the two sections of the poem appear to be oddly disjointed. In the *estribillo* a young girl (the gender of the speaker is still ambiguous, to be sure, but from association with similar poems in the tradition we will see that the speaker is most certainly female) confesses to her mother the fact that she is suffering from love. At the outset, then, the situation presents two characters: mother and daughter; with a third, the lover, implied.

The gloss of the poem represents a totally different scenario. Now someone is addressing a woman who is under an orange tree, exhorting her to come forth, for she is so lovely that the air must (or will) burn her. Since the mother was the one being addressed in the poem's *estribillo*, we must consider the possibility that she is the speaker in the gloss, that this is her response to her daughter's confession. Two factors preclude this interpretation, however. First, while the mother is frequently spoken to in traditional lyrics, almost never does she speak (except in the Galician *cantigas d'amigo*). Her portion of the dialogue is implied by her daughter's or son's response (like hearing one end of a telephone conversation). Second, in the few instances where mothers do speak to their daughters, they never address them as "mi señora."

Young gentlemen pretenders do, however, frequently address the beloved as "mi señora," and in fact, it makes perfect sense that these words should be his. Who would be more likely to flatter her by praising her beauty (for his own ends)? But now one must ask, why this sudden jump in time, place and speaker? The *estribillo* indicates a dialogue between mother and daughter. Unexpectedly the gloss switches the scene and presents an encounter between a man and a woman in an orange grove. The gloss must represent the encounter that sparked the love from which the girl suffers and of which she speaks at the beginning. While the words of the gloss *were* the lover's, in the poem they are spoken by the girl—she is quoting her lover to her mother as a means of explaining the "penas"[11] of the *estribillo*. There appears to be a shift in time and place, but there is really none, other than in the girl's consciousness as she remembers what took place under the orange tree. The entire poem, then, is part of what we initially recognized to be a dialogue between mother and daughter.

The basic plan or structure of this poem is common to a number of confessional lyrics in the tradition: a girl confesses to being in love (usually making the confession to her mother) and then proceeds to recount the circumstances which brought about her fall (...in love!). Let us look at another poem with this same structure, in which a girl, too young to entertain a serious suitor, tells her mother that she has promised herself to a gentleman.

#25 Aquel caballero, madre,   I sent three little kisses,
    tres besicos le mandé;   mother, to that gentleman.
    creceré y dárselos hé.   I'll grow up and give them to him.

The second stanza of this poem's very intersting three-stanza gloss, cited below, employs the same technique of suddenly switching to a direct quotation of the lover's words. In this case the girl repeats the lover's words to her mother in order to illustrate how persuasive he is, and hence how virtuous *she* is in resisting his assault on her virtue. She states firmly at the end of the first stanza of the gloss: "aunque envíe mensajeros/otra cosa no diré:/creceré y dárselos hé." He simply must wait for the fruit to ripen.

Porque fueron los primeros	Because they were the first
en mi niña juventud,	of my early youth,
prometílos por vertud,	I promised it in faith
amores tan verdaderos,	love so true;
aunque envíe mensajeros,	though he send emissaries,
otra cosa no diré:	I'll say no more:
creceré y dárselos hé.	I'll grow up and give them to him.
Señora, si a vos placía	Lady, if it please you
que mi deuda se pagase,	that my debt be paid,
porque luego rematase	so that the damage I've suffered
el daño que padecía,	may be redressed,
y, si en esto consentía,	and if you agree,
gran placer recibiré:	it would please me greatly:
creceré y dárselos hé.	I'll grow up and give them to him.
Los ojos con que le vi	The eyes with which I saw him
han seído causadores,	were the cause of it;
que sean mantenedores,	may the vows I made
los votos que prometí:	sustain it;
la promesa que le di	the promise that I gave him
yo muy bien la guardaré:	I will faithfully keep;
creceré y dárselos hé.	I'll grow up and give them to him.

Notice in the second stanza how tentative and imploring the verb tenses which the lover employs cause his speech to sound. The imperfect subjunctive and indicative, the latter used in a conditional sense with the word "si," combine to produce a tone of improbability to his fantasy expressed in the two *si* clauses—his fantasy which *if* realized *will* make him very happy. But he's passively dependent upon her will in the matter, and she remains firm: "otra cosa no diré:/creceré y dárselos hé." The lover quoted in "Las mis penas" addresses the girl in a completely different tone. He commands her to step forth, and asserts with assurance that the air will burn her.

The lover in this next poem is not directly quoted, but the basic situation is the same: a girl confesses to her mother that she is in love and then describes the circumstances of her meeting with her lover. As in "Las mis penas," the speaker here suffers the after-effects of having already given more than a promise to her suitor.

#26 No me firáis, madre,	Don't beat me, mother,
yo os lo diré:	I'll tell you:
mal d'amores he.	I'm sick with love.

Madre, un caballero	Mother, one of the king's gentle-
de casa del rey,	men
siendo yo muy niña,	begged my promise of love
pidióme la fe;	when I was but a child.
dísela yo, madre,	I gave it to him, mother;
no lo negaré.	I won't deny it.
Mal d'amores he.	I'm sick with love.
No me firáis, madre,	Don't beat me, mother,
yo os lo diré:	I'll tell you:
mal d'amores he.	I'm sick with love.

In this poem the confession of love is hardly voluntary, since the mother seems to need to beat the truth from the girl. One wonders what indication of the girl's state induced the mother to inquire so vehemently. Let us look at the way in which the daughter presents the history of her romance to her mother. She emphasizes, first of all, the social status of her lover, perhaps because a well-positioned lover may seem less offensive to her mother. Then she points out the fact that she was a mere child when this love sprang forth ("siendo yo muy niña"), an assertion which has the same ring of unconscious irony as a ten-year-old talking about "when I was little." Finally she makes certain that the lover is seen as the initiator of the romance ("pidióme la fe"). Yet all these defensive ploys are subtly disguised behind a façade of defiant honesty—"no lo negaré." Her mother, however, is obviously unimpressed by her story, since the repetition of the girl's plea, "no me firáis," indicates that her mother's fury has not abated. Why the renewed violence? Why is the mother dissatisfied with her daughter's story, since the girl's only crime is that of having made a promise—("la fe")?[12] We saw how fearlessly the young girl in "Aquel caballero" told her mother that she had sent her future lover three kisses as a promise of love. Apparently *her* mother did not get angry, but then maybe the only tokens of love she gave were, (in fact), the kisses. Perhaps in this poem, the girl is speaking euphemistically when she boldly admits "dísela yo, madre, / no lo negaré." The verbal promise she gave is not what bothers her mother so, but rather the *physical* token or proof of her "fe."

The poem could be read thus: as an exchange—half verbal, half physical—between an essentially innocent girl who has given her promise of love to a gentleman, and her short-tempered, over-protective, and maybe even jealous (the girl is young) mother. Or it could be that the girl's explanation is specious. Her mother already knows full well the nature of the "fe" that was requested and bestowed. Like the mother's end of this dialogue, it was probably more physical than verbal.

Whether one prefers an innocent or a naughty interpretation, the similarity between this poem and the one we began with, "Las mis penas...," will now prove most interesting. Two symbols appear in the gloss, "naranjale" and "aire," which hold the key to understanding the poem. The symbolism of orange trees, oranges, and citrus fruit in the *cancionero* has been thoroughly studied by Stephen Reckert, who concludes that they symbolize mutual or corresponded love.[13] We can discern this symbolic thrust in the next two poems:

#27	Arrojóme las naranjicas,	Little oranges he threw to me
	con los ramos del blanco azahar;	with clusters of white blossoms;
	arrojómelas y arrojéselas	first he to me, then I to him,
	y volviómelas a arrojar.	and back again to me.

The back-and-forth motion of this game of pitch and catch with little oranges should indicate to the reader the true nature of the speaker's and her partner's ostensibly innocent play. They are flirting. Thus little oranges moving between them are visible representations of an invisible attraction that passes between them. The poem captures a child-like atmosphere implying innocence. The violence of the verb "arrojóme" is immediately cancelled, reversed, de-fused, by the diminutive "naranjicas." Blissful innocence. This is merely mock violence, with tiny green oranges and bunches of orange blossoms as weapons. The air of innocence and joy which permeates this poem is partly due to its expression of timelessness. There is no purpose, no movement toward anything, just joy in the repetition of the game: "volviómelas a arrojar." Orange blossoms and green oranges may hold the promise of ripening into swollen, mature oranges, but the poem makes no allusion to this potential. The game these child-like lovers play may lead to commitment, suffering, responsibility, but that, too, is outside the world of the poem. Perhaps this is the very game our "señora" was playing "so'l naranjale."

The same symbol—the orange—appears again as a promise of love, but in a very different setting. In this next poem we hear a young man advising us to leave his unripe fruit alone. He is in the same situation as the "caballero" who has received "tres besicos" in promise of future pleasures and who used an impersonal language of financial matters (*deuda, pagase, rematase*) to express his impatient desire for sexual union with his unripe beloved. The young man in this poem casts himself in the role of an orchard farmer, yearning for the future harvest which his budding tree promises. These two poems, "Aquel caballero" and the next, present the masculine and the feminine perspectives of the same situation, a situation which has progressed from the innocent tossing back and forth of tiny green oranges in a timeless present, to an intense longing for a future happiness. Since this next lover sees his happiness in the future, he cannot be happy now:

#28	Meu naranjedo no ten fruta,	My orange tree is fruitless now,
	mas agora ben,	yet soon the fruit will come;
	no me lo toque ninguén.	let no one touch it.

Meu naranjedo florido	The fruit has not yet arrived
el fruto no l'es venido;	on my flowering orange tree;
mas agora ben,	yet soon the fruit will come;
no me lo toque ninguén.	let no one touch it.
Meu naranjedo granado,	The fruit has not yet appeared
el fruto no l'es llegado;	on my budding orange tree;
mas agora ben,	yet soon the fruit will come;
no me lo toque ninguén.	let no one touch it.

Here the speaker is a possessive and worried male. He is in love with a girl who has not yet reached sexual maturity, but is about to. She is the tree, but she is also the fruit, though in its newest phase, a mere pip of a fruit (*granado*). She must form and ripen yet. The optimism of the adverb *agora* which qualifies her coming, i.e., the fruit's coming, feels a bit forced and self-deluding. If the fruit is still the size of a grain, he has a while to wait, and hence he is uneasy about whether she will still be his by then. He is also concerned that a thief may rob his fruit before it has ripened. The position of the possessive adjective "meu" at the beginning of each stanza emphasizes his attitude and announces his ownership like a challenge. Each stanza ends with an equally emphatic "ninguén" which prohibits the entire world from touching *his* blossoming orange tree. The speaker in this poem is tense, acutely conscious of time, and suffering the great misery of possession—fear of loss. But in this case the anxiety is worse still, because he may lose what he has not yet fully possessed, just as the speaker in poem #21 did, in fact, lose his unripe fruit. The orange tree is crucial to understanding his fear, for that particular kind of tree implies a promise of corresponded love, just as the two lovers tossing oranges back and forth are signalling to each other that their love is mutual. The virgin girl has already indicated her favor, which is why she is *his* orange tree, so that the prize has been nearly gained. It would be unbearable to lose it now.

In two contrasting poems, one beyond the realm of time, the other intensely conditioned by time, we found that the orange represented the promise of love. Let us return now to the girl still hiding from the air under the orange tree. The gentleman-speaker commands her to leave the shelter of the tree, for (and "que," line 5, must be a logical connective) she is so lovely, the air will or must burn her. There is no conditional sense to the verb he uses: she *will* be burnt, not *might* be burnt. No choice is involved. We must remember that these are the words *she* says—to her mother—that he said. These girls tend to color their stories, and it may be in her best interest not to let on to her mother just how willing she might have been to get burnt.

That brings us to the second major symbol in "Las mis penas" and the symbol we are studying—the air.[14] Besides in this poem, the image of an air that burns is found in only two other contexts. One is a

religious poem in which the air does *not* burn the rose, a symbol of the
Virgin Mary, whose birth this poem celebrates:

#29   Debaxo de la peña nace   Beneath the cliff is born
      la rosa que no quema el aire.   a rose the wind won't burn.

Obviously, the one thing that does not happen to the Virgin, even
though she be fragrant and lovely as a rose, is the loss of virginity.
Nothing could be more vulnerable to a burning wind than a tender
rose born high on a rocky mountain top. The miracle is immeasurable:
the air does not burn this rose, this virgin is never defiled.

But it does burn this next one, who sings her sad confession as she
nostalgically recalls her days of innocence. Notice the position and
tenses of the two verbs, the dative of interest, and the pivotal role of
"y."

#30   Por el río del amor, madre,   By the river of love, mother,
      que yo blanca me era, blanca,   for white I was, so white,
      y quemóme el aire.   and the wind burned me.

The poet feigns real identity with the girl; there is no ironic distance
between poet and speaker. She uses her symbols consciously. This
identification is made perfectly clear by the simple prepositional phrase
"del amor." Clearly the girl intends that her listener understand that
while she may, in fact, have been by a river, not only her skin, but her
whole being burned with love and she now must accept the change
which has really transformed her being, but which she views as a loss
of purity, whiteness. This girl has no need to be punished, since her
punishment is inherent in her transformation—she has become conscious of time, of loss, of change.

This last poem leads us straight back to the girl who *was* under the
orange tree, but now sighs, "Las mis penas, madre/d'amores son."
Significantly, both girls softly complain to their mothers, women who
can understand what pain love brings. Knowledge of good and evil,
awareness of time and its stepchild—death, loss—these are the gifts of
love. Suffering has entered their world and they turn for comfort and
understanding to the one who bore and nurtured them.

The same effect of poignant and painful obsession which the
repetition of "blanca"[15] produces, "que yo blanca me era, blanca,"
surges up yet more wistfully at the end of "Las mis penas" with the
repetition of the last line of the *estribillo*: "d'amores son." When these
words appear at the end of the *estribillo*, they are clearly meant to
modify "penas," and when they re-appear at the poem's end they echo
the *estribillo* and thereby remind us of the sadness it expressed. At the
same time, although the verb "son" does not agree with "aire," there is
still the implication from position alone that "aire," like "penas," is of
love.

The repetition of "d'amores son" then serves two functions: it links "aire" and "penas" by modifying them both; and it brings the poem full circle in time and feeling. The girl begins her song in the present moment full of sorrows, recalls the scene with her lover in a past moment when there was joy and passion, and finally returns to the sadness of the present. Just as in the repetition of "no sé qué me bulle...," the return is never complete. In this case the change is not so much in the girl's consciousness as in the reader or listener of the song. She was already conscious of the change, the contrast between her past happiness and present sorrow. Her song communicates to her mother-audience the depth of her feelings as she laments, "Las mis penas, madre,/d'amores son."

How can we know whether the seductive words of her gentleman-lover achieved the desired effect, and brought her out from the orange tree's protective shade into the hot wind of love? The very fact that she bemoans her misfortune at the beginning is proof enough. She could be the singer of this song, as well:

#31 Con el ayre de la sierra   The wind from the mountain
     híceme morena.   made me dark.

In this poem the girl admits she is *morena*, but blames the mountain air. As we shall see in Chapter III, mountains provide a dramatically virile background for amorous encounters. The next poem also combines the symbols of air and mountain:

#32 En la cumbre, madre,   High in the mountains, mother,
     tal aire me dio,   such a wind did blow
     que el amor que tenía   that the love I was feeling
     aire se volvió.   became the wind.

"Aire" here is specifically and emphatically sexual passion. This girl, too, met her lover on the mountaintop, feeling already pre-disposed toward her young man ("el amor que tenía"), like the girl under the orange tree, and then finds that her feelings undergo a transformation of quality: her love becomes air. She caught the flame of his passion. There is a hint of surprise in her confession—expressed primarily through the adjective "tal," almost as if she had not expected such force of passion. Notice that in both these last poems, verbs of change occur in the preterite ("híceme"; "se volvió"), because the central theme is the same—sudden transformation.

This theme of transformation underlies all the *morena* poems, and indeed most of the poems of the tradition. Except for those which conserve a timeless tone of innocence, like "Arrojóme las naranjicas," the tension which produces song emerges from a new-found awareness of time. Longing, whether for a happier future or past time, dominates the tradition. Occasionally we find a singer who resolutely accepts the conditions of her present time, but even then we hear the faintest undercurrent of bitter regret:

| #33 | Para mí son penas, madre, | For me is this sorrow, mother, |
| | que no para el aire. | not for the wind. |

This girl, who also confides her sorrows to her mother, recognizes that she must bear her sorrow, and bear it alone. Who or what is this air that does not suffer the same sorrow? The winds of sexual passion, possibly, but then one would not expect wind to feel sorrow. More likely it represents the man who carried those winds into her life—the lover. If so, one can hear in her song the bitterness of her resignation. In the following variants of the same poem, the girl-speakers abandon the air symbol, while drawing the focus of the poem to their own suffering:

| #34 | Para mí, para mí son penas, | For me, for me is sorrow, |
| | para mí que vivo en ellas. | for me, since I live in it. |

and,

| #35 | Para mí son las penas, madre, | For me is this sorrow, mother, |
| | para mí, que no para nadie. | for me alone and no one else. |

While the structure of the last is closer to the original—"I suffer, not anyone else"—the emphasis in both is on the speaker. "Para mí" is repeated three times in the first, twice in the second. Each speaker is obsessed with the feeling of separateness, of a suffering which cannot be shared, and like the girl preoccupied with her loss of whiteness, this obsession is made patent through repetition, in this case, of "para mí."

The *morena* poems in which the speaker is the *morena* herself reveal a sense of regret, guilt, sorrow, a need to justify her condition, or a sort of defiant indifference which becomes suspect precisely because of the defiance:

#36	Que si soy morena,	I may be dark,
	madre, a la fe,	mother, I do declare,
	que si soy morenita,	I may be a dark-skinned girl,
	yo me lo pasaré.	but I'll get by.

The change from "morena" to "morenita," and the almost exact repetition of line one in line three, plus the emphatic "a la fe" (by God!) all point to her unexpressed self-doubt. She is worried about her condition; otherwise, why the need to assure her mother that she will get by? Because now she is handicapped. A woman must find a husband, but that becomes more difficult for a *morena* than for a *blanca*. The stigma is social, not moral.

Men do not seem to mind what color a girl's skin is, though. The *morena* poems with men as speakers all offer re-assurance that she is still desirable. But, one wonders, desirable for what?

#37 Morenica, no desprecies la color   Little dark girl, don't despise
     morena,   your dark color,
     que aquesa es la color   for dark is the best of colors.
     buena.

The speaker presupposes a certain attitude in the girl—dislike or
shame of her color. He likes it, but a look at several of these poems that
express the masculine perspective will cast some suspicion on what he
means by "buena." Good for him, perhaps . . . :

#38 Si tienes las piernas   If your legs are
     como la cara,   like your face,
     tú eres la morenita   you're the little dark girl
     que yo buscaba.   I've been seeking.

One wonders just how reassured she feels by an attitude like that!
This gentleman is a bit more subtle:

#39 La morena graciosa   The charming dark girl
     de ojuelos verdes,   with green eyes
     es quien mata de amores,   will kill you with love;
     cautiva, y prende y puede.   she's got the looks, the pull and
                                                  the power.

While the verbs "mata," "cautiva" and "prende" reveal the powers of
her beauty over the speaker, the last verb, "puede," undercuts the
flattery and shows his true attitude toward her. We saw the verb *poder*
before, when our young *vaquera* could not walk ("no puedo andar").
Her use of *poder* implied not only an inability, but also a refusal. Here
poder implies not only the ability, but also a willingness—after all,
thinks he, she is already *morena*.

   Morenas and young men do not have different attitudes toward dark
skin and what it represents. On the contrary, both are aware of its
implications: social shame, loose morals. Men and women are simply
affected differently by the same phenomenon. For the girls themselves
it is the source of sorrow, while for the men it is a source or sign of
hope, even though the hope may not always be fulfilled.

   Even *morenas* have their pride and are not always easy prey to such
transparent flattery.

#40 —Digas, morena garrida,   —Tell me, lovely dark lady,
     ¿cuándo serás mi amiga?   when will you be mine?
     —Cuando esté florida la peña   —When the heights are a-bloom
     d'una flor morena.   with dark flowers.

She uses the paradox of the dark flower to ward off her suitor's
advances. And yet a sad tone underlies her saucy reply. Flowers are
pure and innocent. A flower which is "morena" is an apparent
contradiction in terms. Her reply, then, amounts to a "never." But it
contains a hint of wistfulness—would it not be nice if flowers could be
"morena," if virginity could be regained, if time could be reversed or
stopped?

In this poem, the *morena* deceives herself into believing that her changed condition can be, if not reversed, at least masked. She even tries to convince herself that her darkness is only partial, that the damage, not being complete ("un poco") is reparable:

#41 Aunque soy morenita un poco   Even though I'm a little dark,
     no se me da nada,   it matters not to me,
     que con agua del alcanfor   for with camphor water
     me lavo la cara.   I'll wash my face.

Her nonchalance is as forced as that of the girl who claims that she will get by ("yo me lo pasaré") even though she may be dark-skinned. Other girls seek solace from their misfortune, however, by placing the blame for their condition on some external factor beyond their control:

#42 Criéme en aldea;   I grew up in the village
     híceme morena;   and became dark;
     si en villa me criara   if I'd grown up in town
     más bonica fuera.   I'd be prettier.

A mere accident of birth caused her color. Girls born in town stay white longer because they are less exposed to the elemental forces of nature (elemental passion!).

#43 Aunque soy morena,   Though I'm dark,
     yo blanca nací;   I was born white;
     a guardar ganado   while herding the flocks
     mi color perdí.   my whiteness was lost.

This one points out that she was born white, and that her color change is also due to uncontrollable circumstances—a consequence of her work. Shepherdesses certainly seem to be especially vulnerable targets of the wind, as we shall see later on when we study the mountain as symbol.

Another *morena* simply throws the blame on evil enchantresses, "hadas."[16]

#44 Hadas malas me hizieron negra   Bad luck darkened my skin,
     que yo blanca era.   for I was white.

And in this next variant, "duelos"[17]—pain and sorrow, preceded and caused the change:

#45 Duelos me hicieron negra: Sorrows darkened my skin,
     que yo blanca me era.   for I was white.

In all these poems we see repeatedly the girl's fixation with change, a mournful gazing backward at a time before her fall. This same theme is present implicitly in the *morena* poem we began with—"Las mis penas." The final verse, reflecting as it does the sorrowful opening statement, represents the seed of unhappiness inevitably contained in her moment of passion. Her tale is cryptic, much detail is left in obscurity, but the very beauty of this poetry lies as much in what is left unsaid as in what is stated.

Why do all these *morenas* lament their color so insistently? Because they are *morenas*, and not *casadas*. They've been had, but not kept. The plight of each and every one is the same as that of this angry girl:

#46   Vanse mis amores;   My love is departing,
      quiérenme dejar;   he wants to leave me.
      aunque soy morena   Though I'm dark,
      no soy de olvidar.   I'm not to be forgotten.

If they are seduced and subsequently married—happily—to their gallant seducers, then there is simply no poetry—no tension, no contrast of.happiness-sadness. This is evident in the next *morena* poem, where once again the disillusioned girl worries obsessively about washing away change, while bitterly comparing her condition to that of her married sisters, who wash in lemon water, which symbolizes, like the orange, corresponded love:

#47   ¿Con qué la lavaré   With what shall I wash
      la flor de la mi cara?   my flower-like face?
      ¿Con qué la lavaré,   With what shall I wash it,
      que vivo mal penada?   for I live in great sorrow?

      Lávanse las casadas   Married women wash
      con agua de limones.   in lemon water;
      Lávome yo, cuitada,   while I, full of woe,
      con penas y dolores.   wash in pain and sorrow.

It is evident from the few poems we have looked at thus far that each one presents a particular perspective on a universal theme—love. The poems can be regarded as episodes in one grand story of love, which, like any story, has a beginning, a middle, and an end. Those poems with images of unripe fruit, or of restless motion, represent the beginning of the tale, the first awakenings of sexual passion. Those with images of a wind that burns represent the dramatic climax, the consummation of passion. And those with images of sorrowful *morenas* constitute the tragic anti-climax. It seems natural that time be most consciously felt in the final scene of the drama.

Certain symbols tend to gravitate to certain episodes in the drama. Flowers and fruit and whiteness pertain to the beginning of love's story, the burning wind of passion to the climax, and sorrows and darkness to the ending. Yet the wind permeates each stage of this drama, for its symbolic potential is fluid and multi-faceted. It can awaken desire in the innocent virgin, darken her whiteness with his passion, and finally abandon her to bemoan the consequences of his passing.

The play of the wind in a girl's hair or a tree's leaves presents yet another facet of the symbolic thrust of the air in this story of love. Depending always on the point from which it is viewed, this playful wind can be welcomed or despised.

In the next poem, the wind has already done his damage, but his victim is unsure, as yet, of how to view the consequences. Her lover is asleep, while she—yet another *morena!*—asks herself whether or not to awaken him. The issue at the root of her ambivalence is, of course, whether or not to submit to his passion.

#48 A la sombra de mis cabellos
      mi querido se adurmió;
      ¿si le recordaré o no?

In the shadows of my locks
my beloved fell asleep.
Should I wake him or not?

Peinaba yo mis cabellos
con cuidado cada día,
y el viento los esparcía
robándome los más bellos;
y a su soplo y sombra dellos
mi querido se adurmió:
¿si le recordaré o no?

I combed my locks
with care each day,
and the wind scattered them,
stealing the loveliest.
In the shadows of my blown locks
my beloved fell asleep.
Should I wake him or not?

Díceme que le da pena
el ser en extremo ingrata;
que le da vida y le mata
éste mi color morena;
y llamándome sirena,
él junto a mí se adurmió;
¿si le recordaré o no?

He tells me that I make him suffer
by being most ungrateful,
that this my dark hue
both gives him life and kills him,
and calling me a siren
by my side he fell asleep.
Should I wake him or not?

The second stanza of the gloss is explicit in describing the present moment of the poem. She quotes all the arguments he has used to persuade her to surrender to his passion—the irresistible attractiveness of her color, and the pain which her obstinate refusal causes him and which threatens to destroy him ("le mata"). His final ploy, and the one which may yet work, is to accuse her of being a "sirena" and then poutingly and pointedly fall asleep. As long as he displays his interest by struggling to break her will, she can resist. But indifference is unbearable. If he sleeps he has lost interest, and she has lost her chance to win the ultimate victory—a husband.

These lovers are involved in a battle of wills, and we have interrupted their tryst at the critical moment when she must decide what strategy to follow next. But she has already been defeated. She can still succumb to his passion, but to do so will only signify a temporary moment of happiness, of union. She is aware, by now, that her lover's intentions in this game are diametrically opposed to her own, and the reason is, again, her color, which symbolizes her lack of purity. In case her color alone is not sufficient to suggest the hidden facts of the case, the girl herself hints at them in the first stanza of the gloss.

She recalls the care she took to protect her purity, symbolized by her hair. That a girl's long hair represents her virginity becomes obvious in this poem which is strikingly similar to the *morena* poem in which the speaker, with feigned lack of concern, assures her mother that she will get by just fine, even though she is dark-skinned. Here the speaker, while recognizing the handicap which loss of virginity entails, feels confident that her "donaire,"[18] her charms, will more than compensate her lack:

#49	No tengo cabellos, madre,	I don't have locks, mother,
	mas tengo bonico donaire.	but I've a charming grace.

	No tengo cabellos, madre,	I don't have locks, mother,
	que me lleguen a la cinta;	that fall to my waist,
	mas tengo bonico donaire	but I've a charming grace
	con que mato a quien me mira.	that slays all who look at me.
	Mato a quien me mira, madre,	I slay all who see me, mother,
	con mi bonico donaire.	with my charming grace.
	No tengo cabellos, madre,	I don't have locks, mother,
	mas tengo bonico donaire.	but I've a charming grace.

Just like the morena in poem #36, this girl would feel no need to reassure herself and her mother of her desirability if it were not in question, and here the question involves her hair.

Returning now to the girl who keeps vigil by the side of her sleeping lover, we see that she, too, is concerned about her hair. Despite her efforts to keep her hair neatly combed and organized, a natural force beyond her control—the air—has mussed her hair, soiled her purity, robbed her of her best and most beautiful feature, her virginity. Notice the use of the imperfect tense in this stanza. Her disgrace is history, a history her sleeping lover knows only too well. More than likely, he was the form the winds of passion took when it mussed her hair on past occasions. Now once again, in the present moment of the poem, he expects to enjoy without restriction the pleasure of frolicking in her hair. This time, however, the girl has decided to withhold her favors, in the hope of winning a more lasting prize. But she was not prepared for the new twist events have taken. She expected her lover to persevere until she had extracted a promise of marriage. His lack of persistence confuses her and leaves her wondering what recourse she has left.

The following poem once again manifests the tragic dilemma of woman in the drama of the traditional lyric: damned if you do and damned if you don't. And even if she is determined to resist, the strength of the air is irresistible:

#50	Estos mis cabellicos, madre,	These my locks, mother,
	dos a dos me los lleva el aire.	two by two the wind carries them off.

Depending on the scene we witness, we find differing attitudes toward the ubiquitous and unceasing winds of sexuality. In this little poem, the girl is fascinated by the game the wind plays with her hair, though she recognizes her own lack of control in the situation ("me los lleva el aire"). Two by two the wind carries off strands of hair, just as sexual passion carries lovers off two by two. As in "Arrojóme las naranjicas," the speaker here is beguiled by the apparent innocence of the game ("cabellicos") and does not yet perceive the danger which lurks outside her innocent realm of joy. In the next poem, too, the speaker is unconscious of the destructive potential of the seemingly innocuous "airecillo":

#51 Airecillo en los mis cabellos   The breeze among my locks,
     y aire en ellos.   and the wind in them.

It would seem that what began as a harmless breeze ("airecillo") has quickly gained force, becoming a more substantial, less easily controlled "aire."

Having picked up momentum, the growing passion impels this lover to begin his ever more insistent complaints:

#52 Tienes lindos ojos,   You have pretty eyes
     lindos cabellos,   and pretty hair;
     tiéneslos revueltos   it's all tousled and disturbed
     y a mí con ellos.   and me along with it.

If we recall the boiling turmoil the wind stirred up in other poems, this young man's problem becomes evident. Attracted by her physical charms, he has been playing in his beloved's hair, and now must deal with his aroused passions. His hope lies in the fact that she shares his passion, for her locks, like his feelings, are "revueltos."

If these girls succeed in resisting, they never sing about it. Those who do not succeed, though, have a great deal to sing about:

#53 Soltáronse mis cabellos,   My locks became undone,
     madre mía;   mother dear:
     ¡ay! ¿con qué me los prendería?   Ay! How can I restrain them?

Like countless other girls in the tradition, this one confides her problem to her mother. Her hair escaped, flew freely in the wind. Notice the tense of "soltar" which points to a single occasion, the moment of her downfall. Now she faces the consequences, and like the *morenas*, wishes to undo the damage. How can she now pin back her wildly disordered hair? She cannot, and she knows it, which is why she introduces her question with the mournful cry—"¡ay!," and uses the conditional tense of "prender": if there were some way (which there isn't) how could I undo what has been done?

Her effort to eschew the cold reality of her changed condition will soon give way to the brutal fact that nothing can be done. It is too late, she can only face the inevitable:

#54 Puse mis cabellos   I put my locks
     en almoneda;   up for sale;
     como no están peinados   since they're uncombed
     no hay quien los quiera.   no one wants them.

The symbols are different, but the story is the same. Once again the painful reality of change, the unrelenting chains of cause and effect must be accepted as the condition of existence. Like many of the *morena* poems, this captures the bitterest moment of realization, another birth of consciousness. While the *vaquera* in the very first poem we saw was feeling the tickling stirring of a newfound consciousness of life, with its eternal motion represented as a purposeless coming and going, the tragic females of this and the *morena* poems express in their songs the moment of another shift of consciousness. The motion of life is not a playful to-and-fro game after all—it only *appears* to be. As this girl suddenly realizes, there can be a terrible finality to the motion. The fatal last line of this poem expresses just that: nothingness, death. The logic of the poem is impeccable. She ends up with nobody. Why? Because her hair is uncombed. Why is her hair uncombed? Because she put it up for sale cheaply. At this point the logic seems to break down, until we realize that "Puse mis cabellos / en almoneda" refers not to one past time, but two. The first time she put her hair up for sale she did so because she had a buyer on hand. But this buyer only played for a while with her hair, and then returned the merchandise. As a consequence of that aborted sale, she has been forced to put her locks on sale again, only now the merchandise is used, and consequently, no one wants it.[19]

Repetition in several of the *morena* poems expressed the irony of time and the heroine's obsession with the memory of innocence. Here that obsession is manifested through the double significance of the simple preterite verb *puse*, which refers to two past times, one conditioned by the other.

Seldom do the lyric poems of the tradition give first-hand, immediate accounts of the moment of sexual fulfillment; but we often find it described in past terms. These scenes are remembered, and remembered by those who have at least begun to experience the consequences. For this reason, they are described ironically, for a new consciousness has arisen.

Repeatedly we have seen that the air corresponds to sexual passion. We have also seen the correspondence between trees and young girls in two poems, "Meu naranjedo" and "Aquel árbol que vuelve la foxa." And in the last group of poems we saw the wind playing in a girl's locks. Now let us examine another group of poems in which the wind stirs the tree's locks—its leaves. These two symbols, tree and air, intertwine in a rich symbolic cluster which is multi-functional, recurring throughout the story which the tradition tells.

In the bucolic, garden-like world of the tradition, as in nature, a most amenable spot for a nap is in the shade of a tree.

#55 Con el viento murmuran,   The leaves whisper
      madre, las hojas,   with the wind, mother,
      y al sonido me duermo   and lulled by the sound,
      baxo su sombra.   I sleep in their shade.

This poem exudes a sense of peaceful tranquility, in an eternal present moment beyond time. The only motion of which it speaks is the gentle rustling of the leaves in the breeze. Like the wind playing in a girl's hair, the air's activity in this poem is apparently innocuous. But once we perceive from our reading of other poems that a youth alone under a tree is almost always waiting for his or her lover, then the murmuring wind takes on added meaning. The wind here, then, is still the same aggressive force, it is merely tamer, less potent. Its gentle stirring among the leaves stimulates a suppressed and subdued excitement which promises much. The speaker is lulled into a dream-world of quieted passion as she waits for her lover.

#56 Orillicas del río, mis amoresé,
     y debaxo de los álamos me atendé.

On the banks of the river,
my beloved,
and under the poplars
he waits for me.

In this poem, too, the speaker is aroused by the wind in the treetops, but here the lover waits for her. It is her fantasy of his expectant passion which rustles the leaves in her imagination. The diminutive "orillicas" again indicates her lack of awareness of the potential damage involved in their imminent encounter, while at the same time it expresses her delight at the prospect of their reunion.

Some waiting lovers feign innocence, pretending that the subsequent encounter with the beloved was unexpected. The exuberantly naughty girl in this poem can barely conceal her delight at the "accidental" reunion with her lover, about which she tells her mother in this story of a pilgrimage:

#57 So ell enzina, enzina,
     so ell enzina.
     Yo me iba, mi madre,
     a la romería;
     por ir más devota
     fui sin compañía.
     So ell enzina.

Under the oak, the oak,
under the oak tree.
I was going, mother dear,
on a pilgrimage;
I went all alone
to be more devout.
Under the oak tree.

     Por ir más devota
     fui sin compañía;
     tomé otro camino,
     dejé el que tenía.
     So ell enzina.

To be more devout
I went alone;
leaving my path,
I took another.
Under the oak tree.

     Halléme perdida
     en una montiña,
     echéme a dormir
     al pie del enzina.
     So ell enzina.

I found myself lost
in the mountain woods,
and lay down to sleep
at the foot of an oak.
Under the oak tree.

     A la media noche
     recordé, mezquina;

At midnight
I awoke, wretched one,

halléme en los braços	and found myself in the arms
del que más quería.	of my own true love.
So ell enzina.	Under the oak tree.
Pesóme cuytada,	It pained me so much
de que amanecía,	to see the dawn break,
porque yo goçaba	for I was enjoying
del que más quería.	my own true love.
So ell enzina.	Under the oak tree.
Muy bendita sía	Blessed be
la tal romería.	such a pilgrimage.
So ell enzina.	Under the oak tree.

There's nothing subtle about her consciously employed irony in the lines "Por ir más devota / fui sin compañía." We will look at this poem again when we examine the unusual role of the mother in the tradition, but for now we are interested in the situation the poem describes: the meeting, coincidental or not, of two lovers beneath a tree, where the girl sleeps and awakens to find herself in her lover's arms.

The same scene, explicitly described in the last poem, is implicit in the next, as well:

#58 Daba el sol en los álamos, madre,	The sun played among the poplars,
y a su sombra me recosté;	mother,
dormí, y cuando desperté,	and in their shade I lay down;
no daba el sol, sino el aire.	I slept, and when I awoke,
	the sun no longer played, but
	rather the wind.

In the two poems, a girl begins her tale by explaining to her mother the reason she was under the tree. She goes on to tell how she fell asleep, and when she awoke was surprised to find that things were different. In the first of these poems, the girl confesses openly that she was no longer alone upon awakening, and her unexpected "compañía" was a source of great delight to her. In the second, the girl concludes her tale with a symbol. On one level, she is simply stating that she slept so long that when she awoke the sun was down, and instead of sunlight, what played among the leaves was the wind. But, as we know by now, the wind is sexual passion. This second girl awoke to exactly the same scene as the first girl: an impassioned lover.

Earlier we looked at another poem which told of a meeting under the poplar trees. Our interest at that time was the verb *menear*, as we explored the idea of to-and-fro motion as a symbol of budding sexual impulse.

#7 De los álamos vengo, madre,	I come from the poplars, mother,
de ver cómo los menea el aire.	from seeing them sway in the wind.
De los álamos de Sevilla	From the poplars of Seville,
de ver a mi linda amiga.	from seeing my pretty love.

De ver cómo los menea el aire,   From seeing them sway in the
de los álamos vengo, madre.   wind,
                                  from the poplars I come, mother.

Once again we meet a poem which presents an image of timeless innocence. The verbs capture an eternal present moment of repeated action which goes nowhere. The speaker is returning from his meeting with his "linda amiga," and what he saw, the swaying trees, was an action in the past. And yet he tells it in the present, thereby expressing the timelessness of its repetition—the air sways the trees perpetually. Love is still in its earliest stages, a joyful play in an eternal now, a game without purpose or consequences. There is not even any regret that the happy scene has ended, that he must leave his beloved behind in Sevilla. The feeling is that he will resume his playing beneath the trees tomorrow, and the next day, and forever, just as the wind will sway the branches of the *álamos* on and on in nature's eternal present.

In a related group of poems we come upon the lovers at the moment when they are under the tree together. The drama of the moment is ambiguous. What is made explicit is the fact that one lover sleeps as the other speaks. What is not made clear are the circumstances which surround the moment. Perhaps it is the moment when the absent lover arrives to find that his beloved has fallen asleep while she was waiting for him to come.

#59 No corráis, ventecillos   Slow down, little breezes,
      con tanta prisa,   don't blow so hard,
      porque al son de las aguas   for by the murmuring waters
      duerme mi niña.   my darling girl sleeps.

If our interpretation is correct, then his admonishment to the wind is really no more than an appeal for self-control. The winds of passion, though still harmless breezes, threaten to gain force, gather momentum, which is the reason he exhorts them to slow down.

#60 Mientras duerme mi niña,   While my girl sleeps,
      zéfiro alegre,   happy zephyr,
      sopla más quedito,   blow more softly,
      no la recuerdes.   don't wake her up.

Here, too, the vigilant lover must maintain control over his passion, which is a happy wind—happy at the prospect of union with his beloved. Now she sleeps, so he struggles to contain his desire. Notice that his command to blow more softly is modified by the adverbial phrase which begins the poem, "mientras duerme mi niña." Only while she sleeps does he want the wind to restrain its force.

In the next poem we find not only the wind, but also the verb *andar*.

#61 Ventezillo murmurador   Murmuring little breeze
      que lo andas y gozas todo,   that travels everywhere and
                                  enjoys all things,

hazme el son	make a soft sound
con las hojas del olmo	with the leaves of the elm
mientras duerme mi lindo amor.	while my true love sleeps.

At first glance this appears to be the same situation we have seen in the last two poems. But there are certain subtle differences which link it more nearly with the poem that initiated our excursion into the hair/wind combination, "A la sombra de mis cabellos." In that poem the speaker was a *morena* who, while pretending to repel her lover's advances, really was hoping he would persist. He has fallen asleep (or seemed to) and suddenly she finds herself wanting to awaken him to resume the game. In this poem, also, the speaker is female, the sleeper is male ("mi lindo amor"). While the lovers who watched as the beloved slept exhorted the air to quiet down, this woman wants to be sure the wind persists as a background song while her lover sleeps. It is as if she wants him, even in dreams, to keep his passion alive, and the gentle stirring of the wind in the leaves will serve as a subtle reminder.

Leaves may quiver with another passion besides the sexual. Screams of mourning and despair pierce the air beneath the branches of an olive tree this time, causing its leaves to tremble in sorrowful empathy.

#62	Gritos daba la morenica	Beneath the olive tree
	so el olivar,	the dark girl was screaming,
	que las ramas hace temblar.	making the branches tremble.
	La niña, cuerpo garrido,	The girl with a winsome figure,
	morenica, cuerpo garrido,	the shapely little dark girl,
	lloraba su muerto amigo	wept for her dead lover
	so el olivar,	beneath the olive tree,
	que las ramas hace temblar.	making the branches tremble.

It is not clear whether she screams as she witnesses her lover's death, or whether her screams are in response to the news of his death. Perhaps she was waiting for him when someone came to tell her the tragic news, or perhaps he was waiting for her when he met his end and her screams are precipitated by her finding him dead when she arrives. The details of the scene are not important. What matters in the poem is the empathetic relationship which exists between the girl and the tree. When a person screams, air is expelled from the lungs forcefully, but no amount of screaming can push enough air out to shake the leaves, let alone the branches, of a tree. And yet the poem is explicit—her screaming *makes* the branches tremble. What must be understood about the symbols of the traditional lyric is that they do *not* point to similarities, but rather they indicate correspondence. The wind is not *like* sexual passion, it *is* sexual passion. Girls and trees are one, which is why when the wind plays in the treetop, it is simultaneously playing in a girl's hair. When this phenomenon of identification is understood, then the trembling of the olive tree's branches loses its mystery. The tree feels the passion of the girl because it *is* the girl, and her screams are emotionally identical to the tree's trembling. The intensity of her sorrow stirs the branches of the tree. The intensity of the gentleman's burning desire in "Las mis penas..." will burn his "señora." The stronger the feeling, the stronger the wind.

The last cluster of poems we will look at in which the air functions as the central symbol, has as its theme absence and separation. If the *cancionero* is viewed as a collection of fragments which can be pieced together to tell the story of love, this particular poetic cluster would appear at the end of the story, and would constitute one of two major conclusions offered by this universal tale. We have already seen the other possible dramatic ending in the poems about abandoned *morenas* and mussed-up hair. Following the climactic scene of sexual passion, lovers seem to have only two options, both tragic: they can go their separate ways, usually because the man loses interest in the woman; or they can suffer separation either for unspecified reasons, or because the man is forced to go abroad, possibly to war. The poems we will now look at belong to this last episode in the story. The cause of separation is unimportant. The fact of separation, and the longing it brings, motivates the song.

This is the most common theme of the Galician *cantigas d'amigo*: a girl waits impatiently for the return of her beloved from across the sea. But the air plays only a peripheral role in the Galician songs of separation, in which the major symbol is the sea. We will discuss those songs in the next chapter, which deals with water symbolism. The difference between Galician and Castilian songs of separation reflects the topographical difference between the two regions. Galicia lies on the Atlantic coast, while Castilla is land-locked and windswept.

In many of the Castilian poems of absence, the gender of the speaker is ambiguous, since the particulars of the situation are irrelevant to the main idea: longing. But because the speaker in most cases longs for the homeland as well as the beloved, we can assume he is a man.

#63	Pues que en esta tierra	Since I've no one
	no tengo a nadie,	in this land,
	aires de la mía	breezes from mine,
	vení a llevarme.	come carry me off.
	Pues que en esta tierra	Since I've no love
	no tengo amor,	in this land,
	aires de la mía	breezes from mine,
	lleváme al albor.	carry me off at dawn.

As a symbol of sexual impulse, the real characteristics of air which enter into play are its impulsiveness, unpredictability, and power. In this poem, the air functions as confidante and potential means of transportation. The lonely speaker, devoid of companionship and love, implores the wind to carry him home. The air he speaks to is the air of

his native land, the one element of home which is free to move about
without restriction, the same "ventezillo murmurador / que lo andas y
gozas todo." The air is everywhere, and unlike the earth, cannot be
divided and possessed. The air on one side of the sea is the same air that
blows on the other side—a unified whole which connects all of creation.

Though its principal function in this poem is that of messenger, its
role as sexual impulse does not vanish, but simply recedes to a secondary
level of importance. The speaker is a stranger in a strange land, alone
and yearning for home. But what he misses most from home is love. He
begins his mournful petition by indicating his general loneliness—"no
tengo a nadie," and immediately realizes that his lack is more
specific—"no tengo amor." First he simply begs the wind to carry him
home, and then, having recognized his own specific need for love, asks
to be carried home at dawn. Dawn is, above all, the time when lovers
meet in the *cancionero*, as we shall see shortly. The progression in this
poem is very lovely. Once the speaker has expressed his wish for home,
the thought of being there, in turn, provokes memories or dreams of
certain imaginary pleasures he could be enjoying. If the air can fulfill his
one desire, to be carried home, why not ask it to fulfill another, and blow
him into the arms of a waiting lover at dawn? In the first stanza the air is
only a transporting air, while in the second it accrues a second symbolic
power, closely related to that which it possessed in another poem we
have looked at: "Agora viniese un viento / que me echase aculla
dentro / ... en faldas de mi amiga."

Since separated lovers do a lot of sighing, and a sigh, once it has left
its source, joins the common body of air which surrounds and links all of
creation, it partakes of those characteristics of air which suggest the
messenger role. A sigh becomes a breeze that can travel untrammeled
between the yearner and what is yearned for.

#64	¡Oh dulce suspiro mío!	Oh my sweet sigh,
	No querría dicha más	I wish no greater joy
	que verme donde tú vas	than to go where you go
	y hallarme donde te envío.	and be where I send you.

While one lover sends his sighs to the beloved, she in turn awaits
expectantly the breeze that will bear his message of yearning. The wind
that reaches this next frustrated singer may bring flowers that charm,
but she finds no consolation in nature's beauty:

#65	El viento me trae	The wind brings me
	rosas y flores,	roses and flowers,
	pero no los suspiros	but not the sighs
	de mis amores.	of my own true love.

At times a waiting girl is lulled to sleep beneath the tree designated
as the meeting place with her lover. In this poem, the girl grows

impatient and commands the wind to hasten her lover's arrival by telling him that she is waiting:

#66 Nochecitas de julio   Short nights of July
        y ayres del prado,   and breezes from the meadow,
        dezí a mis amores   tell my true love
        que aquí me aguardo.   that I am waiting here.

If he does not arrive soon, her passion will build, until, with this singer, she cries:

#67 ¡Aires, hola!   Breezes, I welcome you,
        Que me abraso en amores toda.   for all my being burns with love.

The symbolic force of the air in this poem is dual: she cries out to the air as messenger and confidante—'carry the message to my beloved so I can find relief.' But she also invokes the air as the cause of her discomfort. Because the air blows, she burns. It is at once relief and pain.

Finally we find in this same poetic cluster a symbolic equivalence between air and thought which is rooted in their essential freedom of motion. Unlike matter-bound bodies, thoughts can come and go without concern for obstacles and distance.

#68 Lexos se van, madre,   Far away fly my thoughts,
        mis pensamientos,   mother.
        ¡ay, Jesús, quién pudiera   Oh Lord, to be able to go
        partir con ellos!   with them!

Because thoughts share certain traits with the wind, the speaker in this next poem blames the air for robbing her of them:

#69 Los mis pensamientos, madre,   My thoughts, mother,
        pedírselos quiero al aire.   I will seek them in the wind.

The air, as it blows through time, through each moment, robs her of her thoughts. They come from the unknown and return to the unknown in the flash of time which is the present. But why does she want them? Because it is all that she can possibly possess of her lover, now. She is separated from him and thinking of him, but even her thoughts defy possession. The air blows them away, and since she no longer has them, the wind now must. Therefore it seems logical to ask the wind to return them. If she perceives the air as being able to possess something, then she considers the air to be alive, sharing the qualities of being which humanity enjoys. It is, in fact, the same personified thrusting air which stirs passion and burns virgins. It is this wind she must petition for her passion-filled thoughts. The wind in turn manifests itself in the person of her beloved. In "Para mí, madre, para mí son las penas, no para el aire," the beloved is also identified with the wind.

The poem's meaning shifts as the perspective changes. If our focus is on the nature of thought, then the poem first reveals the characteristics common to both air and thought: they are fleeting, ungraspable, and yet perceptible in an intangible, hence mysterious way. If we focus on the relationship between the speaker and her lover, then we must notice that both thought and air span great distances, connect separated lovers in a single moment of time. If it is on the content of her thoughts, then we perceive the symbolic meaning of air as sexual impulse, and understand that her thoughts are desires. She is reaching with the only part of her being that can move about unburdened by flesh—her thoughts. To reach the beloved, thought travels through the air—the air which stirs erotic thought and then absorbs the sighs and thoughts which it engenders into itself. Though the lover may send them to the beloved, their ultimate destiny is unknown. Maybe they return to the sender as the very wind that fanned—and continues fanning—the flame of passion to begin with. In this next poem we find the suggestion of just such an ironic cycle of passion:

#70	Dulces pensamientos	Sweet thoughts
	que vais conmigo,	that travel with me,
	volveréis en el aire	you will return
	de mis suspiros.	on the breeze of my sighs.

Greek mythology portrays thought as winged, traveling through the air. The god of thought and of air is Hermes with wings on his heels, like the *vaquera* with whom we began. Feet are generative and so is the wind, which brings the flower and fruit to the tree, rustles leaves, twists the strands of hair, stirs up passion, and burns virgins' skin. But the joys which the air brings also depart in the wind. The only thing the air leaves in its wake is a bitter consciousness of time and space, the conditions of existence on this earth. Which is why this next traditional lyric *a lo divino* looks to a different wind and complains:

#71	Aires de los zielos,	Heavenly winds,
	vení y llevadme,	come take me away,
	que los de la tierra	for the winds of earth
	son malos aires.	are evil winds.

---

[1] *bullir*: es hervir el agua en el fuego... Un gran concurso de gente ordinaria en plaça, o en otra parte, dezimos, que bulle de gente por estar toda junta y rebuelta, meneandose a una parte y a otra... y bulle bulle, el inquieto que anda de aquí para allí. (Covarrubias)
[2] *bullicioso*: bulle bulle, el inquieto que anda de aquí para allí. Bullicioso sinifica lo mesmo. (Covarrubias)
[3] *menear*: es mover quasi manear, porque comunmente lo que meneamos es con las manos. (Covarrubias)
[4] *descalço*: el que trae desnudo el pie sin çapatos. (Covarrubias)
[5] *seguro*: el que esta quieto y sin recelo. (Covarrubias)

6 *donzella*: la mujer moça y por casar ... y en sinificacion rigurosa, la que no ha conocido varon. (Covarrubias)

7 *andar*: es moverse el animal por sus pies de un lugar a otro. (Covarrubias)

8 *calcanal*: la estremidad del pie, por la parte que cae a la pantorilla. Dixose del nombre Latino Calcaneus, a calcando, porque hollamos con el en la tierra, con mas fuerca que con la punta del pie. (Covarrubias)

9 *falda*: lo que cuelga del vestido que no se pega al cuerpo, como las faldas, del sayo a fallendo; porque en cierta manera nos engaña, cubriendo lo que va debaxo. (Covarrubias)

10 *morena*: color, la que no es del todo negra, como la de los moros, de donde tomó nombre, o de mora. (Covarrubias)

11 *pena*: el castigo que se da en razon de culpa, Lat. poena. Pena vale algunas vezes cuydado y congoxa. (Covarrubias)

12 *fe*: ... algunas vezes vale promesa. (Covarrubias)

13 see S. Reckert, *Lyra Minima*, p. 27.

14 *ayre*: Dizese propiamente ayre aquel espacio que ay entre el elemento del fuego y el de la tierra: aunque en nuestra lengua sinifica el viento, por ser el viento como quieren algunos ayre movido, o por causarse en el ayre. (Covarrubias)

15 *blanca*: color, sinifica castidad, limpieza, alegria. (Covarrubias)

16 *hada*: Los que escriven libros de Cavallerias, llaman hadas a las Ninfas, o mugeres encantadas ... (Covarrubias)

17 *duelo*: el dolor, el llanto, la aflicion, y el trabajo. (Covarrubias)

18 *donaire*: vale gracia y buen parecer en lo que se dize, o haze; porque aire lo mesmo es que gracia y espiritu, promptitud, viveza. (Covarrubias)

19 See Chapter 5 of Edith Rogers' book, *The Perilous Hunt* (Kentucky, 1980), for an excellent survey of the symbolism related to hair and combing (pp. 90-108).

❧ 2 ❧

Water

N ITS SYMBOLIC functions we have seen that the air most often is portrayed as actor, the subject of a verb. It corresponds to the aggressive masculine creative impulse. In contrast, water, in its various symbolic modes, often functions grammatically as direct object, the passive recipient of the action of a verb (e.g., *enturbiar*), or adverbially as richly significant background, the "where" of the poem. The only transitive verb which attaches itself to water symbolism with water as the subject is *llevar*, a verb we also found associated with air, in its role as messenger. Whereas the air bears (*lleva*) the messages of yearning between parted lovers, it is water that carries away the absent lover to begin with. But even in its active role of bearing there is a suggestion of passivity, for the sea carries a boat as a pregnant woman carries a child. The air is active, masculine. Water is passive, feminine.

Many of the poetic elements which gravitate to air symbolism associate themselves with water symbolism also, for the world of the traditional lyric remains a unified whole—merely the focus shifts. Now we enter the mysterious realm of water, of quiet pools, mountain springs, rivers winding seductively beneath swaying branches, and waves pounding on lonely beaches.[1]

Water is engaged in a perpetual cycle of movement and transformation, bubbling out of the earth as a spring, wandering through streams, brooks, and rivers until returning to the vast sea, only to be re-absorbed by the air and returned to the earth as rain. As symbol, water appears in the traditional lyric in all of its earthly guises as bodies of water, but not in the form it takes when it mixes with and is absorbed into the air. Rain and clouds are absent from the world of the tradition for in this poetry water and air cannot mix. This is poetry of longing—the masculine longing for the feminine and the feminine longing for the masculine.

Water moves through and over the earth as blood travels through the human body. Hence it invites association with the vital fluid of life, and when viewed as the moving force of physical matter, it can be seen as symbolic of the libido, the sexual urge, in its feminine aspect. Not surprisingly then, this chapter centers upon the symbol corresponding on the feminine side of existence with the masculine air symbol we last studied. Both symbolize the movement of unknown forces, and the poems we will look at, as the ones we saw in the last chapter, have as their motivating spark the meeting of these two poles. In these poems one sees the masculine introduced into the quiet feminine world of water as a foreign and disturbing element.

The first poem we shall see illustrates this phenomenon perfectly. In this well-known Galician *cantiga d'amigo* we meet again a virgin girl, this time washing clothes, who suffers the effects of the wind.

#72	Levantou-s' a velida,	The maiden arose,
	levantou-s' alva	the dawn-maid arose;
	e vai lavar camisas	she goes to wash shirts
	eno alto:	in the high river:
	vai-las lavar alva.	and white she goes to wash.
	Levantou-s'a louçãa,	She arose so lovely,
	levantou-s' alva	the dawn-maid arose;
	e vai lavar delgadas	and she goes to wash petticoats
	eno alto:	in the high river:
	vai-las lavar alva.	and white she goes to wash.
	(E) vai lavar camisas;	And she goes to wash shirts,
	levantou-s' alva;	the dawn-maid arose;
	o vento lh'as desvia	the wind blows them away
	eno alto:	on the high river:
	vai-las lavar alva.	and white she goes to wash.
	E vai lavar delgadas	And she goes to wash petticoats,
	levantou-s' alva;	the dawn-maid arose;
	o vento lh'as levava	the wind lifted them away
	eno alto:	on the high river:
	vai-las lavar alva.	and white she goes to wash.
	O vento lh'as desvia;	The wind blows them away;
	levantou-s' alva;	the dawn-maid arose,
	meteu-s' alva en ira	anger reddened the dawn-maid
	eno alto:	on the high river:
	vai-las lavar alva.	and white she goes to wash.
	O vento lh'as levava;	The wind lifted them away;
	levantou-s' alva;	the dawn-maid arose,
	meteu-s' alva en sanha	inflamed grew the dawn-maid
	eno alto:	on the high river:
	vai-las lavar alva.	and white she goes to wash.

The most striking feature of this poem is the semantic ambiguity of the word "alva"[2] which can mean "dawn," "white," or "virgin" depending on its context and the perspective of the reader. Furthermore, the phonetic elements of the word are repeated in nearly every key word in the poem—"levantou," "velida," "lavar," "vai," "alto," "vento," etc.

Our concern here is with the play of symbols contained in the poem. Like the poem with which we began the first chapter, this song contains the symbol we are primarily concerned with—water—only by implication. There is no noun in the poem which denotes water, only the verb "lavar" whose meaning is dependent upon the idea of water.[3] A pretty ("velida," 'louçãa") virgin ("alva") girl goes to a mountain ("eno alto") stream or spring to wash her chemise ("delgada," "camisa"). The mountain wind blows her clothes away, and she gets angry. If we condense the poem by eliminating the repetitions, we are left with this:

Levantou-s' a velida (louçãa)	The maiden arose,
levantou-s' alva,	the dawn-maid arose;
e vai lavar camisas (delgadas)	she goes to wash shirts
eno alto:	in the high river:
o vento lh'as desvia (levava)	the wind blows them away;
meteu-s' alva en ira (sanha):	anger reddened the dawn-maid
vai-las lavar alva.	and white she goes to wash.

Alva and *vento* represent the symbolic poles of the poem, and the tension, the movement, and the drama spring from the interplay of these two symbols.

In a sense, the words of the traditional lyric belong to two different languages simultaneously. For example, the words of the first verse, "levantou-s' a velida" signify a thing and an action in the *gallego* language—the pretty girl got up. But at the same time in the symbolic language of the traditional lyric, they signify—or rather suggest (for this is a most tentative language in which "meaning" shifts with the consciousness that perceives it—a phenomenon true of all languages but in less exaggerated form) much more than the meaning denoted by the *gallego* words. If one is aware of the symbols contained in the words—and often, as in this case, they are contained only by association—then the first verse of this poem suggests through the verb *levantarse*, an important symbol in the tradition—dawn. The final word of the second verse, "alva" will substantiate this suggestion. Twice the verb "levantou-se" is repeated, each time indicating the time-setting of the poem. When "alva" appears to emphasize further the fact that it is dawn, that particular meaning of "alva" is already so firmly established that the word can afford a certain semantic ambiguity. "Alva" can signify the girl and the dawn simultaneously—both serve equally well as subject of the verb—and

both rise. The upward motion contained in the image of rising is still
another symbol in the tradition, though this is a more obscure, less
immediate element than dawn, and one that will be discussed later.

Now the fact that a pretty girl is the do-er of the action, that she
got up, tells us that the day, indeed, is dawning, and without any
further information we already know in essence the entire story of
the poem, for when girls awaken at dawn in the tradition, it is
invariably to meet their lovers. The girl in this poem, for example,
asks (commands!) her lover to meet her at dawn:

#73	Al alba venid, buen amigo,	At dawn come, dear friend,
	al alba venid.	come at dawn.
	Amigo, el que yo más quería,	You whom I greatly desire,
	venid al alba del día.	come at the dawn of day.
	Amigo, el que yo más amaba,	You whom I greatly love,
	venid a la luz del alba.	come at daybreak.
	Venid a la luz del día,	At daybreak come,
	no trayáis compañía.	bring no company.
	Venid a la luz del alba,	At daybreak come,
	non traigáis gran compaña.	bring no great company.

This theme of the dawn meeting will be discussed in the next chapter
when we look more closely at the role of the sun.

In the "alva" poem, the second verse, one of the three verses
which are repeated intact in each stanza, tells us in one language that
the dawn also arose, and thus makes explicit what was intimated in
the first verse—the poem's time-setting. Again the words not only
denote, but also connote, and along with the idea of dawn comes the
blending which is characteristic of the way symbols function in the
tradition. The girl and the dawn are one, in the sense of purity, light
(whiteness), freshness and a new birth, a new beginning. This virgin,
like our *vaquera* with the stirring in her heel, is about to be born into a
new consciousness, one which she resists momentarily, just as our
vaquera did.

The third verse, which, like the first, varies in each stanza, tells us
that in the present moment of the poem, the girl goes to wash shirts,
having already arisen. As the poem progresses, the verb "vai," implies
not only the action of going, but also the consequence of the
going—she is there. This temporal ambiguity was seen in the verbs
of other poems and we shall encounter it again often, for in the
tradition, this, too, is a typical means of expanding the poem's
suggestive potential. The complement of "vai," the infinitive "lavar,"
both denotes and connotes water, and here its symbolic connotation
is completed by its direct object "camisas." *Camisas* and *delgadas* are
garments that women wear next to their skin. In a number of poems,

parts have stood for the whole (tree-fruit-flower), and here again the girl's shirt stands in synecdochical relation to the girl. Given that a girl and water at dawn connote an encounter, accidental or arranged, with her love, then the washing of the shirt can be seen on a number of levels: she is purifying and preparing herself for a meeting with her lover; her manipulating of the shirt is a ritualistic, magical way of manipulating the lover—she is calling him, evoking his presence; she is quite simply fulfilling a part of her domestic duty as a female, washing clothes; she is following a plan pre-arranged between her and her lover to meet at dawn, and she uses the washing of her shirts as an 'excuse to visit the spring.[4]

The fourth verse, which remains constant in all stanzas, not only provides information about the setting of the poem, but also introduces into the poem for the first time in explicit symbolic language, an embodiment of the masculine energy. Until now we have only met the girl, the dawn, the water and the shirts, all feminine symbols, in this context, that form a constellation of symbols clustered around the protagonist. On the poem's denotative plane of meaning, the elevated setting suggested by "alto" fits logically with the waters already evoked by the situation described in the first three verses, and also with the lusty wind which will soon blow into the scene, for elevations are notoriously windy. On the connotative plane, the heights foreshadow the masculine force which will disturb the virgin's tranquil world in the guise of the wind.

The last verse of each stanza, like the second and fourth, remains the same throughout: "vai-las lavar alva." In the first two stanzas this verse is basically a semantic repetition of the third verse, with the simple addition of the word "alva," and in the second two stanzas it is a semantic repetition of their first verses which in turn repeat the third verses of the first two stanzas. In other words, no less than eight times in four stanzas, twice in each, we are informed that the purpose of her presence by the mountain waters is to wash her clothes. This emphasis through repetition indicates her determination, perhaps, but suggests more. Is it an ironic use of emphasis? By stating and restating her purpose, the poem, in fact, undercuts the very assertion it is making. In the final two stanzas the irony becomes patent on one level—nature foils her purpose. The wind carries off her clothes, at best obstructing the completion of the task she has undertaken—to wash them, and at worst soiling their whiteness by blowing them about. The girl's reaction, her anger ("ira," "sanha") would appear to be evidence of her innocence—she really did not expect the wind, and she really is upset by the disturbance it creates.

The three verses which remain constant in each stanza reveal the tension produced by the opposition *alva—vento*. In the second and

fifth, the key word is "alva." In the fourth ("eno alto"), there is not
only a symbolic association with wind, suggested by the word "alto,"
but also a phonetic association: *eno alto, ven-to.* While the vowel sound
"a" is fluid, and symbolizes in sound the notion of water, the "o"
sound can be heard as a phonetic symbol of the wind. In this case
"levantou-s' alva," with its accents on both the *o* and the *a* sounds
would contain elements of both principles, *vento* (masculine) and *alva*
(feminine), in sound as well as in meaning. Upward movement was
suggested by the rising, "levantou-se" of the sun and the girl, and by
the girl's movement upwards into the heights, both of which parallel
the wind's movement as it raises and carries off the shirts, "levava."
And even more, the presence of the masculine is contained in
"levantou-s' alva" insofar as her lover is the very purpose of her rising
at dawn.

Having observed the symbolic equivalence of girl-dawn-shirts, we
can now perceive the irony of the wind's action—*desviar.* The shirts
can hardly be said, in logical terms, to have a "via" from which to be
"desviadas." But the girl does have an ostensible "via," a purpose, a
goal—to wash her shirts. The girl then is truly the recipient of the
action *desviar,* while logically the verb which parallels it, *levar,* acts
upon the shirts. But shirts and girl are one, and her anger indicates
that, with the shirts, she is flapping about aimlessly at the wind's
mercy. The girl and the shirts correspond to the dawn as well, and
consequently the reddening of the dawn sky also expresses their
wind-stirred passion.

There are a number of poems that contain symbols relating to
anger—expressions of enmity, battle images, and girls who seem to
resent the intrusion of the masculine into their world, like our "alva."
Always there is a shadow of irony in these protests, however, just as
there is in the common metaphor in courtly poetry of the sexual act
as battle. In the traditional lyric this image of enmity is not conveyed
through metaphor, but rather through symbol:

#74 Arribica, arribica de un verde sauce,	Way up, way up in the willow green
luchaba la niña con su adorante.	the maiden struggled with her suitor.

Here the idea of *luchar*[5] as conflict is undercut before the verb
appears, because the repeated diminutive, and the greenness, the
tree, the very water that is implied by the type of tree ("sauces"—
willows, grow next to water), all have oriented us long before we
reach the verb. Though *luchar* loses its denotation as conflict, it still
denotes the mixing up of bodies and the emotional intensity which go
along with fighting. Sex and battle, both aggressive acts, can be easily
confused. The wind also enters indirectly into this image of the

amorous battle, since the lovers in this poem are up in a tree, shaking the leaves and branches just as the wind in other poems stirs the tree with the breath of sexual passion.

Considering the symbolic implications of enmity in other poems, there is some doubt about the precise nature of the passion which disturbs the "alva" whose wash is blown about by the wind. Is she really angry, or does she only appear angry? Did she only appear to be going to the high waters to wash her clothes, while in fact harboring a different, hidden purpose? Ambiguity such as this is precisely what makes the symbolic language of the tradition move in a completely different direction from the denotative language of the poem. As words, *alva, vento, alto, sanha,* attempt to delimit a meaning for the poem, but as symbols they un-limit the meaning of the poem.

In the next poem we find many of the same symbols found in the last, in an analogous context. Let us observe the similarities and differences between the two poems:

#75 Levou-s'a louçana,   Lovely the maiden arose,

#75	Levou-s'a louçana,	Lovely the maiden arose,
	levou-s' a velida;	the comely maiden arose.
	vai lavar cabelos	Her hair she goes to wash
	na fontana fria,	in cold spring waters.
	leda dos amores,	Joyful with love,
	dos amores leda.	with love joyful.
	Levou-s' a velida,	The comely maiden arose,
	levou-s'a louçana;	lovely the maiden arose.
	vai lavar cabelos	She goes to wash her hair
	na fria fontana,	in cold spring waters.
	leda dos amores,	Joyful with love,
	dos amores leda.	with love joyful
	Vai lavar cabelos	Her hair she goes to wash
	na fontana fria;	in cold spring waters;
	passa seu amigo,	her true love passes by,
	que lhi ben queria,	the one who wanted her so much.
	leda dos amores,	Joyful with love,
	dos amores leda.	with love joyful.
	Vai lavar cabelos	She goes to wash her hair
	na fria fontana,	in cold spring waters;
	passa seu amigo que a muit'ama,	her true love passes by,
	leda dos amores,	the one who loves her so well.
	dos amores leda.	Joyful with love,
		with love joyful.
	Passa seu amigo,	Her true love passes by,
	que lhi ben queria;	the one who wanted her so much;
	o cervo do monte	the mountain stag
	a augua volvia,	stirs the water.
	leda dos amores,	Joyful with love,
	dos amores leda.	with love joyful.

Passa seu amigo	Her true love passes by,
que a muit'ama;	the one who loves her so well;
o cervo do monte	the mountain stag
volvia a augua,	the water stirs.
leda dos amores,	Joyful with love
dos amores leda.	with love joyful.

In the first place there is no mention of *alva* in this poem. And yet the image of dawn is implicit again in the girl's action of rising. The verb "to arise" is the same verb, *levar*, only reflexive, which expressed the action of the wind on the clothes in the last poem—a further proof of the hidden semantic motion upwards in that poem. Here the body of water, "fontana," is made explicit, and the girl's activity by the water has changed slightly—she washes her hair instead of her clothes. Just as dawn is implied without *alva*, so too without *alva* we still have a suggestion of virginity in the image of hair. In the poems discussed in the last chapter the wind blew hair around, defying any efforts to keep it neatly combed. The *morena's* efforts to safeguard the neatness of her hair in "A la sombra de mis cabellos..." were futile. Here the "louçana" is involved in a ritual purification act, preparing herself for the expected encounter with her lover. There is no ambiguity whatsoever about the purpose of this girl's visit to the spring, for from the first stanza on the *estribillo* tells us she is "leda dos amores." The adjective "leda," in the first and last two stanzas, can as easily modify the "fontana" or "augua" as the "louçana." This is the first indication we have of the essential identification of the two which becomes evident in the poem's final stanzas.

In the other poem the virile element first appeared "eno alto" and foreshadowed the entrance of the active masculine energy in the form of "vento." Here, except indirectly through a chain of associations linked to "cabelos," the masculine energy does not enter until the third stanza—"passa seu amigo." If one is tempted through the habits of logical discursive thought to consider the wind in the other poem, for example, as a symbol of the lover, this poem illustrates the fallacy of such a perspective. In this poem one might think that "cervo" symbolizes the "amigo." Yet it is odd that the lover should appear first, and his symbolic representation second. But "cervo" does not symbolize "amigo"; they co-symbolize something which they both embody and which transcends them both—that same masculine creative energy which infuses air symbolism. "Monte," as the place of origin of the stag (mountain stag, mountain air) further contributes to this masculine constellation of symbols.[6]

The lover *passes* and the stag *stirs* the water. *Pasar* denotes linear motion past a point of reference, in this case the girl and the spring. It contains the idea of approaching and departing, but lest we see in that verb the seed of future unhappiness, we are quickly assured in the following line that he loves her well and much, which helps explain why she is "leda dos amores." There seems to be a touch of irony not only in the assertion that he loves her, but in the verb tenses used to express the fact ("queria," "ama"). Perhaps there is some connection between the verb *pasar* and the tense of *querer*. There is a further hint of irony in the verb *pasar* because it makes the lover's action, and his presence by the fountain, appear casual, which it most certainly is not. There is a danger here, however, in emphasizing these ironic touches, for they are simply hints. The very act of alluding directly to them destroys their suggestive quality.

The stag, in contrast to the lover, is not engaged in linear action, but rather circular action—*volver*. Here we have both the idea of stirring things up, an idea already associated with air, and the purposeless back-and-forth circularity of the innocent game of love—"arrojómelas y arrojéselas / y volviómelas a arrojar." It is explicitly the water which is stirred by the stag, but in the same way that the wind in the last poem disturbed both the girl and her shirts, here the girl implicitly feels the effects of the stag's stirring as surely as does the water in which she washed her locks.

In the last poem, *alva* served as the symbolic opposite of *vento*. In this poem we have the obvious antithesis of *velida (louçana)* and *amigo*. There is also the *augua (fontana)—cervo* duality, and yet another set of contrasts in the condition of the water at poem's beginning and end. Water first appears in the poem as *fontana fria*. When it reappears it is being stirred up. The logical opposition one might expect to coldness is heat but the opposition here is not direct, it is oblique. The water is cold at the beginning because it is fresh, pure, and clear. The coldness of the water symbolizes the purity of *a louçana*. She is a virgin who has not yet experienced the heat of passion, the burning of the air. She is in love, as the *estribillo* tells us, but still in that happy phase of innocent love which does not burn—at least not until she meets her lover. *Fria*, then, indicates not emotional frigidity, but rather purity. The churning of the water creates a condition which is opposed to its original limpid, cold condition. The stag stirring the water implies the same activity as the wind stirring locks and leaves. The stag has churned up the passions of both *louçana* and *fontana*, warming them, so that by its final repetition "leda dos amores / dos amores leda" becomes the song of both girl and water.

This next poem contains the same symbols, only now not only the stag, but by extension the doe also is associated with the love scene by the water:

#76	Enas verdes ervas	In the green pastures,
	vi anda-las cervas,	I saw the does a-walking,
	meu amigo.	my love.

Enos verdes prados	In the green meadows,
vi os cervos bravos,	wild stags I saw,
meu amigo.	my love.
E con sabor d'elas	And with the does in mind,
lavei mias garcetas,	I washed my locks,
meu amigo.	my love.
E con sabor d'elos	And thinking of the stags,
lavei meus cabelos,	I washed my locks,
meu amigo.	my love.
Des que los lavei,	After I washed them,
d'ouro los liei,	I wove them with gold,
meu amigo.	my love.
Des que las lavara,	After I would wash them,
d'ouro las liara,	I would weave them with gold,
meu amigo.	my love.
D'ouro los liei	I wove them with gold
e vos asperei,	and I waited for you,
meu amigo.	my love.
D'ouro las liara	I would weave them with gold
e vos asperara,	and would wait for you,
meu amigo.	my love.

The sight of the does and stags walking (again the verb *andar*!) in the green grassy fields reminds this girl of her lover. With amorous thoughts in mind ("con sabor d'elas"), she washes her hair, and then weaves a golden ribbon among her locks as she waits for him.[7] The poem is addressed to her lover, each stanza ending with the vocative, "meu amigo." There is a delightful back-and-forth motion in the alternation between masculine and feminine: *cervas-cervos; garcetas-cabelos*. Once again the timeless moment of new love is portrayed. The swaying motion in this poem moves like a swing in ever longer and wider sweeps, impelled by its wealth of sensuous contrasting images. The sight of the stately stag and the graceful doe enters the speaker with a vividness that she can taste. The impression they make on her is so strong that it permeates all her senses; she is *aware* of the deer as she submerges her locks in the water. Notice the sensuality of the image of the girl fingering her hair, twisting and braiding the long strands as she weaves golden ribbons among them. One is reminded of the wind-hair motif, and consequently this girl's manipulation of the hair she so carefully prepares for her lover's enjoyment appears to be an act of auto-eroticism. The ribbon—golden in lovely contrast to the green of the grassy fields—weaves among her locks in the same way the two lovers' bodies will soon intertwine.

The golden color of the ribbon is yet another symbol which contributes to the image of joyous union which emerges in the poem. It may be considered an emblem of the sun, whose masculine energy fecundates the earth. The following poem illustrates this color symbolism in combination with the symbol of the mountain spring:

#77 Hilo de oro mana   The font begets a thread of gold,
    la fontana,   a thread of gold begets.
    hilo de oro mana.

The water flowing from the spring is golden. Gold corresponds to masculine energy, water to feminine. The symbolic poles unite, just as the lovers meet to share the delights of their love. The thread the spring produces binds them together, weaves itself between and around them like the ribbon woven among the strands of freshly washed hair.

The spring flows only as long as love flows between the lovers. When that love dies, then the spring dries up, as we see in this next *cantiga d'amigo*.

#78   Levad', amigo, que dormides   Arise, love, you who lie abed cold
             as manhãas frias;   mornings;
         todalas aves do mundo d'amor   all the birds of the world were
             dizian: telling of love;
                 leda m'and'eu.   in joy I walk.

         Levad', amigo, que dormide'-   Arise, love, you who lie abed on
             las frias manhãas;   mornings cold,
         todalas aves do mundo d'amor   all the birds of the world were
             cantavan: singing of love;
                 leda m'and'eu.   in joy I walk.

         Toda-las aves do mundo   All creation's birds of love did
             d'amor diziam;   speak,
         do meu amor e do voss'en   my love and yours they had in
             ment'avian: mind;
                 leda m'and'eu.   in joy I walk.

         Toda-las aves do mundo   All creation's birds of love did
             d'amor cantavan;   sing,
         do meu amor e do voss'i   my love and yours they men-
             enmentavan: tioned there;
                 leda m'and'eu.   in joy I walk.

         Do meu amor e do voss'en   My love and yours they had in
             ment'avian;   mind;
         vos lhi tolhestes os ramos en   you cut down the branches on
             que siian: which they perched;
                 leda m'and'eu.   in joy I walk.

         Do meu amor e do voss'i   My love and yours they men-
             enmentavam;   tioned there;
         vos lhi tolhestes os ramos en   you cut down the branches on
             que pousavan: which they rested;
                 leda m'and'eu.   in joy I walk.

Vos lhi tolhestes os ramos en que siian	You cut down the branches on which they perched,
e lhis secastes as fontes en que bevian:	and you dried up the springs at which they drank;
leda m'and'eu.	in joy I walk.
Vos lhi tolhestes os ramos en que pousavan	You cut down the branches on which they sat,
e lhis secastes as fontes u se banhavan:	and you dried up the springs where they would bathe;
leda m'and'eu.	in joy I walk.

"Enas verdes ervas" was essentially a girl's account to her lover of her activities prior to his arrival. Her description was replete with symbols which indicated her eager anticipation. In this *cantiga* the speaker also addresses her *amigo*, also describes the sights and sounds that surrounded her as she awaited his arrival. Here the singing birds serve the same function as the grazing deer in the other—they represent to both girls the love they share with their *amigos*. But the happiness this girl finds reflected in the song of the birds is ironically undercut by her lover's disdain.

The first word of the poem is the girl's command to her lover to arise. As in the first two *cantigas* studied in this chapter, the verb *levar*, meaning to get up, indicates dawn, and by association the conventional dawn encounter. This association is reinforced by the fact that the speaker in this poem is a girl who addresses her *amigo*. Though the situation is ambiguous at first, she seems to be waiting for him at their designated meeting place, and exhorting him with her song to arise and hasten to her. "Que dormides as manhãas frias" may be a statement of fact, but it sounds like a complaint, and an admonishment: "get up, you've overslept!" Her description of the cold morning is significant—she focuses on the singing of the birds. This is the great attraction of the morning that he is missing, for the singing of the birds stands in synecdochical relation to the beauty and seductiveness of the morning. And what is their song? Her song: "leda m'and'eu." Her song and the birds', through semantic ambiguity, merge in the first four stanzas. But the singing of the birds is, by her own description, symbolic of, and essentially identical with the cold morning itself.

Why is the morning cold? On one level, *frias* points to autumn, the dying season, which in turn is the first hint that the poem is about dying love. But *frias* is a word, like all the others, which is semantically ambiguous in the symbol language of the tradition. *Frias* can also be understood in the sense discussed before in relation to *fontana fria*. The girl, the morning and the birds are one, aspects of the same essence. The coldness of the morning, like the coldness of the water, points to the girl's virginal state. They have not yet been warmed by the sexual passion of the burning wind. The coldness of the morning, in that sense, is due to the fact that the lover still sleeps. Not until the second half of the poem does one realize retrospectively the particular irony of that adjective. The initial meaning of *fria*—"virginal"—which the temporal ambiguity of the first half affords, is cancelled by the second half, and a second meaning emerges which was already present but with a different shade of meaning. From the start it was clear that the coldness of the morning had to do with the absence of the lover, apparently because he overslept. Not until the second half does one realize fully the relationship between the coldness and the lover's absence. He has not overslept, and his absence is not accidental. It is voluntary. He does not want to be there, he does not love the waiting girl. "Frias" connotes rejection.

But, of course, while the girl was waiting with happy confidence for her lover, she remained ignorant of his disinterest, just as we do at first. Her song was full of expectant joy—a song of love which she projected into the song of the birds. From her perspective, it seemed not only that the birds, too, were in love and singing the same joyous song as she, but that their song was triggered by the love she shared with her lover. The birds had these human lovers in mind as they sang, just as the girl of "enas verdes ervas" had the deer in mind ("a sabor d'elas") as she washed her hair. Again we see that the symbols of the tradition are not elements of the natural world that represent elements of the human world, but instead they are elements of both worlds simultaneously, for in the tradition no distinction exists between the two.

Because of this essential identity, the lover's sudden and cruel change of heart can be expressed as a cruelty perpetrated upon nature. His victims are many—the girl, the birds, the tree in which they perch, and the spring from which they drink. But in the poem—which is the girl's song—the primary victims are the birds. The birds had *her* in mind as they sang their happy love song; now she has *them* in mind as she sings her sorrowful complaint.

The lover's cruelty takes on a special bitterness when compared with the lover in this next poem, who also victimizes birds, but only those that do not sing:

#79   Vaiamos, irmãa, vaiamos dormir   Come with me, sister,
                        to sleep on the shores of the lake
        en nas ribas do lago, u eu andar vi   where I saw hunting
                        the birds my love.
        a las aves meu amigo.

        Vaiamos, irmãa, vaiamos folgar   Come with me, sister,
                        to play on the shores of the lake
        en nas ribas do lago, u eu vi andar   where I saw hunting
                        the birds my love.
        a las aves meu amigo.

En nas ribas do lago, u eu andar vi,	On the shores of the lake where I saw walking,
seu arco na mãao as aves ferir,	his bow in hand to wound
a las aves meu amigo.	the birds my love.
En nas ribas do lago, u eu vi andar,	On the shores of the lake where I saw walking,
seu arco na mãao a las aves tirar,	his bow in hand to shoot
a las aves meu amigo.	the birds my love.
Seu arco na mãao as aves ferir,	His bow in hand to wound and those that sang
a las que cantavan leixa-las guarir,	to leave unharmed,
a las aves meu amigo.	the birds my love.
Seu arco na mãao as aves tirar,	His bow in hand to shoot and those that sang
a las que cantavam non as quer matar,	he will not kill,
a las aves meu amigo.	the birds my love.

Their song of love protects these birds from the lover's arrows, but the singing birds and girl of our other poem have no defense against the indifferent cruelty of that lover. When he cuts the branch, he harms not only the birds, but the tree itself, which likewise corresponds to the girl. When he dries up the water so that the birds cannot drink, he dries up the love which bubbles in his *niña*, as well.

What is most impressive in this poem is the way in which certain conventions of the traditional lyric transcend their conventional function. For instance, verb tenses in traditional lyrics are often non-specific and ambiguous. The imperfects of the first four stanzas, consequently, do not necessarily indicate that the girl is speaking of a scene in the past. They could be used equally well to describe a present scene, and thus we understand them at first. Not until the fifth stanza is it clear that, in fact, they describe the past. They take on a retrospective irony. And it is precisely this temporal ambiguity which lends the *estribillo*, with the verb *andar* (again!) in the present tense, its bitterly ironic tone.

Other girls, like Leanor in this one, have been stood up at the spring by their lovers:

#80 Na fonte esta Leanor	In spring waters bathes
lavando a talha e chorando,	Leonor and weeps,
os amigos preguntando:	asking of her friends:
vistes lá o meu amor?	have you seen my own true love?

The fact that she asks her friends if they have seen her love indicates that she resists accepting what her crying indicates that she has already realized—her lover is not coming. Her tears are a consequence of his disdain.

In this next poem, the tears of the speaker are in anticipation of the rejection she fears:

#81   Ai cervas do monte, vin vos preguntar:
       foi-s'o meu amigu' e, se alá tardar,
           que farei, velidas?

       Ai cervas do monte, vin vo-lo dizer:
       foi-s'o meu amigu' e querria saber
           que farei, velidas?

O mountain does, I've come to ask:
my own true love has gone, and if there he dallies,
    what will I do, my fair ones?

O mountain does, I've come to say:
my own true love has gone and I would like to know,
    what will I do, my fair ones?

The lover is temporarily absent, but the beloved fears the absence will be prolonged or permanent. She seeks advice and consolation from her sisters, the deer. The stag, as the embodiment of the masculine sexual, creative energy, invades the feminine world, and his presence there allows the female of the species to participate in that world through association. The "cervas," also "do monte," are a toned-down manifestation of the same energy, but in its feminine phase. They are symbols of the sexual impulse in woman, and as such the speaker here addresses them. They represent the urge within herself for union with the beloved, and so she speaks to them as she frets over her lover's absence. They *are*, in fact, her pain.

While in many *cantigas* the *cervas* appear as confidantes of the girl who usually waits for the return of her lover, in this Castilian lyric the doe embodies the feelings of the girl herself, which in turn is the function which permits the confidante role.

#82 Cervatica, que no me la vuelvas,
     que yo me la volveré.

     Cervatica tan garrida,
     no enturbies el agua fría,
     que he de lavar la camisa
     de aquel a quien di mi fe.
     Cervatica, que no me la vuelvas,
     que yo me la volveré.

     Cervatica, tan galana,
     no enturbies el agua clara,
     que he de lavar la delgada
     para quien yo me lavé.
     Cervatica, que no me la vuelvas,
     que yo me la volveré.

Little doe, stir it not,
for I will stir it myself.

Little doe so charming,
do not muddy the cold spring water,
for I must wash the shirt
of the one who has my faith.
Little doe, stir it not,
for I will stir it myself.

Little doe so lovely,
do not muddy the clear spring water,
for I must wash my petticoat
for the one for whom I've bathed.
Little doe, stir it not,
for I will stir it myself.

This little doe who yearns to stir up the water is, of course, an externalization of the yearning of the girl herself, so that when she

commands it not to stir the water, she is attempting to control her
own impatient desire. Here the adjectives "fría" and "clara" are used
to describe the pure spring waters. Because of the essential identification of *agua*, *niña* and *cerva*, those two adjectives indicate, again, the
girl's virginity—as does also the diminutive applied to the doe, who
embodies the girl's sexuality. This *niña* washes not only her own
shirt, but also that of her lover, to whom she has already given a
promise of love, and for whose arrival she has bathed in preparation.
The activity of preparing for their tryst has stirred her desire, a
natural force, like the *cerva*, beyond her control.

In contrast, in the next poem the speaker is a girl who is reluctant
to enter these same waters of sexual love. She, too, has given a
promise of love to one whose shirt she washes like the last girl did,
but she is fearful of fulfilling her promise:

#83	A mi puerta nace una fonte;	By my door bubbles a spring;
	¿por dó saliré que no me moje?	how will I leave without getting wet?
	A mi puerta la garrida	By my pretty door
	nasce una fonte frida,	bubbles a cold spring
	donde lavo la mi camisa	where I wash my shirt
	y la de aquel que yo más quería.	and that of my own true love.
	¿Por dó saliré que no me moje?	How will I leave without getting wet?

Her initial statement reveals a great deal about her situation, again
through the connotation of the word-symbols used, rather than
through the denotative function of the words. The spring which is
born at her door we recognize as the symbol of the girl's sexuality.
As such, the verb "nace" suggests the newness of this sexual feeling,
and tells us that this girl is young, virginal, and sexually inexperienced. Her question, in this light, is rhetorical. She knows perfectly
well that there is no way to avoid wetting her feet in these waters,
unless she chooses to remain a prisoner in her own house. Passage
through that door represents a change in her condition. In the house
she is protected from the experience of the world, involving an
awareness of time, suffering, loss, and yet the attraction of experience is so great, as represented by her lover ("aquel que más quería"),
that she recognizes the inevitability of her immersion in the waters.
Her situation is similar to that of the *vaquera*, whose stirring sensation
in the heel is symbolically equivalent to the spring bubbling by this
girl's door. The *vaquera*, too, resisted accepting the change taking place
within her by attempting to remain in a state of ignorance: "no sé
qué me bulle/en el carcañal."

The symbolic import of the door is double. As the point of passage
from one place to another, it symbolizes the change of consciousness

this girl must undergo to enter the world of experience, and in order to pass through the door, she has no choice but to get wet in the newly bubbling spring. The spring and the door, in this sense, are mutually dependent, the one symbol conditioning the other.

On another level, the door can be seen as corresponding to another point of entry in the female anatomy.[8] Its meaning in this sense becomes obvious in poems where the girl denies or permits her lover to enter. This girl, for instance, could be the same virgin of the last poem, finally confronting the sexual experience:

#84 Alma mía, entre quedo,   Enter softly, my dear,
    que me estoy muriendo de   for I am dying of fright.
    miedo.

And this one presents a woman who, for whatever reason, rejects her suitor's advances:

#85 Caballero, bien podéis iros,   Good sir, well you may depart,
    que en verdad no puedo abriros.   for in truth, I cannot let you in.

She does not sound unwilling, but rather constrained by circumstances. Perhaps, like the girl in this poem (whose presence is implicit, precisely through the word "puerta"), she is being guarded:

#86 Aunque ando y rodeo   Though round and round I circle
    nunca falta a la puerta un perro.   and pace
                                 there's always a dog by her door.

Notice the verbs this young man uses to describe his amorous efforts—the now familiar *andar*, and *rodear*, which describes a movement very much like the *volver* associated with water and stags.

"Perro" here indicates that she is being restrained against her will by her mother, the mother whose attempts in this next poem to protect her daughter from sexual experience, were in vain:

#87 Aunque me vedes   Even though you see me
    morenica en el agua,   dark-skinned in the water,
    no seré yo fraila.   I won't be a nun.

    Una madre   The mother who raised me
    que a mí me crió,   loved me greatly
    mucho me quiso   and guarded me badly;
    y mal me guardó: at the foot of my bed
    a los pies de mi cama   she tied the dogs;
    los canes ató;   first she tied them,
    atólos ella;   then I untied them,
    desatélos yo;   to invite in, mother,
    metiera, madre,   my own sweet love.
    al mi lindo amor;   I won't be a nun.
    no seré yo fraila.

    Una madre   The mother who raised me
    que a mí me criara,   loved me greatly

mucho me quiso	and guarded me badly;
y mal me guardara;	at the foot of my bed
a los pies de mi cama	she would tie the dogs,
los canes atara;	first she tied them,
atólos ella,	then I would untie them,
yo los desatara,	to invite in, mother,
y metiera, madre,	my own true love.
al que más amaba;	I won't be a nun.
no seré yo fraila.	

In the *estribillo* the girl openly admits that she has experienced sexual involvement because she describes herself as "morenica en el agua." Both her color and the fact that she is already in the water tell us in symbolic language what the gloss makes clear: "metiera, madre, / al mi lindo amor." In this poem the dogs with which her mother tried to protect her were tied to her bed, rather than by her door—but in symbolic language bed and door serve the same suggestive function.

In the following poem, the girl has neither a mother nor dogs standing between her and sexual fulfillment, but instead she must contend with her lover's infidelity:

#88 Buscad, buen amor,	Do something, dear love,
con qué me falaguedes,	to please me,
que mal enojada me tenedes.	for you've got me good and mad.
Anoche, amor,	Last night, love,
os estuve aguardando,	I waited for you,
la puerta abierta,	the door open,
candelas quemando:	the candles shining,
y vos, buen amor,	and you, dear love,
con otra holgando.	with another frolicking.
Que mal enojada me tenedes.	You've got me good and mad.

The burning flame and the open door are symbolic reinforcements of an eagerness which she openly admits. Her door stood open all night, but her lover never came.

In contrast, this lover stands hopelessly before a closed door, and recognizing the rejection which it expresses, he weeps:

#89 A la puerta está Pelayo	Pelayo's at the door,
y llora.	and he's weeping.

In a sense, Pelayo corresponds to the spring bubbling outside the other girl's door. He represents an invitation to experience love, but the girl behind this door has firmly decided not to wet her feet.

Once the lovers have met, the spring becomes symbolic of their sexual union. In certain poems the lovers bathe together in a ritualistic "baño de amor." This delightful poem once more captures the timeless joy of new love through the familiar back-and-forth motion.

#90 En la fuente del rosel	In the rosebush-spring,
lavan la niña y el doncel.	bathe the maiden and the young man.

En la fuente de agua clara	By the rosebush-spring,
con sus manos lavan la cara,	with their hands their faces wash,
él a ella y ella a él,	he, hers and she, his,
lavan la niña y el doncel.	the maiden and the young man
En la fuente del rosel	bathe.
lavan la niña y el doncel.	In the rosebush-spring
	bathe the maiden and the young
	man.

The tone of the poem, conveyed through the symbols, suggests innocence. This spring is not high in the mountains, but rather next to a rose bush. The rose, as we shall see again later, suggests purity. Furthermore, the water is "clara," it has not yet been "enturbiada," despite their washing activity. We come upon these lovers as they ritualistically prepare each other for the immersion that will follow. The reciprocity expressed is reminiscent of the child-like lovers who tossed tiny green oranges back and forth to each other.

This next poem is an elegant sequel to the last:

#91 Mano a mano los dos amores,	Hand in hand, the lovers,
mano a mano.	hand in hand.
El galán y la galana	The lad and lassie
ambos vuelven ell agua clara,	together stir the waters clear,
Mano a mano.	hand in hand.

In this simply exquisite poem there are two elements which suggest consummated sexual love: the clasped hands and the stirred waters. In the last poem, preliminary to the moment of union, the hands, although engaged in the same activity, acted individually. Now they are interlocked and acting jointly. Their clasped hands, once again through synecdoche, represent their clasped bodies. This poem captures the very moment when they are passing through the door which divides innocence and experience. It is their first experience, for the water which they are just now in the act of stirring is still "clara." The most striking feature of this poem is the way in which it presents the two lovers as an undifferentiated unity. In the *estribillo* they are "los dos amores" and in the gloss they are assigned equivalent labels—"galan" and "galana," masculine and feminine forms of the same noun. Neither acts alone, neither is more active nor passive than the other. Together as one they stir the water of love, achieving that for which all the other lovers in the tradition yearn—unity. They have merged into a single being.

Having spied upon the lovers in the act of making love, we now hear the girl's cries as she reaches the climax of passion in this enigmatic little poem:

#92 Cuando de mi dueño	When my lord's
se escapa el alma,	soul escapes,
como cierva herida	like a wounded doe
me arrojo al agua.	I plunge into the waters.

While it seems plausible that this poem could be understood as
referring literally to death, that is, that the girl is asserting that when
her lover dies, she will drown herself, a more likely reading would be
that she is expressing the drowning feeling of sexual climax. Notice
first of all that the verb of the adverbial "cuando" clause is in the
present indicative. She is not, therefore, thinking of a hypothetical
moment of death in the future, but rather is alluding to an action, in
her present world, which recurs. Her own action of throwing herself
in the water is not in the future tense, but rather expresses a
repeated action in the present—"everytime this happens, I do that."

She refers to her lover as her "dueño," one who possesses and
rules her, and compares herself to a wounded doe. The female deer,
we saw, represents female sexuality, and hence it is easy to perceive
that a wounded deer signifies the same thing as stirred up waters, or
leaves and locks fluttering in the breeze. Her passion has been
aroused. This notion of the wound not only as pain, but also as
arousal of the amorous-sexual feeling, along with the association of
wound and water, emerges in this poem:

#93 Enviárame mi madre	My mother sent me
por agua a la fonte fría:	for water to the cold spring:
vengo del amor ferida.	I have come back wounded with love.

The innocence in which she approached the spring has been wounded
by what she met there—the wind, the stag. Now she must suffer the
pain of longing. It seems that her mother, having recognized the
inevitability of her daughter's loss of innocence, arranged the girl's
rendezvous with experience.

The frequent image of the hunt as a metaphor for love in courtly
poetry appears only peripherally in the tradition, and usually in
relation to the heron, *garza*,[9] a bird which nests by the *water*. In this
haunting poem, the heron has been wounded, and we watch her as she
swoops along the water alone, crying out.

#94 Mal ferida va la garza;	Smitten is the heron,
sola va y gritos daba.	alone she soars and weeps.
Donde la garza hace su nido,	Along the banks of the river
ribericas de aquel río,	where the heron makes her nest,
sola va y gritos daba.	alone she soars and weeps.

The key word in this poem is "sola." She has been wounded, she is in
love, her desire has been aroused, but for whatever reason the lover she
longs for is not with her, and consequently she cries out in anguish. The
pain of her solitude is made more acute by the location, the waters of
love.

The situation of the *garza* may help to explain this little poem, sung
by a girl who, like the heron, lives on the shores of the water:

#95 Orillas del mar
    me vine a vivir,
    ¡cuánto mejor dixera
    que vine a morir!

By the edge of the sea
I came to live;
better to say
I came to die!

As we shall see shortly, girls go to the ocean shore to await the return of their lovers from across the sea. This girl, then, alone like the *garza*, is dying of longing. In the tradition, her song merges with the mournful cries of the heron.

The marvelous ambiguity of the idea of wounds and the death which threatens the wounded lover is pivotal in this next delightful *cantiga*:

#96 —Tal vai o meu amigo
    con amor que lh'eu dei
    come cervo ferido
    de monteiro del-rei.

My own true love is in such a state
because of the love I gave him,
like a stag wounded
by the king's own huntsman.

    Tal vai o meu amigo,
madre, con meu amor
come cervo ferido
de monteiro maior.

My own true love is in such a state,
mother, for love of me,
like a stag wounded
by a great huntsman.

    E, se el vai ferido,
ira morrer al mar;
si fara meu amigo,
se eu d'el non pensar.

And, if he is wounded,
to the sea he'll go to die,
he swears he will,
if I should forget him.

    —E guardade-vos, filha,
cá já um atal vi
que se fez mui coitado,
por guaanhar de mi.

Be careful, daughter,
for I've seen one like that
who seemed so smitten
just so he could win me.

    E guardade-vos filha,
ca já un vi atal
que se fez mui coitado
por de min guaanhar.

Be careful, daughter,
for one like that I've seen
who looked so smitten
my favors for to win.

In this poem a lover has been wounded by his love of a girl who converses with her mother. Since he corresponds to the wounded stag of her simile, she corresponds to the "monteiro-maior del-rei," a position of great distinction. She thinks well of herself and is quite confident of the effect her charms have on her lover. If she disdains him, he will drown in his own passion, but then if she grants him the favor for which he longs, she will drown. Her mother realizes that the girl's concern for her lover's safety is merely a camouflage for her passion, and that the danger that the lover claims threatens him is a ploy he uses to persuade her to succumb to his desire. From the mother's perspective, based on her own experience, the one who is in danger of drowning is her daughter.

The symbolic association of orgasm and death stems from the loss of identity which is felt at the moment of orgasm and which the ego fears is a condition of death. When the individual dies, so does the individual identity. When the individual merges with another in the sexual act, individual identity is likewise lost. Hence orgasm and death symbolize transformation. This association between sexual love and death is most evident in these two poems:

#97   Ora amor, ora no más;   Hurry, love, hurry up now,
      ora amor, que me matáis.   hurry, love, for you slay me.

#98   Ya no soy quien ser solía,   I am no longer who I used to be,
      mozuelas de mi lugar,   sisters of my village;
      que no es para cada día   it's not for every day
      morir y resucitar.   this dying and reviving.

While, in the first, the girl awaits this loss of identity, in the second she has already undergone the transformation brought about by sexual union and finds it a most special experience, "que no es para cada día," which she delightedly confides to her inexperienced sisters. Her poem expresses her awareness of the radical change of consciousness which she has suffered. She has died and been returned to life. The etymological root of the verb suggests that *resucitar* really means to re-awaken, and hence she has awakened from the sleep of sexual innocence, into a new life.

This death of the old self is paradoxically frightening and exhilarating simultaneously. Hence the ambivalence the singer expresses in this little poem:

#99   En tan hermosa mar   In such a lovely sea,
      ¡ay Dios!   dear God,
      ¿si me he de anegar?   am I to drown?

The verb which denotes drowning "anegar," connotes, through its etymology, the idea of being negated, cancelled out—the loss of self. But the ocean in which the speaker both fears and longs to drown is "hermosa," desirable despite the threat it poses to the self.

This poem focuses on the fearful side of drowning in the sea of love:

#100 Aguas de la mar,   Waters of the sea,
      miedo hé   I do fear
      que en vosotras moriré.   that in your midst my death will be.

While the next one captures the delightful aspect of the experience:

#101 Hola, que me lleva la ola,   Look, the wave has taken me;
      ola, que me lleva la mar.   wave, I've been taken by the sea.

A wave is nothing more than the product of the wind's action upon the surface of the water. The wind may burn a girl's skin, but it also stirs up the ocean, and having done so, threatens to carry off any unwary lovers who chance to be on the shore. The energy of the wind is communicated to the sea and reveals its power through the pounding waves. A frothy ocean is really just a large version of the spring's *aguas turbias*. Consequently, lovers occasionally meet on the ocean beach, rather than by the mountain spring:

#102	El céfiro sopla	The west wind gusts
	orillas del mar;	on the edge of the sea.
	allá voy, mi madre,	There I shall go, dear mother,
	por verle soplar.	for to watch it blow.

Here the girl's desire to see (in reality, to *feel*) the wind blow, like the young man who went to Sevilla to see the poplars sway in the breeze, is symbolic of her desire to experience the effects of her lover's passion.

This use of the verb *ver* (or *mirar*) recurs throughout the tradition. Perceiving with the eyes can stand in place of perception with any or all of the other four senses, as this poem demonstrates.

#103	En la huerta nasce la rosa:	In the garden a rose blooms;
	quiérome ir allá	it's there I wish to go
	por mirar al ruiseñor	to watch the nightingale
	como cantabá.	as he was singing.
	Por las riberas del río	Along the banks of the river
	limones coge la virgo:	the maiden gathers lemons;
	quiérome ir allá	it's there I wish to go
	por mirar al ruiseñor	to watch the nightingale
	como cantabá.	as he was singing.
	Limones cogía la virgo	Lemons the maiden gathered
	para dar al su amigo;	to give to her own true love;
	quiérome ir allá	it's there I wish to go
	por mirar al ruiseñor	to watch the nightingale
	como cantabá.	as he was singing.
	Para dar al su amigo	To give to her own true love,
	en un sombrero de sirgo;	gathered in a silken hat;
	quiérome ir allá	it's there I wish to go
	por mirar al ruiseñor	to watch the nightingale
	como cantabá.	as he was singing.

Here the lover's words, confined to the last three lines of each stanza (the rest is spoken by a narrator), state that he wants to *see* the nightingale singing. Of course the song is heard, not seen, but since the singing in symbolic language corresponds to the girl's lemon picking, and the girl herself corresponds to the rose (a symbol of virginity made explicit by the epithet "la virgo") there is much to see in this garden by the water. The lemons she picks, as we already know from the oranges discussed previously, constitute her favorable response to the lover's expression of desire and affection. That she feels the same desire as he is further established by the sensuous texture of the silken hat which she bestows upon him as a token of her love. He wants to hear the birds, taste the fruit, feel the silk, smell the rose, and see it all—he wants to enjoy his beloved with all five senses.

The "ribera" along which the virgin picks lemons is as delightful as the one described in this poem:

#104	Que no hay más fresca ribera en todo el extremo como aquesta era.	There's no sweeter river bank in all the land than this one here.
	En esta ribera hay lindos pradales, son las aguas frías y muy especiales: las hierbas son sanas a los animales, y el ganado puede hartarse do quiera.	Along this bank lie lovely meadows, with waters cold and rare; lush and green the grasses grow where the flocks do graze, all they want the cattle eat, roaming here and there.

If we understand that the river whose bank holds such delicious treasures is the river of love, and that rivers have two banks, then we can understand the dialectic of this poem:

#105	Pásame por Dios, barquero, d'aquesa parte del río, duélete del dolor mío.	For the love of God, boatman, take me over to the other shore; have mercy on my sorrow.
	Que si pones dilación en venir a socorrerme, no podrás después valerme, según mi grave pasión. No quieras mi perdición, pues en tu bondad confío, duélete del dolor mío.	If you wait too long in bringing me aid there'll be no way to save me, so great my passion has grown. If you don't wish to see me lost, since I trust in your kindness, have mercy on my sorrow.
	Que d'esa parte se halla descanso de mis tormentos, y en aquesta la batalla de mis tristes perdimientos. ¡Oh ventura! Trae los vientos homildes, mansos, sin brío, duélete del dolor mío.	For on that shore I'll find at last rest from my stormy sorrows, while on this shore all I find is conflict and great losses. Oh fortune, bring me breezes humble, meek and mild, have mercy on my sorrow.

The suffering lover in this poem is trapped on the opposite bank of the river from the bank so lusciously described in the last poem and referred to here as the place where "se halla descanso de mis tormentos." He calls upon the wind to blow gently, for "pasión" and "tormentos" are the forms it takes now, on this shore.

The lover in the following poem, caught in the mountains where the wind blows mercilessly, begs the *serrana* (who is the cause of his torments) to guide him to the river.

#106	Paséisme aor'allá, serrana, que no muera yo en esta montaña.	Take me over, highland lassie, for I'll not die in these mountains.

> Paséisme aor'allende el río,   Lead me across the river,
> que estoy triste, mal herido,   for I am sad and badly wounded,
> que no muera yo en esta   and I'll not die in these mountains.
> montaña.

Again we find the lover wounded and fearing death, but here he fears dying of unrequited love. The "serrana," in other poems of the tradition which we shall see in the next chapter, often functions as the guide who shows the lost traveler a way out of the treacherous windy mountains. Only she can save him from being destroyed by the passion which torments him. But in this poem, he does not just want a way out—he wants to be taken to the river and carried to that other shore where his desires can be fulfilled.

Perhaps he is the same lover who sang this song, and who, having been seduced by the *serrana's* beauty, followed her into the mountain and lost his way:

> #107 Encima del puerto   High on the mountain pass
> vide una serrana: I saw a mountain girl:
> sin duda es galana.   without doubt she is lovely.
>
> Encima del puerto,   High on the mountain pass,
> allá cerca el río,   beside the river,
> vide una serrana   I saw a mountain girl
> del cuerpo garrido;   with such a lively figure;
> sin duda es galana.   without doubt she is lovely.
>
> Encima del puerto,   High on the mountain pass,
> allá cerca el vado,   beside the river,
> vide una serrana   I saw a mountain girl
> del cuerpo lozano;   with such a graceful figure;
> sin duda es galana.   without doubt she is lovely.

If she guides him to the river but refuses to cross to the other side, he may sing with this lover:

> #108 Al río me salgo   I go to the river
> y en su ribera,   and on the bank
> escribo en el agua   I trace in the water
> toda mi pena.   all my sorrows.

The river, in the cyclic journey of water on earth, stands midway between the mountain spring and the sea, and shares symbolic qualities of both. In many poems it is the same *locus amoenus* as the spring—a place where lovers meet, where virginal girls wash their clothes or their hair, or where the rejected lover bemoans the loss of what was once enjoyed in the very same place. In other poems, as we have just seen, it is a barrier which stands between torment on one shore, and bliss on the other. And finally, the river functions interchangeably with the sea as the place from which lovers depart for other lands.

This next mysterious little poem exemplifies the intermediate role of the river in the tradition. Here it is both *locus amoenus* and point of departure simultaneously:

#109   Vi los barcos, madre,   I saw the boats, mother,
       vilos y no me valen.   I saw them and they did me no
                                            good.
       Madre, tres mozuelas,
       non de aquesta villa,   Mother, three maidens
       en aguas corrientes   who aren't from here,
       lavan sus camisas,   in fast-running waters
       sus camisas, madre.   wash their shirts,
       Vilos y no me valen.   mother, their shirts,
                                            I saw them and they did me no
                                            good.

The gender of the speaker is the first mystery the poem presents, since
the *yo* of the poem is present only in the pronoun *me* and the verb form *vi*.
The fact that the poem is addressed to the mother is of no help in
identifying the speaker, since both young men and women confide their
feelings and adventures in the mother. If we look at the situation of the
poem, the confusion grows, because the *estribillo* would suggest that the
speaker is feminine, since women are the ones who watch for a boat that
will return the lover to them. But the gloss would suggest that the
speaker is a young man, for men are the ones who look on admiringly as
women wash.

The second mystery of the poem resides in the one-line
refrain—"vilos y no me valen " The verbal complement "los" refers, of
course, to the boats both times it is repeated, since "mozuelas" and
"camisas," also seen by the speaker, are both feminine. And yet, the
refrain at the end of the gloss has shifted its meaning, so that the "los"
now includes not only the boats, but the girls, the shirts and even the
running waters. Both times the refrain appears, that which "los" refers
to is also the subject of "valen." The refrain functions as a lament—the
implication of the combination of affirmation followed by negation
being that some result was expected from the sight of the ships, but this
expectation was not fulfilled. "No me valen," then, rings with
disappointment. What must be deciphered from the symbology of the
poem is precisely what effect was anticipated from the sight. Let us
attempt to solve these two mysteries by examining this poem's relation
to another poem in the tradition:

#110   Vi eu, mia madr', andar   Mother dear, I saw the boats
         as barcas eno mar;   sailing on the sea,
           e moiro-me d'amor.   and I'm dying of love.

         Foi eu, madre, veer   I went, mother, to see
         as barcas eno ler;   the boats at the shore,
           e moiro-me d'amor.   and I'm dying of love.

         As barcas eno mar   The boats on the sea
         e foi-las aguardar: and I went to await them;
           e moiro-me d'amor.   and I'm dying of love.

As barcas eno ler	The boats at the shore
e foi-las atender:	and I waited for them;
e moiro-me d'amor.	and I'm dying of love.
E foi-las aguardar	And I went to await them
e non o pud'achar:	but I couldn't find him;
e moiro-me d'amor.	and I'm dying of love.
E foi-las atender	And I waited for them,
e non o pudi veer:	but I couldn't see him;
e moiro-me d'amor.	and I'm dying of love.
E non o achei i,	But there I didn't find
o que por meu mal vi:	the one I was unlucky enough to see;
e moiro-me d'amor.	and I'm dying of love.
E non o achei lá,	I didn't find there,
o que vi por meu mal:	the one I was unfortunate enough to see;
e moiro-me d'amor.	and I'm dying of love.

The similarities between the *estribillo* of the other poem and the first stanza of this one are striking. Both begin with the verb "vi" and their complement is the same except that in one the boats are feminine and in the other masculine. Both contain the vocative, "madre." Both consist of a statement of fact, followed by a statement of feeling conditioned by the fact. The first part of each is identical, except that the *cantiga* is more redundant ("as barcas *eno mar*"; "*mia* madre") and explicit (where the boats are, what they are doing). In contrast, the Castilian lyric seems terse, shunning the detail of the *cantiga*. The first word of the second verse condenses that same statement of fact yet further, while repeating its content ("vilos"). The repetition here functions as an echo of her thoughts which are fixated on the sight of the boats. It expresses her clinging to that moment of hope when she first saw them. In the same way, the repetition built into the very structure of the *cantiga* lends it an air of nostalgic cavilation, of returning again and again in memory to an extremely painful experience, reconstructing each detail. Slowly she moves in thought from the moment when she sighted the boats in the sea, to her and the boats' arrival at the shore, her waiting for them to anchor, her search for her lover, the failure of her search, and finally to the conclusion that it was an unhappy hour when she first met him, for love of him has brought her this suffering: "e moiro-me d'amor."[10]

The two phrases "y no me valen" and "e moiro-me d'amor" alike express the subjective reaction of the speaker to the situation, yet the words they choose to express their feelings are indicative of the principal difference in focus between the two poems. While in the *cantiga* the refrain tells explicitly about the "I" of the poem, the position of the "I" in the other remains peripheral to the statement, as indirect object (no *me* valen). Somehow the boats, as subject of *valer*, are made responsible: "they are worthless—to me"; "they are of no comfort—to me." She expected them to bring her relief from her sorrows, and they let her down. Of course the reason she needs comfort is because she, too, is dying of love for the absent lover whose arrival she hoped for. But for her the boats are imbued with life, she personifies them, in a sense, by placing the blame for her disappointment on them. The combination of terseness, the recurring explosive "b" sound, and her choice of words to express her feelings, combine to create a tone of resentment. This resentment is expressed in the *cantiga* as well, "o que por meu mal vi." It is as if an association occurs in the girl's mind between the sight of the disappointing boats and the sight of her lover. The verb *ver* in this context implies not only seeing but falling in love—the two actions are identical—to see him was to love him. One sight brought joy—the sight of her beloved; the other—the sight of the boat—brought sorrow, with the sorrow being a consequence of the joy. Had the sight of her lover not captured her love, the sight of the boats would not make her suffer. Through this contrast, the terrible irony of love emerges, an irony made explicit in this bitter little poem:

#111   Por mi mal te vi,   It was my misfortune to see you,
         el bien que tenía   the happiness which was mine
         en ti lo perdí.   I lost in you.

The "bien" which the speaker once possessed, but lost at the sight of the beloved, is, of course, the innocent unconsciousness of love. Love brings a desire in the lover to hold on to the beloved. Once love is found, the lover wants time to stop, wants the present joy to extend unchanging into the future. But the inexorable march of time cannot be stopped, change continues. However, if one is innocent, has not yet loved, then there is no clinging to the present, there is no fear of losing today's happiness, and consequently no painful suffering when change occurs, no bitter contrast between joy and sorrow, for neither has been experienced.

The radical shift of situation in "Vi los barcos" between the *estribillo* and the gloss disorients the hearer/reader, creating a confusion not unlike that experienced after suffering a great disappointment. There seems to be no relation whatsoever between the situations of the two parts of the poem, except in the mind of the speaker. The gloss describes a scene we have already encountered—virgin girls washing shirts in the river. Thematically the gloss is related to a number of poems in the tradition, but unlike the others, it appears from the situation of the *estribillo* just discussed, that the speaker is a woman. The other poems which describe one or more girls washing in the spring, are spoken by men:

#112 Las tres Maricas de allende,   The three little Marys from over
      cómo lavan y cómo tuercen,   there,
      y tienden tan bonitamente.   see how they wash, see how they
                          wring,
                          and see how they spread in such a
                          lovely way.

The similarities between this poem and the gloss of the other are striking. In both we find *three* women washing, and in both the women are strangers in town. In this one the "Maricas" perform three actions: *lavar*, suggestive through association with water and the ritual preparation for an encounter with the lover; *torcer*, with the suggestiveness of *volver*, of mixing and twisting—like the girl in "Enas verdes ervas" who weaves golden ribbons in her hair; and *tender*, which, when we recall the action of the wind on the girl's shirts in "Levantou-s-a velida," suggests that these girls spread out their washed clothes and themselves in expectation of the wind's involvement. The three verbs indicate the primary interest of the speaker, who in observing the washing girls, is enchanted by their movements. That last verse, "tienden tan bonitamente," makes explicit this effect which their actions have on the speaker through his expression of his subjective reaction to the sight—he finds it delightfully seductive.

While the situation described in the gloss is identical, that is, the speaker witnesses the scene of three girls from another town washing in the stream, the focus of the poem is radically different. Perhaps through examining the focus of the speaker, the incongruity between the situation and the gender of the speaker can be reconciled. Again there are three girls washing who are called "mozuelas," indicating their youth and virginity, and who are "non de aquesta villa," a descriptive phrase with a semantic import identical to "de allende" of the other poem. But "de allende" is a positive description, and one which suggests mystery—they are from beyond, from some unknown place. That phrase seems to reinforce the mysterious attraction which the girls' movements have on the speaker. "Non de aquesta villa," though signifying the same thing, suggests something different. Being a negative statement, it emphasizes the "not-belonging" of the girls, their foreignness. Furthermore, the last word, "villa," produces a phonetic echo of the repeated "b" sounds of the *estribillo*, which contributed to the tone of resentment heard in the first part. "Non de aquesta villa," then, sounds like a prolongation of this resentment, paralleling the negation of "no me valen."

The gloss goes on to state, in the third verse, the location of the scene being described. The three "mozuelas" wash in running waters. In the other poem, the speaker's attention was focused on the provocative activity of the "Maricas" and he expressed no interest in the place where

he saw them. The running waters of this poem are emphasized by the
speaker because they are significant to her. The waters themselves
suggest sexuality, and here the fact that they run or flow points to rapid,
excited motion. Remember the "arroyuelo bullicioso" which splashed
the girl who in that poem assures her mother that she will not go back to
it. Bubbling water connotes the same thing as a strong wind—sexual
excitement, churned-up passion.

In the fourth verse of the gloss, the speaker finally describes the
action of the three girls—they wash their shirts. Here the verb is merely
a statement of fact, and their actions hold no particular attraction for
the speaker. But what they perform the action upon is of great interest,
for she repeats it: "lavan sus camisas,/sus camisas, madre." Like the
repetition of "vilos" in the *estribillo*, this repetition of "camisas" indicates
where the speaker's consciousness has been snagged—the image of the
shirts obsesses her. In several poems we have seen girls washing their or
their lovers' shirts. This activity alludes to an imminent encounter with
the lover, for whom they ceremonially prepare. She repeats "sus
camisas" as she repeated "los barcos" (implicit in "-los"). Both are
significant visual images which obsess her. They are similar sights, in a
way—the shirts are white, the sails of the boat are white; the shirts float
in the water while being washed, the boats floated in the water. Perhaps
both shirts and sails are also impregnated by the wind. The sight of the
shirts leads her thoughts in opposite directions simultaneously—
towards the happy memory of occasions when she, too, like the
"mozuelas" washed in preparation for the arrival of the beloved; and
towards the bitter memory of her dashed hopes, aroused and destroyed
by the sight of the boats. The ironic contrast between these two
memories provokes her bitter repetition of the refrain "vilos y no me
valen." The object of "vi" no longer refers only to the boats, but now to
this other sight, which in its joyfulness, makes her pain harder to bear.
The resentment contained in "no me valen" has grown stronger, for not
only was the sight of the boats painful, but the sight of someone else's
happiness is unbearable. Mixed with her resentment, now, is envy of
the three fortunate girls—who are not even from around here!

This bitter contrast between another's joy and one's own misery is
the theme of this poem, as well:

#113 Dos ánades, madre,   Two geese, mother,
        que van por aquí,   that pass by here
        mal penan a mí.   cause me great sorrow.

        Dos ánades, madre,   Two geese, mother,
        del cuerpo gentil   with graceful shape
        al campo de flores   in the flowering meadows
        iban a dormir;   were going to sleep;
        mal penan a mí.   and cause me great sorrow.

Here the sight of the two happy water fowl, graceful in their mutual love, going off to sport in a field of flowers, reminds the speaker of her own lover and her own loneliness, and consequently "mal penan a mí." The speaker here, as in the refrain of the other poem, implicitly blames the birds for her misery, making them the cause of her sorrow. In both poems the painful scene is described externally, with the speaker functioning as an observer outside the action. Having concluded her description she then expresses the effect it has had on her: "mal penan a mí," "no me valen."

The importance of sight, by far the most frequently mentioned of the five modes of perception, will be discussed shortly. It can provoke love, sorrow or joy, and it can provide solace, as suggested by *valer*:

#114	De las dos hermanas, dose,	Of the two sisters, two,
	válame la gala de la menore.	may the beauty of the younger do me good.

Here the speaker hopes that the enticing sight of the younger sister will bring him relief from his yearning for love. From the festive tone of the poem, it seems he has cause for hope and will not be forced to complain, with the speaker of our other poem, "no me vale."

Returning now to "Vi los barcos", we can summarize our interpretation of the poem thus: the speaker is indeed a girl who, upon returning home, describes to her mother the sights she saw on her excursion to the shore to look for her lover among those arriving on the boats. The *estribillo* sounds like the answer to a tacit question posed, verbally or not, by a mother who knew where she was going and eagerly awaits the outcome of the trip. The girl's answer amounts to "Well, I saw the ships but they did not do me any good." While talking, the memory of the boats triggers an association with another sight she has just witnessed on her way home, a sight which she resents because of the contrast it forces her to make with her own unhappy situation—a contrast not only between their happiness and her own misery, but also between her own former contentment and its loss. Here again we find that relentless movement of time, with the change it inevitably brings, dragging its bitter irony into the once-tranquil consciousness of a once-innocent girl.

The beauty and power of this poem derive from the juxtaposition of two associative clusters related to water: the spring or river as the place where lovers meet; and the ocean as the place where lovers separate. The contrast between the two produces in the consciousness of the speaker and the reader/hearer the painful realization of time's effect, through the tension of opposition.

The excruciating pain of separation is beautifully expressed in the following poem, from the departing lover's point of view. He experiences the separation as a split, a dismembering of himself.

#115 Apartar-me-hâo de vos,   They'll take me from you,
      garrido amor!   dearest love.

      Eu amei hûa senhora   I loved a lady
      de todo meu coraçâo;   with all my heart
      quis Deus a minha ventura   but God willed it to be my fate
      que nâo m'a querem dar nâo,   that they won't give her to me,
      garrido amor!   dearest love.

      Nâo me vos querem dare,   They won't give you to me;
      irme hei a tierras agenas,   to strange lands I will go
      a chorar meu pesare,   to bemoan my fate,
      garrido amor!   dearest love.

      Ja vedes minha partida,   You watch my departure;
      os meus olhos ja se vâo;   my eyes must now go,
      se me parte minha vida,   my very life is going,
      ca me fica o coraçâo.   here remains my heart.

Here the situation is very specific: the beloved's parents refused to
allow her to marry him, and hence he departs to bemoan his sorrow in
foreign lands. But the emotion is universal among those who suffer
separation. The eyes with which he saw her, which relished her
beauty, are leaving. The eyes of the beloved watch as his eyes depart,
but his heart, no longer his own, remains behind. The severing of the
bond between eye and heart becomes more painfully acute when we
realize their relationship—the eyes speak to the heart, while the heart
speaks through the eyes.

Many of the lyrics associated with the departure-by-sea motif
partake of a delicious ambiguity afforded by the image of the sea as the
dangerous depths of love.

#116 ¡Plegue a Dios que te anegues,   I hope to God you sink,
      nave enemiga!   you wicked enemy ship!
      Pero, no, que me llevas   But no, for you are carrying
      dentro la vida.   my life on board.

Here the speaker is, on one level, a woman watching the departure of
the boat which carries her lover. The boat, then, is the enemy, and she
wishes for it to sink, as a punishment for robbing her of her lover. But
suddenly she realizes that if the boat sinks, her lover, too, will go
under. At the same time, the speaker could be a man who sees his
beloved as the ship on the sea of love which has robbed him of his
heart. She does not return his love, and hence he wishes to see her
destroyed, but then her destruction would also be his own.

The double meaning of the sea is made explicit in this poem, in
which the *estribillo* points to an actual separation that causes forgetfulness, while the gloss utilizes this image metaphorically, to complain of
the beloved's disdain:

#117 Después que la mar pasé,   Now that I've crossed the sea,
      vida mía, olvidástesme.   my love, you've forgotten me.

Después que en el mar de amor	Now that I've entered the sea of
entré a ser tu servidor,	love
dasme tan gran disfavor	to be your loving slave,
que pienso no escaparé.	you treat me so unkindly
	I think I can't escape.

The sea causes separation and separation causes forgetfulness; hence this complaint:

#118 Frescos ventecillos	Sweet little breezes,
favor os pido,	I beg you for kindness,
que me anego en las olas	for I'm drowning in waves
del mar de olvido.	on the sea of forgetfulness.

In the next poem the threat the sea poses is not of being forgotten, but of being overpowered by the passion of love. Having embarked on this sea of love, a traitorous wind arises—the winds of his sexual desire—which threaten to drown him, to destroy him in the way we discussed before—loss of self.

#119 Embarquéme en mar de amar;	I embarked on the sea of love;
en el golfo estoy de amor,	in the gulf of love I sail,
un viento llevo traidor:	blown by a traiterous wind:
¡ay Dios, si me he de anegar!	Oh God, am I to drown!

And in this poem the sea is identified with the beloved:

#120 Alta mar esquiva	Fickle high seas,
de ti doy querella,	of you I complain;
házesme que viva	you make me live
triste y con gran pena.	in sorrow and pain.

Sea and woman alike are deep and fickle. His beloved causes the same suffering which the sea brings to separated lovers. The poem functions equally well in the voice of the lonely waiting girl and in the voice of the rejected lover.

Not all of the many poems that play upon this double meaning of the sea are complaints. In the next, the situation would also seem to suggest sorrow, portraying again the beloved who remains behind watching her lover depart, but the tone of the poem belies this interpretation. Maybe it is the other end of the separation—the moment of return:

#121 Alcé los ojos,	I raised my eyes,
miré la mar,	looked at the sea,
vi a mis amores	my lover sailing
a la vela andar.	I did see.

From whichever end one wishes to view it, the poem functions on another level altogether if one understands the sea again as the sea of love, and remembers the covert suggestiveness of the verb *andar*. And the sail which permits this "walking" of course, does so because it catches the wind! He walks "a la vela," filled with passion.

Similarly the tone and content of this next poem do not appear to fit, if one understands it as another departure poem.

#122 La barca de lo mi amore, 　　lo farirá, 　　la barca de lo mi amore, 　　que esta noche partirá.	The ship of my love, my love and my heart, the ship of my love tonight will depart.

The speaker states that her lover's boat sets sail tonight, but she uses such a gleeful tone that one suspects she is really talking about a much more pleasant event she expects will occur tonight. A departure, perhaps, from the shore of torment, through the waters of love, to that other sensuously luxuriant shore described in poem #104 of our study.

When the departure by sea is understood thus, as a symbol of the sexual act, as immersion in the waters of love, then the oar takes on a special significance as a phallic instrument dipping into the waters of female sexuality, churning and stirring in the back-and-forth movement by now familiar to us. Observe the symbolism of the oar in this trio of lyrics:

#123 ¡Cómo retumban los remos, 　　madre, en el agua, 　　con el fresco viento 　　de la mañana!	How the oars resound in the waters, mother, with the fresh breezes of morning.
#124 Vaste, amore: 　　¡Quién fuera agora el remadore! 　　Amor y vaste: 　　¡Quién fuera agora el que 　　　remase!	You're leaving, my love. Would that I were the oarsman! My love and you leave. How I wish I were rowing!
#125 Salen de Sevilla 　　barquetes nuevos, 　　de una verde aya 　　llevan los remos.	Brand new skiffs sail out from Seville waving oars of green ash.

All three of these poems, of course, can be read as departure songs sung by the girl left behind. In the first, the dreadful roar of the oars in the water could be heard as a contrast to the fresh morning breeze. The departure of the lover, then, would stand in ironic opposition to the seductive morning, the time of day when the lovers come together. But at the same time, read as a symbolically sensuous description of the morning's power to awaken amorous feelings, the sound of the oars churning the water, like the stag stirring the clear spring waters, merges with the blowing of the fresh morning breeze.

In the second, the symbolic import of "remo" as masculine instrument is secondary to the more obvious meaning—the abandoned girl yearns to be aboard her lover's ship. But when we switch the gender of the speaker, then the poem reads as a naughty *piropo*. An admiring young man catches sight of a lovely girl and wishes he could be the rower who churns her waters.

If, in the last poem, the oar is, indeed, a symbol of virility, then there arises a new associative potential in tree symbolism. The tree possesses a symbolic ambiguity, afforded primarily by its shape, that permits it to function at both the masculine and feminine symbolic poles of this tradition. The poem can be read, then, as an admiring description of both the attractive new boats and the lusty young—and sexually inexperienced (green)—men they carry. Perhaps implicit in the emphasis placed on their youthfulness is a wistful regret that such young men must go off to war, and possible death. From the feminine perspective, they are wasted.

Our study of water symbolism in the tradition has led us from the mountain spring where love begins, to the sea, where very often love ends with the separation of the lovers. The sea as a body of water, as the vast repository of the life fluid which emanates from the earth and flows over and through its contours, enjoys all the associative potentials of the other water symbols. Like the spring and the river, it, too, can be the meeting place of lovers at dawn. It can even be the site of the highly significant washing activities associated with the spring and the river. Furthermore, we have seen its function as the great separator of lovers and how, consequently, its shore becomes symbolic of the long waiting and hopeless despair of the girl left behind. The merging of its two primary symbolic roles—waters of love, waters of separation—affords the sea its associative potential as death. But we have seen that this death is, at the very least, highly ambiguous in its meaning. Because, in fact, the sea does swallow countless lovers, young and old, the death it represents is, on one level, the termination of life. Yet on another level, drowning by sea represents not actual death, but transformation of the self through love. The virgin girl's submersion in the spring waters as a ceremonial preparation for her lover is in itself a symbolic act which corresponds to this drowning by sea (and also relates to the symbolism of baptism). When she steps into the spring she is manifesting her readiness for this transformation. As we have seen repeatedly, the impulse to submit to this experience which will transform her being often runs counter to her will. But the force of this relentless natural urge is beyond her control, and she ultimately submits.

One last aspect of the sea—its power—remains to be examined, and this aspect will link the sea with a symbol which is its apparent opposite. From the beginning of this chapter we have regarded water as an archetypal representation of the feminine: it surges from the breast of the earth, it is deep, dark, mysterious, cold; before being stirred by the wind or the stag it is clear and pure. When all these passive, feminine waters run together into the great sea, their various symbolic levels likewise merge and empty into a symbol which suddenly acquires a characteristic that was hidden, lying latent and scattered beneath the individual symbols—the vast *power* of water. To be sure, we recognized that the attraction of the waters was greater than the virgin's conscious resistance, but nowhere has the immensity of its power revealed itself as majestically as it appears in this next poem.

Because of the sea's many associative potentials, the *situation* of this poem can be interpreted in various ways. The levels of meaning in the poem, however, should not be seen as alternative interpretations, but as congruent and complementary suggestions which fuse into a single expression of an essentially ineffable human feeling. The poem communicates this feeling—or experience—through their simultaneous apprehension by the hearer.

#126   Sedia-m'eu na ermida de San Simion
    e cercaron-mi as ondas, que grandes son:
        eu atendend'o meu amigo,
        eu atendend'o meu amigo!

I was visiting the chapel of Saint Simeon
when waves that were immense surrounded me.
    My own true love I did await,
    My own true love I did await.

    Estando na ermida ant'o altar,
e cercaron-mi as ondas grandes do mar:
        eu atendend'o meu amigo,
        eu atendend'o meu amigo!

In the chapel I was standing before the altar
and was surrounded by immense waves of the sea.
    My own true love I did await,
    My own true love I did await.

    E cercaron-mi as ondas, que grandes son,
non ei i barqueiro, nen remador:
        eu atendend'o meu amigo,
        eu atendend'o meu amigo!

When waves that were immense surrounded me,
neither boatsman nor oarsman had I to rescue me.
    My own true love I did await,
    My own true love I did await.

    E cercaron-mi as ondas do alto mar,
non ei i barqueiro, nen sei remar:
        eu atendend'o meu amigo,
        eu atendend'o meu amigo!

And was surrounded by immense waves of the sea;
I have no boatsman and know not how to row.
    My own true love I did await,
    My own true love I did await.

    Non ei i barqueiro, nen remador,
morrerei fremosa no mar maior:
        eu atendend'o meu amigo,
        eu atendend'o meu amigo!

Neither boatsman nor oarsman had I to rescue me;
I will die, beautiful, in the great deep sea.
    My own true love I did await,
    My own true love I did await.

    Non ei i barqueiro, nen sei remar,
morrerei fremosa no alto mar:
        eu atendend'o meu amigo,
        eu atendend'o meu amigo!

I have no boatsman and know not how to row;
I will die, beautiful, in the great high sea.
    My own true love I did await,
    My own true love I did await.

No matter how the poetic situation is understood, certain aspects of the poem remain common to all its various possible levels of interpretation. The speaker is a girl ("fremosa" by her own description) who waits for her lover on the edge of a stormy sea, at the shrine of St. Simeon. Though we know she waits for her lover, we do not know just how imminent his arrival is, nor the cause of his absence. This lack of detail affords the poem its semantic ambiguity, and hence its expressive wealth.

The situational vagueness stems mainly from the opening line of the poem, which is, in essence, repeated in the first verse of the second stanza. The experience which the poem describes occurs while the speaker is visiting the shrine of St. Simeon, and this location contains several possible associations. She may be there to pray for the safe and speedy return of her lover who is across the sea. But more likely, she has probably arranged to meet her lover at the shrine, since in the tradition religious festivities provide excellent cover-ups for clandestine trysts between youthful lovers who are not free to meet openly and at will. Remember the young girl who recounted in great detail to her mother the adventures of the pilgrimage which she had undertaken in solitude ("por ir más devota"), and which ended with a most devotional encounter under the "encina." This idea of the pilgrimage as a meeting place for lovers is most pronounced in the *cantigas*. It is noteworthy that the mothers of these eager girls are accomplices, willing or not, to their daughters' encounters with the sexual experience:

#127 Pois nossas madres vam a San Simon
de Val de Prados candeas queimar,
nos, as meninhas, punhemos d'andar
con nossas madres, e elas enton
 queimen candeas por nós e por si
 e nós, meninhas, bailaremos i.

Nossos amigos todos lá iram
por nos veer e andaremos nós
bailand'ant'eles, fremosas, en cós,
e nossas madres, pois que alá van,
 queimen candeas por nós e por si
 e nós, meninhas, bailaremos i.

Nossos amigos iram por cousir
como bailamos e poden veer
bailar moças de mui bon parecer,
e nossas madres, pois lá queren ir,

Since our mothers are going to Saint Simon
at Meadow Valley to light votive candles,
let's us, young things, try to walk along
with them, and then our mothers
 can burn candles for us and for themselves
 while we, girls, go off and dance.

All our suitors will be there
to see us and we will dance
before them, beautiful, in chemises, without capes,
and our mothers, since they're going there
 can burn candles for us and for themselves
 while we, girls, go off and dance.

Our suitors will go there to watch
how we dance and they can see
very good-looking girls perform,
and our mothers, since they want to go,

| queimen candeas por nós e por si | can burn candles for us and themselves, |
| e nós, meninhas, bailaremos i. | while we, girls, go off and dance. |

The expectantly festive tone of this *cantiga* provides an excellent and importantly suggestive contrast to the tone of the poem we are now concerned with. If indeed the girl who fears death from the pounding waves has come to St. Simeon to meet her lover, one wonders why she does not express the joyous excitement appropriate to her expectations of union with the lover. There are two equally valid explanations: she may indeed expect his arrival momentarily, and as the moment of truth approaches, she is overwhelmed by a realization of the seriousness of the transformation she is about to undergo; or perhaps her anxious excitement has slowly been replaced by a deepening sense of despair as she comes to realize that her lover is not going to appear— that she has been abandoned.

It is extremely important for the reader to understand that the poem does not offer us a choice between two valid interpretations, but rather that their simultaneous existence heightens the expressive force of the poem which really is not concerned with a situation. It is concerned with a feeling, or better yet, with the intensity of that feeling. Whether the feeling stems from hope or despair is unimportant. Of far greater importance is the fact that it *can* stem from either. In other words, hope and despair are merely two ends or poles of the same passion, a passion represented by the immense power of the sea. Overwhelming, powerful passion is the poem's subject and the situational ambiguity enhances its expression, in the same way that temporal ambiguity expands the expressive potential of traditional poetry. In fact, notice the elegant progression of verb tenses in this poem—the movement from the past tenses through the present, into the future—which indeed intensifies the immediacy of the feeling the poem expresses, while at the same time contributing to the important vagueness of the situation. Time and space are transcended in the inner world of emotion.

The emotion is the focus of the poem, and the heart of the emotion is expressed through the two semantic units which float and crest four times each in the heart of the poem: "cercaron-mi as ondas..." and "non ei i barqueiro, nen..." Each time these units appear their completion either varies slightly or alternates like successive waves, the same yet different. Three of the endings to "cercaron-mi as ondas" express the size, the power of the waves with the adjective "grandes." But the last time the unit occurs, it ends with "do alto mar." Syntactically this ending is closest to that of the second line of the second stanza "...ondas grandes do mar," and phonetically it echoes the first verse of that stanza "ant'o altar." It is as if structurally the repetition builds and peaks in this verse "e cercaron-mi as ondas do alto mar"—the last pounding crash after which the speaker's consciousness admits the inevitability of her death.

The notion of death pulls like an undertow from the very first lines of the poem. St. Simeon himself draws our attention to death, for he symbolizes in Christian tradition the death of the old order which, before it expires, welcomes the new. Ancient Simeon would not die until he held the infant Messiah in his arms. Significantly, he points simultaneously to death and new life. The altar before which the girl in the poem stands does the same thing, for as the sacrificial table it is where the dead or the sacrificed is transformed or made sacred. So while the poem's fatal undertow is death, it is also new life.

When the waves reach their peak in the first line of the fourth stanza, their power is described through a word so richly suggestive that it transcends the duality of life's current, a word which touches the notion of primordial power—the force that infuses the masculine and the feminine, the wind and the water, the mountain and the sea. That word is "alto,"[11] here an adjective modifying "mar." Frequently, however, it stands alone with the same semantic import of high turbulent, and simultaneously, unfathomably deep seas. But remember how crucial that same word was in a context diametrically opposed to the sea—the mountain, "eno alto," where our virgin girl met the force of the lusty wind. Height and depth are not opposed, they are the extremes of one notion—vertical space. Hope and despair are not opposite emotions, they are the extremes of one emotion—desire. Thus when our singer tells us that she is surrounded by waves "do alto mar," she is telling us of her impotence, her fear, her excitement, the great force of the passion in which she sees death, whether that death springs from the peaks of pleasure, or from the depths of despair. She is the sacrificial victim on the altar, and despite her fear, she is able to glimpse the transformation, the new life on the other side of experience. She hints at this realization through the beauty which lies embedded like a seed in her acceptance of death—"morrerei *fremosa* no alto mar." Again semantic and syntactical ambiguity, like a prism, scatter a rainbow of suggestions onto the poem. If she is suggesting an awareness of the beauty of this death, then "fremosa" indicates her excitement at the prospect of union with her lover. If it is strictly an adjective which indicates how she views herself in this storm of despair, then her awareness of her own beauty is an awareness of the bitter irony of love—that her beauty has no power over the inexorable flux of life.

When we look carefully at the other major semantic unit in the poem "non ei i barqueiro, nen sei remar (nen remador)," we have to notice again how critical the situational ambiguity is to the expressive power of the poem. On the one hand the girl has told us that she is at a shrine on the ocean shore. Suddenly she tells us that she does not have anyone to save her ("non ei i barqueiro") and she cannot save herself ("nen sei remar"). Is she sitting on a rock which she reached when the tide was low, but now the tide is moving in and she is stranded? Does she want a boat as some means of reaching her lover who is on the ocean's other shore? Again the vagueness permits a variety of inter-pretations, but the essential notion is that she has no resources, within or without, which might save her from this sacrificial death. Her insistent repetition of this sense of helplessness creates the vital contrast with the ocean's might which is the source of the poem's expressive energy. Small, helpless and beautiful she can only wait passively ("eu atendend'o meu amigo,/eu atendend'o meu amigo"— repetition upon repetition, wave after wave) for the awesome moment of transformation to be wrought by the immense power "do alto mar."[12]

---

[1] Egla Morales Blouin has written an excellent study of the symbolic function of both water and deer in her recent book, El ciervo y la fuente (Madrid, 1981).

[2] alva: es lo mesmo que la aurora, que es el resplandor del sol que alumbra el aire y las nubes, antes de echar sus rayos en el emisferio, en donde amanece... los Gentiles hazian a la aurora una deidad, figurandola como una ninfa muy hermosa vestida de blanco y rociada de aljofar con gran gallardia y gentileza. (Covarrubias)

[3] The word "alto" could be considered a synonym for "río," as M. Alvar López demonstrates in his excellent study, Cantos de boda judeo-españoles (Madrid, 1971), p. 90 n. 33. Macedo points out in his discussion of this poem in Do cancioneiro de amigo, p. 58 n. 4, that "alto" often means "high seas" in medieval Galician poetry. He rejects such a reading of the word in this context as being semantically incongruous, since the maiden would hardly wash her clothes in salty ocean water. He, therefore, prefers "heights" as the meaning of "alto" in this poem. While I, too, have chosen to read "alto" as "heights," I believe that "river" offers an equally valid interpretation (see poem #245). It would, however, limit the sense of upward motion which is implicit in the poem.

[4] On the implications of washing or sewing a shirt, see S. G. Armistead and J. H. Silverman, Judeo-Spanish Ballad Chapbooks, p. 303, n. 14.

[5] lucha: una suerte de exercicio gymnastico, en que abraçandose dos, cada qual procura dar con su contrario en tierra. (Covarrubias)

[6] Alan Deyermond has written a perceptive study of this symbol of the stag in his article, "Pero Meogo's Stags and Fountains: Symbol and Anec-dote in the Traditional Lyric," RPh 33 (1979). p. 280. See also Morales Blouin, El ciervo y la fuente, Chapter 6.

[7] See again Edith Rogers, The Perilous Hunt, p. 92, on washing and plaiting the hair.

[8] On the door and its symbolism see Aguirre's article in N. D. Sher-gold's Studies of the Spanish and Portuguese Ballad, pp. 53-72.

[9] garça: es ave conocida comunmente de plumaje blanco, y en si hermosa. (Covarrubias)

¹⁰ In her article on "Parallelism in the Medieval Portuguese Lyric," *MLR* 50:3 (1955), p. 281-87, Dorothy Atkinson discusses the emotional intensity achieved through the apparently limiting structure of the *cantigas de amigo*, and cites this poem as an example of sorrowful emotion intensified through repetition.

¹¹ *alto*: el lugar levantado, como monte, peñasco, torre: y lo demás que tiene en si altura: Transfierese al animo, y sinifica cosa escondida, profunda, como alto misterio, alto pensamiento... Alto se toma muchas vezes por profundo como en alta mar; otras vezes se toma por el cielo, como el de lo alto, el Dios de las alturas. (Covarrubias)

¹² See also Reckert's comments on this poem in *Do cancioneiro de amigo*, pp. 131-37. Bruce Wardropper discusses the subtle implications of meaning achieved through the poem's parallelistic structure, in his article, "On the Supposed Repetitiousness of the *Cantigas d'amigo*," *RHM* 38 (1974-75), 1-6.

❧ 3 ❧

Fire

IN ORDER TO UNDERSTAND the symbolism of the fiery essence, let us pause a moment to reflect upon what has been observed thus far in our studies of wind and water. The quality of motion is crucial to their symbolic roles, because they are vehicles of change, transformation. But motion implies space, movement from one point to another. In the case of the wind, we saw that its objective is either the virgin girl or one of the other symbols that correspond to her—shirts , hair, trees, sea. But from where does that wind which seeks the feminine emanate? Since the air envelops the space surrounding the earth, it links sky and earth, and from its power to burn we may discern its source in the sun. The relationship between sun and wind as emitter and emissary—breather and breath —is evident in a *cantiga* already discussed at length, "Levantou-s'a velida."

The first two lines of the poem established a correspondence between the dawn and the virgin girl, since both arise simultaneously and the same word refers to them both (*alva*). We discussed the fact that the very notion of dawn in the tradition implies the rising of the virgin, but we did not mention an equally inevitable rising which dawn implies. That is the rising of the wind, naturally and symbolically inherent in the rising of the sun. When the sun comes up, its warmth stirs the air and precipitates the movement known as thermal currents. Any peasant girl is well aware of this phenomenon and consequently, she chooses to do her washing at dawn in order to take advantage of the wind's activity to dry her clothes. Having realized, then, that the "velida" was conscious of the presence of the wind on the mountain top at dawn, her anger with it becomes playfully ironic. The wind and the girl are engaged in a mock battle, but how can they really be in conflict, for their encounter is the result of a mutual attraction? The sun need never appear in the poem, and yet from the very first word, "Levantou," its presence is felt, and indeed conditions the action of the whole poem. The sun rises, and when it does, all of creation is set in motion. Thus begins the eternal play of apparent opposites in a series of games involving two energy poles: hide and seek, pitch and catch, or like this poem, mock battle. But the sun stands behind it all. When the sun gets up, its warmth attracts the girl like a magnet, and she is pulled irresistibly to the mountain. There she encounters the emissary of the sun—the wind—which transmits to her the sun's energy, either by communicating to her its own quality of motion ("yéndome y viniendo") or by burning her skin. Hence we see that the wind is really not a force in itself, but rather is a vehicle or messenger who bears the masculine energy to the feminine, its objective. The sun's masculine energy seeks completion in the feminine, and the wind is that which bridges the two, the sun and the earth. The wind transforms the girl by infusing her with the sun's energy, so that she, too, is set in motion and yearns for completion. Passion is contagious. The sun, pure activity, stimulates the air, which in turn stimulates the girl, and union is sought by both.

And how is this union represented in the tradition? By the sea. Water lies buried deep within the earth from whence it springs to eventually meet the air. And where do these springs of water first appear? High in the mountains, where the wind is born under the sun's heat. The movement of both wind and water begins on the mountain top, but their union is not effected on the heights. Once born, expelled from the depths of its mother earth, the water begins its travels over and through the sundry landscapes of the mother's breast till it reaches the ocean. The air, once set in motion by the sun's heat, travels swiftly and freely. Water, however, once exiled from the earth's womb, remains tied to the mother source, hugs her tightly as it flows to the sea. Perhaps in this natural order lies the germ of the unique relationship between mother and daughter which will be explored in the final chapter. Water, like wind, is in constant motion, but water moves passively, and ultimately receives the action of the wind. When the energy the sun imparts to the wind is great, huge waves are created on the ocean's surface, waves which engulf lovers, bringing a death which is really transformation. This union of opposites, of male and female, is represented by drowning, by immersion in water.

The point of this brief review of what has been discussed about wind and water is to note that these symbols are essentially *effluences*, that which flows out from the two poles of existence: the masculine and the feminine. Wind emanates and flows from the sun, bearing its energy and actively seeking completion in the feminine. Water emanates and flows from the earth, bearing its energy and passively attracting fulfillment from its opposite. Masculine energy moves vertically from the heights, the sun, the mountain, to the earth's depths. Feminine energy moves horizontally, spreads itself out, waiting for the sun's energy to be brought by the wind.

The wind and the water are the most common masculine and feminine symbols in the tradition, but they are not the masculine and feminine essences. These are the sun and the earth. However, though they are the magnetic poles around which symbols gravitate, and the energy sources which set the symbols of the tradition in perpetual motion due to the tension they create, the sun and the earth are not themselves symbols. All the symbols of the tradition are in flux, imbued with now more, now less masculine or feminine energy. None is pure. But the sun and the earth are pure as principles, and consequently do not enter into the back-and-forth motion—the game—which results from the tension between active and passive energies which they embody.

Though the sun itself hardly engages in the game of life played out by the tradition's symbols, it is represented in that game by a very complex symbol—the eye. The eye, like the sun, emits energy. This correspondence between the two has been evident to man in all cultures and at all times, and can be seen in his perception of the sun as the all-seeing eye of god. When the eye of god opens, when the sun emits its energy, its light, the very opening, the very emission of light permits the perception of earthly activity. Its activity permits its passivity.

The simultaneously active and passive roles of the eyes are evident in this poem which presents a situation oddly reminiscent of the situation in the last poem discussed, "Sedia-m'eu na ermida..." In both poems a woman stands alone by the sea which reflects her inner, emotional condition.

#128   Miraba la mar   On the sea gazed
          la mal casada   the sorry bride,
          que miraba la mar   who gazed on the sea
          como es ancha y larga.   so deep and wide.

What first strikes us from the juxtaposition of this poem and the last is the contrast in tone. This sea is as placid as the other was turbulent. The repeated "m" and "a" sounds imbue the poem with a murmuring air of quietude. Whereas the stormy sea was masculine, this tranquil sea is feminine. Crashing waves are produced by strong winds that blow from the mountain—the winds from "o alto" create a sea which is "alto." But in this poem the wind is quiet, the breath of the masculine aggressive power remains on the mountain top. And that is precisely the problem, what makes this woman a *"mal* casada."

The sea is spread out—wide and long—waiting for the wind, like the shirts spread out by the mountain stream. Horizontal dimensions are of interest in this poem, whereas in the last the direction was vertical—deep seas, high crashing waves. It is hardly surprising that verticality should be associated in the tradition with sexual force, creative energy, or simply power, since the erection of vertical monuments, overtly phallic or not, universally symbolizes just this force. In this poem both the feminine passive sea and the unfulfilled young wife yearn for some vertical force to disturb their smooth waiting surface.

Again, the sea may suggest separation, and her gazing upon it may indicate her frustrated hope to witness her husband's return. Its flat expanse, then, would deepen her despair, since nothing—no hoped-for oar—stirs its waters.

But our attention now is drawn to the verb *mirar*.[1] Besides participating in the phonetic suggestiveness of the song, *mirar* is the first word of the poem, and also its only verb of action. In a certain sense it is a linking verb, not a verb of action at all, for the gaze is really a bridge between the "mal casada" and the spacious sea. Her gaze not only links them, it equates them, it melds them into a single whole, so that girl and sea become the yearning, feminine void awaiting fulfillment. The placid expanse of water fills her tranquil gaze, so that the sight of the sea, expressed in the opening verse, is then repeated—reflected—in the wide placid pools of her eyes, like the repetition of the first verse in the third. Girl, eyes, and sea partake of the same qualities—"ancha y larga."

There occurs a marvelous circularity in the first three verses—the girl who looks at the sea looks at the sea. She is described in the adjectival clause "que miraba la mar" by the very action which she performs in the main clause. But "que" is another ambiguous word. It is indeed a relative subject pronoun of an adjectival clause, yet it could equally well be that mysterious, indefinable "que" which begins so many traditional lyrics, and which gives the impression that the speaker is beginning her song in the middle of an ongoing train of thought.

#129	Que mis penas parecen	For my sorrows are like
	olas de la mar	the waves of the sea,
	porque unas vienen	because some always come
	cuando otras van.	when others recede.

In both these sea poems "que" suggests a pensive, almost meditative repetition in harmony with the images of the sea that they present.

The eyes of the "malcasada" reflect the sea, whose energy enters her being through the eyes. In *looking* she performs an action and receives its effect. This is the stupefyingly complex role of the eyes. Like suns they exhale the procreative energy—the wind,—and like the sea they spread themseles wide to receive that energy. What a narcissistic and paradoxical symbol!

The "malcasada," by the action of looking at the sea, permits the image of the sea to enter her eye. The sun by looking at the earth, sends her its energy, which returns having been reflected by her. The circularity of the eye's activity is dizzying.

#130	Soles claros son	Shining suns
	tus ojuelos bellos,	are your lovely eyes,
	oro los cabellos,	hair of gold,
	fuego el corazón.	heart of fire.

This is the song of praise of a young man enchanted by the charms of his beloved. Her eyes, whose innocence and purity are expressed by the diminutive, are radiant like the sun. Her hair, too, emits golden rays. Eyes and hair send forth an energy, which penetrates the singing lover through his eyes. He never mentions his own eyes and yet it is clear that they must be the point of entry of this energy, for the sources of the energy are features of her physical being which he *sees*. The final verse, with its image of fire, parallels the image of heat and light contained in "soles" and "oro." But what is aflame is *his* heart, as well as hers. He is not describing in the last verse a third sight—her heart—but rather he expresses the effect which the sight of her eyes and hair have had on his heart. The energy which flows from the radiance of her eyes and hair, while it may have emanated from the flames of passion in her heart, has been absorbed by his own eyes and transmitted to his heart, which catches fire. The fire which her eyes emit is communicated to him through his own eyes. What is communication? The act of making two individual entities common, of binding them into one, so that they share one essence, one experience.

The speaker in this poem recognizes the communicative power of the eyes when she exhorts them:

#131	Ojos, dezíselos vos	Eyes, tell him these things
	con mirar,	with your look,
	pues sabéys también hablar.	for you, too, are able to talk.

She feels love and desire and wants the lover to understand and respond to her passion. Being a woman she ought to be passive. She cannot command the object of her desire to come out and let her passion burn him, so instead she resorts to the silent but nonetheless expressive language of the eyes to communicate her longing.

The singer of this next song likewise recognizes the power of her eyes to express her desire. But in this case, she also recognizes the consequences of doing so: that is, that the heat of her passion, once kindled in her lover, will return to burn her. Hence she struggles to control the urge to *express* (and the meaning of that verb is perfect in this context: to press out) her passion:

#132	¡Ay, que non oso	I don't dare look,
	mirar ni hacer del ojo!	nor wink my eye;

| ¡Ay, que no puedo | I cannot tell you |
| deciros lo que quiero! | what I want. |

But the eyes are not easily controlled, for, as this poem states,

| #133 Allí miran ojos | There gaze the eyes |
| a do quieren bien. | where they love well. |

Again the paradoxical activity of the eyes—they focus on what they yearn for because their energy is pulled to the object of their desire as if to a magnet. Once they are trained upon it, however, they transmit their desire, and consequently become the object of the other's desire:

#134 Vuestros ojos negros	Your eyes so black
por mi mal los vi.	I saw to my sorrow.
¡Ay de mí, que en verlos	Poor me, for in seeing them
no fui más de mí!	I was no longer my own.

The speaker's love was sparked by the beloved's eyes. The sight of her eyes entered his eyes and enslaved him. Whether or not she was conscious of speaking through her eyes, they have introduced desire into the lover's consciousness, for now he feels no longer complete in himself. I speak about the beloved as the owner of the eyes, and the lover as the see-er of those eyes. But it could be just the other way around. In this game that lovers play with their eyes, the two participants become equal—the male in the activity of looking, makes himself passive, open to the sight, the presence of the beloved. And the beloved, passive though she may be in terms of action, is the passively active agent of the sight he sees. By simply being what she is, she provokes an effect in the lover through his eyes. The very terms *active* and *passive* become paradoxical in relation to the eyes.

Her black eyes, simply by becoming a *sight*, conquer the seeing eyes and hence the see-er. The see-er, then, becomes a possession of the sight, so that the opening *vuestros* by poem's end modifies the see-er as well as the eyes he saw. Those black eyes have conquered the eyes that perceive them.

#135 Vencedores son tus ojos,	Victorious are your eyes,
mis amores,	my love,
tus ojos son vencedores.	your eyes are victorious.

The image of the eyes as engaged in some sort of conflict becomes evident through the word "vencedor." Eyes are victors but they are also victims:

#136 Libres alcé yo mis ojos,	Free were the eyes I raised,
señora, cuando os miré;	lady, when first I looked at you;
libres alcé yo mis ojos	The eyes I raised were free,
y captivos los bajé.	And those I lowered enslaved.

Let us abstract the terms of this conflict. The beloved is the person who is desired, be it male or female, and the lover is the person who does the desiring. The lover is the active term of the relationship and the beloved is the passive. But what happens when the game moves into the eyes? The beloved's eyes are the ones that conquer, that wound, and that have the power to destroy. The lover's eyes are passive recipients of the damage the beloved's eyes inflict. It is as if the eyes of the two lovers reflect the normal order of subject-object, and like every reflection, turn things around in the process.

In the last chapter we encountered the image of battle, of conflict, of wounder and wounded in relation to the doe who, when wounded by the lover's passion, hurls herself into the sea to be finally destroyed through immersion in the lover. Whenever there is contact with an already kindled passion, that passion is transmitted, and the one to whom it spreads perceives this transfer as a wound, as death, or as enslavement. If there is joy in love, very little of it associates with the eyes. It is as if opening the eyes and seeing corresponds to the stirring changes that accompany adolescence and to the ritual bathing of the virgin in preparation for her sexual transformation. When the eyes open and see, they are inviting the other—the sight, that which is seen—to enter the consciousness of the see-er. In the recognition of the other is born desire and a sense of incompletion. That awareness of something missing creates the desire to again feel complete, but now that the other has been experienced, completion can only be obtained through union with the other. By merging with the other, consciousness experiences the wholeness, the peace of lost innocence. But that new wholeness is not the same as the sense of wholeness which preceded awareness of the other, for that was an illusion of wholeness, the innocence of ignorance, of unconsciousness. The perfect completion is one which is achieved by knowing the other, by becoming one with it, a completion which transforms both parts.

And the eyes are the vehicle *par excellence* of perception, that which introduces an awareness of the other into the consciousness of the perceiver. The perception brings pain through desire, and hence the perceived becomes the wounder, and the perception the wound:

#137 Si de los ojos nace   If sight and desire
        ver y desear,   from eyes are born,
        no quiero tener ojos   I want no eyes
        para no penar.   so as not to mourn.

The speaker here may not want to enter into this game of life and love expressed through the eyes, but the currents of wind and water are relentless.

#138 Véante mis ojos,   May my eyes see you
        y muérame yo luego,   and then I'll expire,
        dulce amor mío   my sweetest love
        y lo que más quiero.   whom I most desire.

The bittersweet call of love's transformation, awesomely frightening and desirable, is expressed again in the notion of death. Apparently one may drown as well in the beloved's eyes as in the "hermosa mar."

The verb that most often appears in the "wounding eye" cluster is *matar*. In the last poem the speaker longed for death as self-surrender. But more often, the lover views himself as an unwilling victim, as being killed by the sight of the beloved. Or rather he *pretends* to be an unwilling victim, for remember, if one does not look one does not see.

#139 Abaja los ojos, casada;
      no mates a quien te miraba.

Bride, look away,
or your former admirer
you will surely slay.

Casada, pechos hermosos,
abaja tus ojos graciosos.
No mates a quien te miraba;
abaja tus ojos, casada.

Bride, lovely breasts,
lower your charming eyes
or your former admirer
you will surely slay;
Bride, look away.

The speaker who once looked ("quien te miraba") before his beloved was "casada"—and could that looking imply sexual communion?—kills him because she continues to play with his affection by sending him silent messages with her eyes. A cruel and fickle game she plays, to be sure, yet how sympathetic can one be when he clearly does not lower his own eyes, elsewise how would he notice those "pechos hermosos," or even pick up the messages of her flirting eyes? No, his protests sound as feeble as the "velida's" anger with the wind on the mountain top. If his "casada" stops looking at him, then he will surely complain:

#140 Los ojos que matan a mí,
      días ha que no los vi.

The eyes that are killing me,
for days I have not seen.

When he sees her but she refuses to look at him, he complains:

#141 Menina dos olhos verdes,
      por qué me nâo vedes?

Girl with eyes of green,
why don't you see me?

for he perceives in her refusal to look her lack of interest. Then again, if she does share his affection and looks at him, he still complains:

#142 Tenedme los ojos quedos,
      que me matáis con ellos!

Keep your eyes still,
you're killing me with them.

No wonder the girl in this poem proudly proclaims the value of her eyes to her mother:

#143 Mis ojuelos, madre,
      valen una ciudade.

My dear little eyes, mother,
are worth a city.

Mis ojuelos, madre,
tantos son de claros,
cada vez que los alzo
merescen ducados,
ducados, mi madre;
valen una ciudade.

My dear little eyes, mother,
are so very bright,
each time I raise them
they earn gold coins,
coins of gold, mother;
they're worth a city.

Mis ojuelos, madre,
tanto son de veros,

My dear little eyes, mother,
are so very true,

cada vez que los alzo	each time I raise them
merescen dineros,	they earn money,
dineros, mi madre;	money, my mother;
valen una ciudade.	they're worth a city.

One cannot help but wonder if she is not receiving money to raise more than her eyes, but be that as it may, her eyes are definitely more expressive communicators than words, for their message comes from deep within:

#144	No me mires, moreno,		Don't look at me, dark sir,
	cuando te miro,		when I look at you,
	que se encuentran las almas		for our souls meet
	en el camino.		on the way.

The very act of looking is an invitation, an expression of desire. And vertical movement becomes associated once again with desire, for eyes that are raised announce their openness, their interest. They represent to the lover the same thing as the beloved's association with the orange tree—a willingness to participate in love's game. When the beloved's eyes are lowered, they express disinterest. But her disinterest may be as much a pretence as his complaints:

#145	No paséis, el caballero,		Don't pass, gentleman,
	tantas veces por aquí;		so often by here;
	si no, bajaré mis ojos,		otherwise, I'll lower my eyes
	juraré que nunca os vi.		and swear I never saw you.

In this poem the speaker recognizes the gentleman's passion in his restless pacing before her house, and also recognizes the danger that others may understand his pacing in the same way she does. Hence she threatens to close herself off from him, by lowering her eyes (eyes which have been avidly following his steps).

But her gazing upon him is as clear a sign to the world of her affection as his pacing is of his:

#146	Por una vez que mis ojos alcé,		Because one time I raised my eyes
	dicen que yo lo maté.		they say that I killed him.
	Ansí vaya, madre,		As truly may I go, mother,
	virgo a la vegilia,		a virgin to the vigils,
	como al caballero		as truly as I did not
	no le di herida.		wound the gentleman.
	Por una vez que mis ojos alcé,		Because one time I raised my eyes
	dicen que yo lo maté.		they say that I killed him.

What naughty irony! This hypocritical young girl swears on her virginity: as truly as she will undertake her pilgrimage in a state of innocence, she never wounded the gentleman. Since she has already admitted having raised her eyes to see him, she has as good as admitted having wounded him. And since her emphatic denial of that accusation is false, her assertion that she is a virgin is equally false. But the action of raising her eyes not only has had its effect on the lover— people say it killed him—but has also robbed her of her virginity.

The Latin root of the verb "matar" suggests the notion of sacrifice, of a death which brings transformation: wholeness-holiness. Before the transformation is complete, before union is achieved, there prevails in the lover a sense of confusion, of loss.

#147 Perdíme por conoceros,   I lost myself by knowing you,
        ojos morenos,   dark eyes,
        perdíme por conoceros.   I lost myself by knowing you.

The speaker in this song blames the eyes of the beloved for this sense of loss, for they seduced him, drew him irresistibly. In the next song, the singer swears by her eyes, the eyes that looked and saw, that she loves her gentleman, but, at the same time, she stresses her sense of being lost:

#148 Por vida de mis ojos,   I swear by my eyes,
        el caballero,   gentle sir,
        por vida de mis ojos,   I swear by my eyes,
        bien os quiero.   I love you well.

        Por vida de mis ojos   I swear by my eyes,
        y de mi vida,   and by my very life
        que por vuestros amores   because of your love
        ando perdida,   I am now lost.
        Por vida de mis ojos,   I swear by my eyes,
        el caballero,   gentle sir,
        por vida de mis ojos,   I swear by my eyes,
        bien os quiero.   I love you well.

We have encountered this sense of loss before on various occasions: for instance, the loss of whiteness lamented by the *morena*; and the loss of self associated with drowning in the sea of passion.

Eyes are also closely associated with poems lamenting the absence of the beloved, since the eye is the point of contact between lovers. When the beloved is absent, the eyes suffer loss:

#149 Vaisos, amores, de aqueste lugar;   You are going, my love, from this
        ¡tristes de mis ojos, y cuándo   place;
        os verán!   oh my sad eyes, and when will
                                            they see you again!

Since perception is concentrated symbolically in the eyes, and since they establish the bond between lover and beloved, they are considered the source from which love flows. Hence the departing lover regards his beloved's eyes, which he claims for his own, as the seat of her memory.

#150 ¡Ay, ojuelos verdes,   Ay, green eyes,
      ay, los mis ojuelos!   ay, my little eyes,
      ¡Ay, hagan los cielos   heaven grant
      que de mí te acuerdes!   that you remember me.

Possession of the beloved's eyes is possession of her affection. Consequently when the beloved bestows her eyes upon her lover, she grants
him complete possession of her being. And when he leaves, he carries
away all that connects her with the world.

#151 A la guerra van mis ojos;   My eyes are going to war;
      quiérome ir con ellos,   I want to go with them
      no vayan solos.   so they won't go alone.

Having given her eyes, her affection to the lover, he becomes identified with them. Hence his betrayal is experienced as a betrayal of her
own eyes, and rightly so for they were the eyes that caused her to
surrender to him in the first place:

#152 Apartaram-se os meus olhos   My eyes have left me,
      de mi tâo longe...   gone so far away...
      Falsos amores,   False love,
      falsos, maus, enganadores!   false, bad, and lying.

Absence of the lover represents dismemberment of the self, since
the eyes belong to him. Consequently, his death, too, is a death of the
eyes:

#153 En Avila, mis ojos,   In Avila, my eyes,
      dentro en Avila.   there in Avila.

      En Avila del Río   In Avila by the river
      mataron a mi amigo,   they killed my true love,
      dentro en Avila.   there in Avila.

This girl's lament is addressed to her eyes, because the lover is
identified with them.[2] They were the vehicles of her initial perception
of him, bringing him into herself; they may have witnessed his death
in Avila; and they are the focus of her sorrow, for bereaved of his
sight, she weeps. Although I definitely prefer reading this poem as a
lament, stark and poignant, for the murder of her lover, the symbolic
ambiguity that is afforded by combining eyes with the verb *matar* can
carry the semantic direction of the song toward the other pole of the
separation/union motif, also. His death could be symbolic of sexual
union.

The eyes, too, are the sufferers of insomnia, for once the other has
been seen and desired by the raised eyes, those eyes can no longer
close until their desire is fulfilled. Loving eyes cannot sleep, and even
when they do, the inner eyes of dreams continue to perceive images
which remind the dreamer of her passion:

#154 No pueden dormir mis ojos,   My eyes cannot sleep,
      no pueden dormir.   they cannot sleep.

Y soñaba, mi madre,	And I dreamt, my mother,
dos horas antes del día	two hours before dawn
que me florecía la rosa:	that the rose was blooming;
ell pino so ell agua frida:	the pine beneath the crystal
No pueden dormir.	waters.
	They cannot sleep.

Though this girl claims she cannot sleep, she must have slept in order to dream about the virginal rose (herself?) flowering next to the pool of cool water over which towers, and in which is reflected, the pine, a masculine symbol because of its shape.[3] But her sleep was not felt as rest, it only prolonged her restless yearning.

The dawn, the moment when the world awakens, is paradoxically the moment when lovers can finally sleep. It is the time when lovers meet, when the eyes can stop their yearning:

#155	Que ni duermen los mis ojos	My eyes do not sleep
	ni descansa el corazón	nor does my heart rest
	hasta que venga el albor.	until the dawn arrives.

Dawn poetry in the Spanish traditional lyric is so lovely, fraught with all manner of delightful symbolism, for it alludes to the one happy moment in the drama of love—the moment when youthful lovers come together. The protagonists of this poetry are little more than children—natural impulses—who live under the controlling rules and regulations of parents or society, rules which keep them apart during the night. Dawn is the time when they can escape these restrictions and meet the object of their desires.[4] When the sun rises and the activity of the day begins, these children are sent out to perform their duties to society. Girls go off to wash clothes, and sometimes to tend flocks, and these tasks take them to solitary places where they can enjoy the game of love unrestricted by society's gaze.

#156	—Desciende al valle, niña.	—Go down to the valley, maiden.
	—Non era de día.	—It was not light.
	—Niña de rubios cabellos,	—Maiden with golden locks,
	desciende a los corderos	go down to tend your flocks,
	qu'andan por los centenos.	for they roam among the rye.
	—Non era de día.	—It was not light.

Embedded in this charming little poem is a multitude of associations which sparkle with an array of colors when the light of dawn touches it. The sun's rays are hidden in the girl's golden locks, in the stalks of golden rye, and in her very denial that dawn has arrived. There are two opposing but equally plausible ways to interpret this poem, and again we must keep in mind that opposite really means complementary and that the ambiguity of the poem is its expressive objective. The poem is a dialogue in which one speaker, that of the refrain, is the girl with golden hair. Her response to the exhortation that she descend to the valley to tend her sheep is a protest: "Non era de día." From what point of time is she speaking? Her voice reaches us from beyond time, from a dream world, as though she were still half asleep and not yet awakened to the time of the other speaker, the exhorter. She hears that voice as though it were a memory, and responds in the past tense.

The ambiguity of the poem stems from the vagueness surrounding the voice of the one who addresses the sleepy *vaquera*. Since the command, ostensibly, is that she get to work, that she undertake her daytime responsibility of tending the flocks, it appears to be spoken by a parent or other representative of society who reminds her of her social task. If this is the case, then perhaps she has spent the night in her lover's arms, high in the mountains, and resents the arrival of dawn as the time when she must leave her lover and return to the valley. Rarely is dawn associated with the separation of lovers in the tradition. This next poem, however, lends support to the interpretation of the *vaquera's* protest against the arrival of the day as reluctance to leave the pleasures of her lover's arms:

#157	Ya cantan los gallos,	The cocks are crowing,
	buen amor, y vete,	sweet love, and be gone,
	cata que amaneçe.	for see, daylight has come.

But the fact that the *vaquera* is addressed as "niña de rubios cabellos" indicates that the speaker is acutely aware of her charms. Could the speaker be the lover, pretending to be concerned about her neglect of her task? Could he be exhorting her to awaken and tend to her flock not because he really cares whether the lambs graze in the rye, but because he is waiting to see her? The lambs in the rye provide both a convenient excuse for waking her even before the appointed hour, and at the same time they serve as a lovely symbolic image of his expected pleasures among her golden locks. Her response can be read variously as stemming from her mistaking his voice for that of an authority because she is still half asleep, or as stemming from the shy reluctance of a virgin fearful of wetting her feet in the spring waters by her door, who refuses to admit that dawn has arrived.

A variant of this highly suggestive poem narrows its semantic potential by clearly indicating the significance of the command: she is to descend to the valley for the express purpose of seeing and being seen by the lover.

#158	Descendid al valle, la niña,	Go down to the valley, maiden,
	que ya es venido el día.	for already day has arrived.
	Descendid, niña de amor,	Go down, maiden of love,
	que ya es venido el albor.	for already dawn has arrived.
	Veréys a vuestro amador	You will see your own lover
	qu'en veros se alegraría,	who will rejoice to see you,
	que ya es venido el día.	for already day has arrived.
	Descendid al valle, la niña,	Go down to the valley, maiden,
	que ya es venido el día.	for already day has arrived.

This poem contains the same idea as the insomnia of love, but from a different angle. Nighttime means the closing of the day's eye, the separation of the young lovers. Since at night both society and absence of light prevent the eye from being filled with the sight of what is loved, the eye is empty, hungry, desirous, unable to sleep. The return of light with the rising sun heightens passion, stirs the wind, and returns the sight of the beloved to the longing eye.

Yet sight is much more than perception through the eyes. All five modes of perception condense into one, and seeing therefore symbolizes knowledge of the beloved through the five physical senses—sexual union. Let us look back at the highly sensuous poem in which seeing connotes tasting, smelling, feeling, and hearing:

#103	En la huerta nasce la rosa:	In the garden a rose blooms;
	quiérome ir allá	it's there I wish to go
	por mirar al ruiseñor	to watch the nightingale
	cómo cantabá.	as he was singing.

Here is another poem with a singing nightingale:

#159	Recordades, niña,	Wake up, maiden,
	con el albore,	with the dawn,
	oiredes el canto	and you will hear
	del ruiseñore.	the nightingale's song.

Suddenly it becomes clear that the richly symbolic scene in the garden by the river is taking place at dawn. It is the virginal hour of the day when eyes are raised and see, drinking in the image of the beloved. The eyes participate in the general movement upward which the rising sun precipitates.

Yet always lurking behind the seductive pleasures of the senses, represented by the activity of the eye, remain the pain and sorrow that are only momentarily eclipsed by the sun's fresh morning rays. We have encountered a series of complaints related to the eyes, wounded and wounding. The singer in this poem adopts a tone strongly reminiscent of the *morenas'* laments:

#160	Aquel gentilhombre, madre,	That gentleman, mother,
	caro me cuesta el su amor.	his love costs me dear.
	Yo me levantara un lunes,	I would get up one Monday,
	un lunes antes del día.	one Monday before dawn.
	Viera estar el ruyseñor.	There I would see the nightingale.

On the one hand she expresses her pain in financial terms, like the girl who sold her hair at bargain prices and once the goods are returned, is unable to find another buyer. On the other hand, she speaks through dawn symbols—the verb *levantar*, the nightingale, and the seeing all combine to formulate a confession to her mother that she has lost her virginity. And once again the ambiguity of the verbal tense, here the imperfect subjunctive, heightens the suggestive potential of her song, for thus does she express both regret and a wistful longing for the dawn encounter to be repeated.

Like many another lover, her eyes were her downfall. But so were the eyes of her lover the cause of his downfall:

#161 Vos me matastes,
    niña en cabello,
    vos me habéis muerto.

    Riberas de un río
    vi moza virgo.
    Niña en cabello,
    vos me habéis muerto.

    Vos me matastes,
    niña en cabello;
    vos me habéis muerto.

You slew me,
girl with flowing hair.
You have made me die.

On the river shore
I saw a virgin lass.
Girl with flowing hair,
you have made me die.

You slew me,
girl with flowing hair.
You have made me die.

Here again is the notion of a sight entering the eyes and wounding or killing, in the same way the sun at dawn begins to emit an effluence—the wind, which burns and stirs. In the poem "Levantou-s'a velida" the verb *desviar*, we concluded, was a more apt description of the effect of the wind's action on the virgin than of its effect on the shirts. This verb relates to another action which is frequently mentioned in descriptions of love's effect on the lover—*prender*. And *prender* is in turn related to the idea of *matar*. If the sight of the beloved is imagined to be capable of entering a small point like the eye and passing from there to the heart, the center of life, where it kills—i.e., transforms—the lover, then the imagination's eye visualizes the sight as some pointed object like a dart or an arrow. The beloved is the emitter of this fatal weapon. But she, too, experiences love as a wound inflicted by a sharp instrument:

#162 ¡Ay, mezquina,
    que se me hincó una espina!
    ¡Desdichada,
    que temo quedar preñada!

Ay, foolish me,
for a thorn has pierced me!
Unhappy me,
I fear getting pregnant!

The thorn is inherent in the rose just as the wind on the mountaintop is inherent in the dawn. The two epithets, "mezquina," "desdichada," which this girl applies to herself indicate that she views herself as the unwitting—though not necessarily unwilling—victim of the thorn. But surely she was as aware as this next girl of the dangers involved in picking roses:

#163 Dentro en el vergel
    moriré;
    dentro en el rosal
    matar m'han.

    Yo m'iba, mi madre,
    las rosas coger;

There in the garden
I will die;
there in the rosebush
I will be slain.

I went, mother,
roses to pick,

hallé mis amores   my love I found
dentro en el vergel.   there in the garden.
Dentro en el rosal   There in the rosebush
matar m'han.   I will be slain.

The death this girl expects in the rose patch is the transformation of
love. The transformer is the male principle, the thorn, the lover.

The beloved's hair, too, partakes of this power to wound, precisely
because it is, as seen in our discussion of the wind, so powerfully
attractive. It was the salient feature of her appearance which "killed"
the lover in poem #161. In this next poem the color of the girl's hair
relates to the passionate energy of fire and sun:

#164 Los cabellos de mi amiga   The locks of my beloved
      d'oro son;   are made of gold,
      para mi lançadas son.   they pierce me like lances.

And once again the sight which wounds introduces passionate desire
into the consciousness of the lover, who in turn yearns to wound the
beloved with his passion:

#165 ¡Ay, Dios, quién hincase un   Oh God, how I wish to sink a dart
      dardo   into that dark little deer!
      en aquel venadillo pardo!

This cluster of symbols associated with instruments of death
attracts another symbol—the bull—which, in turn, because of the
horns they have in common, relates to the stag. The bull, through its
role as sacrificial victim (even though the sacrifice has come to be
regarded as a sport, its roots lie deep in religious sacrificial practices—
as do most games), is identified with the lover who suffers the wounds
of desire:

#166 Por una morenita   Because of a little dark-skinned
      corren un toro,   girl
      las garrochas de plata,   a bull is pierced
      los clavos de oro.   by pikes of silver
                                          and spikes of gold.

The lover may suffer like a wounded bull, but if he gets a chance, like
any brave *novillo*, he will impale the one who is sticking him with
"garrochas" and "clavos." He seduces the object of his desire with the
promise that he will be tame and let her touch his dangerous horn!

#167 Zagaleja del ojo rasgado,   Shepherdess with slanted eye,
      vente a mí, que no soy toro   come to me, for I'm no wild bull.
      bravo,
      Vente a mí, zagaleja, vente,   Come to me, shepherdess, come,
      que adoro las damas y mato la   for I adore ladies and slay people.
      gente.

Zagaleja del ojo negro,
vente a mí, que te adoro y quiero;
dexaré que me toques el cuerno,
y me lleves si quieres al prado;
vente a mí, que no soy toro
  bravo.

Shepherdess with eye of black,
come to me, who loves and adores
  you;
I will let you touch my horn
and lead me to pasture, if you
  wish;
come to me, for I'm no wild bull.

This bull-lover focuses his eyes on the eyes of the "zagaleja" and from his description of those eyes, "rasgados" and "negros," one may surmise that she is another *morena*. A still more sexually suggestive song is this:

#168 Aste a la rama,
      niña, verás;
      aste a la rama
      y no morirás.

Sharpen the branch,
girl, and you will see;
sharpen the branch
and you won't die.

In an earlier poem the *remo*, symbol of the male genitals, was made from the tree's branch, "verde aya." Here the lover bids his beloved to seize his branch, while promising her that she will not die. Whether or not he keeps his promise depends on how one interprets death. She may welcome that death, if she shares the admiring attitude of this girl:

#169 Ay, amor, como sois puntuoso,
      la darga dandeta.

Oh, love, how pointed you are,
dandy dart.

Whether they are interpreted on the physical or conceptual level, these pointy symbols can snag as well as kill, and this is one of the ideas suggested by *prender*.[5] This verb conveys the idea of interrupting the free movement of something, and hence its relation to the wind's action—*desviar*, and likewise, to the notion of capturing, an activity also performed by the eyes.

In this next poem, the singer tells us that the lover captured her and subjected her to his will all night, not letting her sleep:

#170 Prendióme el amor,
      aquel traidor,
      aquel engañador,
      aquel porfiado,
      que en toda aquesta noche
      dormir no me ha dexado.

Love pricked me,
that traitor,
that liar,
that stickler,
all night long
he hasn't let me sleep.

But *prender* permits other interpretations as well. Perhaps it was the sight of him which captured her and desire has kept her awake. More likely, however, he did indeed hold her captive all night, and what is more, perhaps *prender* does not only refer to the initial action by which he took her prisoner, but also to the activity which kept her awake all night.

#171 Más prende amor que la çarça,   Love sticks more than the
      más prende y más mata.   bramble,
                                          it pricks more and kills more.

The bramble, like the rose, is full of thorns which prick. But love, the
last poem tells us, has more thorns than the bramble. Nevertheless,
this next ardent lover wishes to be captured and even killed:

#172 La dama que no mata o prende   The lady who doesn't kill or
      tírala dende.   capture,
                                          throw her out of here.

Men may be free to regard love's prick so lightly, for they need not
worry, like the girl in poem #162, about getting pregnant. The
situation is different for women. Once more, in this symbolic cluster,
just as in nearly every other, one hears the sorrowful lament of the
girl who has learned too late about love's painful consequences:

#173 Prendióme el amor, prendióme,   Love pricked me, pricked me,
      ¡ay de mí!   oh poor me;
      prendióme y dejóme ansí.   pricked me and left me like this.

Prender here has the double meaning of being pricked and of being
captured, the latter being the semantic import of this analogous poem:

#174 Del amor vengo yo presa,   Caught by love I come,
      presa del amor.   caught by love.

Once the prey has been captured, her captor frequently demands a
prize, some symbol of his dominance. The *prenda*[6] he demands may be a
piece of her clothing, often a ribbon, a kiss, or in this case, the ultimate
proof of affection:

#175 Que no me desnudéis,   Don't undress me,
      amores de mi vida;   love of my life:
      que no me desnudéis,   don't undress me
      que yo me iré en camisa.   for I would go in my slip.

      Entrastes, mi señora,   You entered, my lady,
      en el huerto ajeno;   in another's orchard;
      cogistes tres pericas   You picked three pears
      del peral del medio;   from the middle pear tree;
      dexaredes la prenda   you must leave a token
      d'amor verdadero.   of love so true.
      Que no me desnudéis,   Don't undress me,
      que yo me iré en camisa.   for I would go in my slip.

This scene is reminiscent of the garden by the river with the roses,
the lemon-picking virgin, and the nightingale. But this garden belongs
to the lover, and because the girl has trespassed, she must pay the
consequences. The "huerto ajeno" which she unwittingly entered is
probably nothing more than the scope of his vision—her real crime is
having allowed herself to be seen by him. And not only seen, but seen

engaged in a highly suggestive activity—picking the golden-colored fruit. In the first of our *morena* poems, the singing girl quoted the demand of her lover that she come out from under the orange tree. Perhaps she, too, was caught by the eyes of her lover in the act of picking oranges, and hence his demand for the same *prenda*, in that poem expressed through the symbol of the burning air.

This next poem suggests that the picking of fruit symbolizes a more irresistibly stimulating activity than simply presenting a seductive sight to the eyes of the lover. The elements of the last poem recur in this, but vary their symbolic import:

#176 Perdida traigo la color;   I've lost my color;
      todos me dicen que lo he de   everyone says it's because of love.
        amor.

      Viniendo de romería   Coming from the pilgrimage
      encontré a mi buen amor;   I met my own true love;
      pidiérame tres besicos;   he asked me for three little kisses;
      luego perdí mi color.   then I lost my color.
      Dicen a mí que lo he de amor. They say it's because of love.
      Perdida traigo la color;   I've lost my color;
      todos me dicen que lo he de   everyone says it's because of love.
        amor.

In the *morena* poems we saw how love can affect the color of a girl's skin—the winds of passion darken and burn. But it can also cause a girl to lose her color. In this case we find once more the virgin associated with a religious celebration which immediately indicates that a meeting with the lover is involved. In the last poem the girl picked three little pears. In this one she bestows three little kisses upon her lover at his request. The price the first girl had to pay for this was her virginity, and the symbolism of the loss of color suggests the same notion of loss of virginity in this poem. Consequently, both girls are paying the same price for the same crime—picking fruit corresponds to the bestowal of kisses. Both activities arouse the lover's passion, setting a force in motion which is beyond their control.

Not only men request some *prenda* to requite the passion which the beloved has inadvertently (at times) aroused. In this poem, the picker of fruit is a young gentleman and the garden in which he picks belongs to nuns:

#177 Gentil caballero,   Gentle sir,
      dédesme hora un beso,   give me now a kiss,
      siquiera por el daño   if only in return for the damage
      que me habéis hecho.   that you have caused me.

      Venía el caballero;   The gentleman was coming,
      venía de Sevilla;   coming from Seville,
      en huerta de monjas   in a garden of nuns
      limones cogía,   lemons he picked,

y la prioresa
prenda le pedía:
"Siquiera por el daño
que me habéis hecho."

and the prioress
asked him for a token:
"If only in return for the damage
that you have caused me."

And if perchance he should be reluctant to surrender the *prenda* she requests, she will show him a sight which will convince him to comply:

#178 No me las enseñes más,
que me matarás.

Estábase la monja
en el monesterio,
sus teticas blancas
de so el velo negro.
Más
que me matarás.

Show me them no more,
for you will slay me.

The nun was in
the convent,
her small white breasts
beneath her black veil.
More,
for you will slay me.

The role of the nun in the tradition will enter our discussion in the next chapter when we explore social restrictions placed upon budding virgins. Right now our interest lies primarily in the effect which the sight and actions of the desired object have upon the beholder. In this poem, the sight of her lovely little breasts slays the lover, but it is a death he would not miss for anything:

#179 Si n'os hubiera mirado
no penara,
pero tampoco os mirara.

Veros harto mal ha sido,
mas no veros peor fuera;
no quedara tan perdido,
pero mucho más perdiera.
¿Qué viera aquél que n'os viera?
No penara,
pero tampoco os mirara.

If I hadn't seen you
I wouldn't grieve,
but I also wouldn't have seen you.

To see you has been plenty bad,
but not to see you would be
     worse;
I wouldn't be so lost,
but much more I would have lost.
What does one see who doesn't
     see you?
He wouldn't grieve,
but also he wouldn't have seen
     you.

Notice here the function of the verb *perder*. What exactly has he lost by seeing his beloved? The implications are multitudinous. He has lost his peace of mind, his sense of wholeness, for now he yearns for completion through sexual union. He has lost dominion over himself— he has been enslaved by her beauty, or rather by his desire to possess her beauty.

And lovers seem to feel that they have the right to demand recompense for this loss:

#180 Ell amor que me bien quiere
agora viene.

Ell amor que me bien quería,
un'empresa me pedía.
Agora viene.

The lover who loves me well
is coming now.

The lover who loved me well,
asked me for a favor.
He's coming now.

If this singer relinquishes the "empresa" he demands, then she, too, will experience a loss. This next poem may be an expression of her reluctance to give him this sign of affection:

#181 Por un cordoncillo verde   For a little green cord
     no quiero yo perderme.   I don't wish to be lost.

The "cordoncillo" is at once the ribbon he demands as a prize, and the ties that will bind her if she surrenders her virginity to him. She does not want to lose herself, her virginity, her peace of mind for a green ribbon. Ribbons bind things together, like the golden thread that twisted among the freshly washed locks of the virgin, and they represent the twining together of bodies in the sexual act. Consequently in this poem, the green ribbon may also represent the same thing as the green oar that stirred the morning waters.

Reluctant though she may be, she will surely surrender, for soon she sings:

#182 Cordón, el mi cordón,   Cord, my own cord,
     ceñidero de mi lindo amor.   binder of my sweet love.

She delights in her power over the lover. But the bestowal of her ribbon can work both ways—it may give her the illusion of victory for a while, but later she recognizes that she has been as subjugated by the gift as he:

#183 Por mi mal me lo tomastes,   To my sorrow you took it,
     caballero, el mi cordón.   gentle sir, my own cord.

The same symbol, seen by the same character, the virgin girl, can point to bliss and misery. In one poem she sees her ribbon as a symbol of her power over the lover, and in the other as a symbol of his power over her. Chains and ribbons are symbolically identical:

#184 Bien haya quien hizo   Blessed be he who made
     cadenas, cadenas;   chains, chains:
     bien haya quien hizo   blessed be he who made
     cadenas de amor.   chains of love.

and

#185 ¡Ay, cadenas de amar,   Ay, chains of loving,
     cuán malas soys de quebrar!   how hard you are to break.

Here again is the same contrast we saw with ribbons. The same viewer can regard these symbols from two entirely different perspectives, in exactly the same way that the air can be simultaneously a wind that burns and a breeze that stirs and carries messages of love, and the sea is both a storm of passion and a placid expanse of endless waiting.

The chains lead us link by link, full circle back to the eyes and their narcissistic game of love. The effluences emitted by the eyes may be darts or chains, for both "prenden." Eyes that see closely resemble hunters, for they follow their prey until they have it in sight. Then they shoot their arrows, or trap the victim in the twisted threads of a net thrown by the eyes.

#186 En el lazo te tengo,   In the snare I have you,
      paloma torcaz,   wild-dove,
      en el lazo te tengo,   In the snare I have you;
      que no te me irás.   and you won't get away.

But if the hunter's eyes think they have caught the prey they were after, remember they run a great danger of being snagged in their own net:

#187 Al revuelo de una garza   At the twisting flight of a heron,
      se abatió el neblí del cielo,   the falcon was brought down
      y por cogella de vuelo   from the sky,
      quedó preso en una zarza.   and because he wanted to catch
                                            her in flight
                                        he was snagged in the blackberry
                                            bush.

We too are going around in circles as we pursue these symbols. Not only do we find again that stirring, circular motion of the stag and wind, now performed by the *garza* in her flight, but also the prickly bramble and the notion of captivity.

In an earlier poem the garza was seen to make her nest by the river:

#94   Mal ferida va la garza;   Smitten is the heron,
      sola va y gritos daba.   alone she soars and weeps.

      Donde la garza hace su nido,   Along the banks of the river
      ribericas de aquel río,   where the heron nests,
      sola va y gritos daba.   alone she soars and weeps.

This poem presents the paradoxical situation of the heron who, while associating herself with love by building her nest on the riverbank, maintains her solitude. She is wounded, but has not been caught or killed:

#188 Montesina era la garça   Mountain wild was the heron,
      y de muy alto volar,   and high was her flight,
      no hay quien la pueda tomar.   there's no one who can catch her.

Again she eludes the arrows of her pursuers, and her elusiveness is related to the *height* of her flight. The notion of height in the poem is further suggested by the mountain. She has suddenly become a mountain bird in the eyes of the one who wishes to catch her, because of the *high* passion she occasions in him. Again and again symbols have been seen to reverse direction, and the *garza*, too, in her very elusiveness becomes both a symbol of the object of desire, the prey, and a symbol of the pain of unfulfilled desire, since she, too, has already been wounded:

#189 Si tantos halcones
la garza combaten,
por Dios que la maten.

If so many falcons
engage the heron,
by God let them kill her.

La garza se queja
de ver su ventura,
que nunca la deja
gozar del altura.
Con gozo y tristura
la garza combaten,
por Dios que la maten.

The heron bemoans the sight of
her fate,
that never lets her
enjoy the heights.
With joy and sorrow
they engage the heron,
by God let them kill her.

While the *estribillo* alone could be interpreted as the words of the hunter who hopes his falcons will take the prey, the gloss suggests that the speaker, whether the hunter or not, wishes that the lonely, suspended *garza* could reach the heights she strives after. She is the one who, perhaps unconsciously, longs to die. *Matar* in this poem draws together the notion of death as orgasm, and the idea of sacrifice. *Matar*, signifying sacrifice, carries the suggestion of bringing something low, as well. Therefore, her high circular flight is seen by the lover-hunter as an indication of her need and unconscious desire for love. Consequently he exclaims, "By God may they kill her!"

This lovely symbol of the lonely *garza* who hovers between the two poles of passion takes us into the mountains once more. If the *garza* was having difficulty attaining the heights she longs for, she is not alone, for the mountain, while powerfully attractive, is at the same time a troublesome place. It is as hard to climb as the chains of love are to break ("malas soys de quebrar"):

#190 Aquellas sierras, madre,
altas son de subir;
corrían los caños;
daban en un toronjil.

Those mountains, mother,
are steep to ascend;
canals carried water
as far as the fragrant mint.

Madre, aquellas sierras
llenas son de flores;
encima dellas
tengo mis amores.

Mother, those mountains
are full of flowers;
at their top
I have my love.

The mountains are full of flowers—virginal love, because they are the birthplace of water, which here is channelled in *caños* so that it will nourish the "toronjil." Having scaled the mountain, the girl will drink the waters of love with her waiting lover, just as the flowering "toronjil" drinks in the earth's precious waters, flowing from the "caños."

"Aquellas sierras, madre"—the mountains loom in the distance, filling her vision and her mind. She presents them to the attention of her mother and then describes them as she perceives them. Her perception—"altas son de subir"—seems to be conditioned by a memory she has of them. She describes in the imperfect tense the long irrigation channels that carry water to the "toronjil" because she is describing both what she *saw* and what happened when she was there. So what does she mean when she says "altas son de subir?" For one thing, the words she chooses reproduce the whistling of the wind she has heard up there. For another, the adjective "altas" refers as much to the irresistible power of the mountain as to its height. But here their height is relative to the action of climbing them. She knows their height and their power because she has gone up, she has met her lover who is there at the summit. They are high and difficult to climb, but the pleasures that await her at the top make the journey worth the pain.

As with every other symbol, the mountain, too, can point in several directions simultaneously. The ambivalent attitude which the singer of the last song expressed corresponds to the ambiguity of the symbol. At times it is seen as the setting for the joyful union of lovers:

#191 Montaña hermosa,   Beautiful mountain,
      alegre y muy leda;   happy and gay;
      la tu arboleda   your grove—
      ¡cómo es deleytosa!   how delightful!

In this song the mountain and the trees merge, thereby blending their symbolic associations—mountain and trees suggest wind, water, birds, flowers, dawn and lovers, as well. No wonder there is such an effusion of adjectives: "hermosa," "alegre," "leda," and "deleytosa."

#192 En esta montaña   In this mountain
      de gran hermosura   of great beauty
      tomemos holgura.   let's take our pleasure.

"... de gran hermosura." The singer is only going to emphasize the delights of the mountain, for he is attempting to entice his beloved to come with him into the deserted heights where they can enjoy the pleasures forbidden them by society.

Her answer is straightforward:

#193 A las montañas, mi alma,   To the mountains, dearest love,
      a las montañas me iré.   to the mountains I will go.

Her decision to go to the mountains is a statement of her willingness to enter love's game.

#194 Lá detrás los montes   There behind the hills
      nascen meus amores.   my love is born.

Love is born behind the mountain. It seems that every time the verb *nacer* appears, no matter to what symbol it is attached, it always indicates the birth of desire: "si de los ojos nace ver y desear..."; "A mi puerta nace una fonte..." From desire is born transformation, as well as the suffering that unfulfilled desire stirs in the breast of the one who desires.

The hunter heard the *garza's* cries and saw her high spinning flight as signs of the longing for completion. Girls, too, hear cries—now coming from the mountain—which they take to be longing cries of passion. They are drawn to those cries out of a sympathetic yearning to relieve the pain of the mountain sufferer.

#195 Gritos daban en aquella sierra; Cries came from that mountain;
   ¡Ay, madre!, quiero m'ir a ella. Oh, mother! I want to go there.

   En aquella sierra erguida   On that high mountain
   gritos daban a Catalina;   they were crying out for Catalina;
   ¡Ay, madre!, quiero m'ir a ella. Oh, mother! I want to go there.

The source of the cries is unknown, and this mystery enshrouds the poem like mist enshrouding the mountain. Perhaps the girl who insistently repeats her desire to go to the mountain believes the cries to be those of her lover. Yet again, the situation is less important than the feeling—an irresistible desire to go to the mountains, as though being pulled by a magnet.

The girl who hears the cries in this next poem is convinced that she is being called, since after all, she is "la más garrida!"

#196 ¡Si me llaman!; ¡a mí llaman!; But they're calling me! me they
   ¡que cuido que me llaman a mí! call!
               I think they're calling me.
   En aquella sierra erguida
   cuido que me llaman a mí.   In that high mountain
   Llaman a la más garrida;   I think they're calling me.
   que cuido que me llaman a mí. they're calling the most graceful;
   ¡Si me llaman!; ¡a mí llaman!; I think they're calling me.
   ¡que cuido que me llaman a mí! But they're calling!; me they call!
               I think they're calling me.

This singer knows herself to be the object of desire, and in the next poem the singer knows the identity of the one who is crying out, and fears that he will die of longing:

#197 Gritos daba el pastorcico   The young shepherd was crying
   en las sierras donde está,   out
   ¡Dios mío!, ¿si morirá?   in the mountains where he stays,
               My God! will he die?

In all these mountain poems there seems to be something or some-one obstructing the union of the lovers, a force which keeps them apart. These songs sound like an attempt to convince the obstructor, most likely the mother, of the dire need for the singer's presence in the mountains.

Once she manages to elude the protective restrictions of the mother, the girl will head directly for the mountains, where she is certain her lover will seek her:

#198 Naquela serra   To that mountain
   irei morar,   I will go to live,

quem me bem quiser   whoever loves me well
lá me irá a buscar.   will go there to seek me.

It might have looked very hospitable when she was down in the
valley hearing the seductive cries of passion, but once she ventures
into the thickly wooded mountain,[7] she finds it dark, cold and
frightening:

#199 Por el montecico espeso   Through the thick wooded hill
      ¿y cómo yré,   how will I go?
      que me fatigaba la sed?   for I was dying of thirst.

She is. no longer sure how to regard the mountain. On the one hand
it is still the site of innocent love, "montecico." On the other, it is
dark and treacherous—"espeso." How can she make it through when
she is dying of thirst? What will quench her thirst? The waters that
bubble forth from the high mountain spring, and in reaching the
waters that will extinguish her thirst, she will also reach the lover
who alone can put out the flames of her desire.

If it is not death by thirst that threatens her, it is getting lost.
Once more we come upon that ubiquitous verb, *perder*:

#200 Por el montecilla sola,   Through the mountain alone,
      ¿y cómo yré?   how will I go?
      ¡Ay, Dios, si me perderé!   Oh God! will I be lost?

The mountain is lovely ("hermosa," "leda," "deleytosa") only when
lovers are snuggled safe together under a tree. But when a girl
wanders through the mountains alone, they become awesome and
dangerous. There is an inherent incongruity in the juxtaposition of
virgin girl and mountain, from which a tension arises that demands
an outlet. The speaker here is mystified by what he sees, a young girl
alone in the "montecico."

#201 ¿Adóla, adóla,   Where, where are you going, girl,
      por el montecico sola,   through the mountain alone,
      sola por el monte?   alone through the mountain?

The repetition of "sola, sola" reminds us once again of the lonely
garza. Like the *garza*, the virgin is drawn to love's lair but she resists
the death which awaits her there, for she fears love's transformation.

#202 Por las sierras de Madrid   Through the mountains of
      tengo d'ir,   Madrid
      que mal miedo he de morir.   I have to go,
                                       for I greatly fear that I will die.

Now that she actually faces the journey, she no longer asserts her
desire to go, "quiero m'ir a ella," but rather the *compulsion*—"tengo d'ir."

And she is right to hesitate before climbing to the heights,
because once she arrives, the reception she will receive is by no
means certain:

#203 Dame acogida en tu hato; Give me shelter in your hut;
      pastorcico, Dios te duela; young shepherd, God cause you
      cata que en el monte yela.   to take pity;
                                  for it's freezing in the mountain.

She begs the young shepherd to give her shelter, to take her in, for
the mountain, alone at night, is an inhospitable place—cold, in contrast to the warm winds that will stir at dawn. But the "pastorcico" in
this poem seems to be related to a whole group of hard-hearted
shepherds who exile themselves in the mountains in order to escape
love's clutches. We will meet these recluses shortly, but first let us
see how vulnerable "caballeros," too, can be in the unfamiliar mountain. The situation is the same as that of the last poem—a lost and
weary traveler seeks warmth in a cabin, but now the terms are
reversed. The traveler is a man, and the mountain-dweller is a
"serrana," here called "zagala."

#204 Dame acogida en tu hato; Give me shelter in your hut;
      zagala, de mí te duela; *vaquera*, have pity on me;
      cata que en el monte yela, for it's freezing in the mountain;
      que en el monte yela. it's freezing in the mountain.

The mountain travelers are unwanted and vulnerable.

When asked what brought him to the mountain in the first place,
the "caballero's" reply is as vague and fatal as the mysterious cries
that probably drew him there:

#205 ¿Quién te traxo, el caballero, Who brought you, gentle sir,
      por esta montaña escura? through this dark mountain?
      ¡Ay, pastora! ¿Quién? Oh shepherd girl! Who?
      Mi ventura. My good fortune.

And with this poem, too, we find another, almost identical, but with
the terms once more reversed. The one who wanders lost and alone
in the "hyermos" (a word that corresponds semantically to "montaña"
as an isolated, deserted place) now is the same "niña de rubios
cabellos" who slept while the errant lambs grazed in the rye. Is she
wandering astray like the lambs?

#206 Mi ventura, el caballero, My fortune, gentleman,
      mi ventura. my fortune.

      Niña de rubios cabellos, Girl with the golden locks,
      ¿quién os traxo aquestos who brought you to these wild
        hyermos?   places?
      Mi ventura, el caballero, My fortune, sir,
      mi ventura. my fortune.

Both these lost travelers, *caballero* and *niña*, recognize the fatal pull
of the mountain and their own impotence to resist. Herein lies the
inexorable reality that the tradition portrays in each cluster of associated symbols. Love is everyone's "ventura." Where there is life,
there is water, and where there is life, there is air. Life depends on air
and water, symbols of masculine and feminine libido. They cannot be

escaped. If one is not slain by a pair of eyes, if one does not drown in
the sea, then surely one will meet one's fate high in the mountains.

The mountain is the setting *par excellence* for the drama of love in
the traditional lyric. To be sure we find a variety of other highly
symbolic geographical locations: the shore, the garden by the river,
the groves of citrus trees, the valley, the pasture. Yet even these are
linked in one way or another with the mountain. Some are specific
parts of the mountain: the pasture where sheep graze, implies the
presence of the shepherd who is always found in lonely exile in the
mountains; the citrus grove can be located in the mountains where it
drinks the spring waters; the river which flows through the garden is
fed by mountain waters. The valley and the ocean, while standing in
apparent opposition to the mountain heights, in reality acquire their
symbolic meaning through the contrast they represent to the mountain. Insofar as the mountain heights emit masculine energy, they
correspond to such other masculine symbols as the wind, the stag,
the oar and the thorn. Each of these symbols acted in some way
upon, or implied the existence of a complementary feminine symbol:
virgin, water, whiteness, hair. In just the same way, the mountain
implies the existence of a complementary feminine symbol—the valley. In this poem we see how valley, virgins, roses and greenness
merge into one sensuous feminine essence:

#207 ¡Por el val verdico, mozas,   To the little green valley, girls,
      vamos a coger rosas!   let's go pick roses.

Over and over the same fatal flaw is found. All this virginal purity is
just begging to be stained, darkened by the wind. The suggestive
activity these *mozas* are engaged in—or are about to be engaged in,
will inexorably call forth their masculine complement. For the voice
of the girl who calls the others to join her produces the same effect as
the mysteriously seductive cries echoing mournfully from the mountain top. The voices reach us from opposite ends of the spectrum, one
steeped in hope, one steeped in longing despair, but both filled with
desire, and both calling others to enter the game of love. Both are
irresistible.

While the girls pick roses in the valley, the young men decide that
it is time to harvest the grain that grows there. In an earlier poem
the golden rye corresponded to the golden hair that in turn corresponded to the virgin girl. And work activities in these songs merge
with sexual activity. These two symbolic currents flow together so
that the threshing and crushing movements of the harvest suggest
movements that we found represented earlier by the verb *luchar*:

#208 Este pradico verde,   This little green pasture,
      trillémosle y hollémosle.   let us thrash and trample.

The "pradico," with its horizontal dimensions, corresponds to the
virgin girl. But if that "pradico" gets married some day, her husband
may be in for quite a shock:

#209 Por el val que habéis de arar,
el desposado,
por el val que habéis de arar
ya estaba arado.

The valley you are to plow,
bridegroom,
the valley you are to plow
was already plowed.

Surprisingly enough, there appears a happily married man, symbolized in the next poem by an unusual shepherd, who finds his valley untouched by a trespassing plow. When one thinks of how many "plowed valleys" we have crossed, this is nothing short of miraculous:

#210 Tan buen ganadico,
y más en tal valle,
placer es guardalle.

Such a good little flock
and what's more in such a valley,
a pleasure it is to guard.

Ganado d'altura,
y más de tal casta,
muy presto se gasta
su mala pastura;
y en buena verdura,
y más en tal valle,
placer es guardalle.

Flock from the heights,
and what's more of such
breeding,
very quickly exhausts
the bad pasture land,
and what's more, in such a valley,
a pleasure it is to guard.

Ansí que yo quiero
guardar mi ganado,
por todo este prado
de muy buen apero:
con este tempero,
y más en tal valle,
placer es guardalle.

This is how I want
to guard my flock,
through this good pasture
with a fine sheepfold,
with this pleasant weather,
and what's more, in such a valley,
a pleasure it is to guard.

Está muy vicioso
y siempre callando,
no anda balando
ni es enojoso;
antes da reposo
en cualquiera valle:
placer es guardalle.

They are very well fed
and always quiet,
they never bleat
nor give me trouble;
rather they give me rest
in any valley:
a pleasure it is to guard.

Conviene guardalla
la cosa preciosa,
que en ser codiciosa
procuran hurtalla,
Ganado sin falla,
y más en tal valle,
placer es guardalle.

It's important to protect
something precious,
for if it is enviable
people try to steal it.
Flawless flock,
and what's more, in such a valley,
a pleasure it is to guard.

Pastor que se encierra
en valle seguro,
los lobos te juro
que no le dan guerra.
Ganado es de sierra
traspuesto en tal valle,
placer es guardalle.

The shepherd who closes himself
off
in a safe valley,
the wolves, I swear to you,
won't cause him trouble.
A flock from the mountains
brought down to such a valley,
a pleasure it is to guard.

Pastor de buen grado	A shepherd willingly
yo siempre sería,	I always would be,
pues tanta alegría	for so much joy
me da este ganado:	this flock gives to me:
y tengo jurado	and I have sworn
de nunca dejalle,	never to leave it,
mas siempre guardalle.	but always to guard.

This valley is reminiscent of the "fresca ribera" where the water sparkled and the cattle could "hartarse." The snugness and security of this valley suggest the assurance of possession that only marriage can appear to provide. The shepherd here delights in this security because he has already experienced the excitement of passion on the mountain: "Ganado *d'altura* / y más de tal casta, / muy presto se gasta / su mala pastura." The bad pastureland is quickly exhausted because it is "*d'altura*," the place where the "ganado" originated. But the mountain cattle have been *brought down* (as the *garza* longs to be) to the valley: "Ganado es de sierra / traspuesto en tal valle." What does this "ganado" represent? If they roamed loose in the mountains where sexual passion peaks, and now they graze contentedly in a snug little valley, then it seems they must be the shepherd's—the lover's—sexual drive. It is the "ganado" he describes in the third stanza of the gloss, which seems to have quieted down in the valley, just like the wind, wild in the mountains, gentle in the valley. His "ganado" he calls in the fourth stanza "la cosa preciosa," his masculine energy, his virility. If that energy, that "cosa preciosa" is "codiciosa," if it tries to protect itself from an encounter with the feminine, "they" will only try to rob it. Who are *they*? Why, they are all those virgins lost in the mountains who call at his door and ask for shelter. They are the very emissaries of love's pain which he had hoped to elude in the deserted mountains. So now he has surrendered, come down to the valley with his precious energy, where he keeps it safe and sound from the howling wolves ("gritos"?) that would rob it. It is a pity, but can one help feeling cynical about his snug, smug assurance? In the next chapter we will see that where there is marriage there is a "mal casada" in the picture, too, and she is usually eager to let some new shepherd graze in her valley.

But let us return to the mountains where passion runs loose and nobody is happily married. When you ask a mountain shepherd for his feelings about marriage, you will get a simple answer:

#211 —Di, pastor, ¿quiéreste casar?	—Say, shepherd, do you want to get married?
—Más querría pan;	—I'd rather have bread;
más querría pan.	I'd rather have bread.

In the mountains social law has no place. There life is centered on survival, needs are basic, sexual forces are natural, uncontrolled.

#212 En el monte do no hay favor,   In the mountain where there's no
     pan y vino es lo mejor.   favor,
                                  bread and wine is best.

Let us turn our attention now to the protagonists of the mountain drama. There are two separate but parallel pairs who play the game of love in the mountains. In one pair, the feminine part is played by the *niña* who is in love with the lonely shepherd. In the other pair of protagonists, the actress is the *serrana*, the one who dwells on the mountain, and the actor is a *caballero*, a stranger to the mountains, who has been smitten with love of the *serrana*. The two protagonists of these parallel dramas who are mountain-dwellers, the *pastor* and the *serrana*, are alike the objects of desire. The *niña* and *caballero*, the low-landers, come to the mountain to seek sexual experience. They usually feel lost and confused and often they are spurned or abused by their mountain lovers.

In the last chapter we met the *serrana* who alone could requite the passions of the young man pleading with her to guide him to the river. She was experienced in love; he was a novice. He was afraid of dying in the mountains; she knew her way around.

We have seen a poem where a young girl tells her mother about her adventures beneath the "encina" while traveling to a "romería." In this next poem, a young man tells his mother about his adventures in the mountain while hunting:

#213 Yo me yva, mi madre,   I was going, mother,
     a Villa Reale,   to Villa Reale,
     errara yo el camino   I lost my way
     en fuerte lugare.   in a deserted spot.

     Siete días anduve   Seven days I travelled
     que no comí pane,   and I ate no bread,
     cevada mi mula,   nor hay my mule
     carne el gavilán.   nor meat my sparrow-hawk.
     Entre la Zarçuela   Between Zarçuela
     y Daraçutan,   and Daraçutan
     alçara los ojos   I raised my eyes
     hazia do el sol sale;   to where the sun was rising;
     viera una cabaña,   I saw a cabin
     della el humo sale.   from which smoke was rising.
     Picara mi mula,   I spurred my mule
     fuyme para allá;   and headed over there;
     perros del ganado   sheep dogs came out
     salenme a ladrar;   to bark at me;
     vide una serrana   I saw a mountain lady
     del bello donayre,   of lovely charms.
     —Llegaos, caballero   —Come near, gentleman,
     verguença no ayades;   don't be ashamed;
     mi padre y mi madre   my father and mother
     han ydo al lugar,   have gone to town,

mi caro Menguillo	my dear Menguillo
es ydo por pan,	has gone for bread,
ni vendrá esta noche	he won't come tonight
ni mañana a yantar;	or tomorrow for dinner;
comeréys de la leche	you will eat some custard
mientras el queso se haze.	while the cheese is a-making.
Haremos la cama	We will make a bed
junto al retamal;	next to the broom field;
haremos un hijo,	we will make a son
llamarse ha Pasqual:	who'll be called Pascual:
o será Arçobispo,	he'll either be an archbishop,
Papa o Cardenal,	a pope or a cardinal,
o será porquerizo	or he'll be a pig-keeper
de Villa Real.	in Villa Real.
Bien, por vida mía,	Well, on my life,
devéys de burlar!	you must be teasing!

This *serrana* does not care a bit about any notions of fidelity that might be implied in marriage, if indeed her "caro Menguillo" is her husband, or soon-to-be husband.

In this next poem, the *serrana* is not only unfaithful to her husband, but to her lover as well. She is probably one of those bad pasturelands the happy husband in the valley tried out before he settled down:

#214 Serrana, ¿dónde dormistes?	Mountain girl, where did you sleep?
¡Qué mala noche me distes!	What a bad night you gave me!
A ser sin vuestro marido,	Had you been without your husband,
u sola, sin compañía,	or alone, without company,
fuera la congoxa mía	then my suffering would not have been
no tan grande como ha sido.	as overwhelming as it has been.
No por lo que habéys dormido,	Not because of the hours you slept,
mas por lo que no dormistes,	but because of those you didn't sleep,
¡tan mala noche me distes!	such a bad night you gave me!

Serranas, probably from their long residence in the virile mountains, are nothing if not direct in pursuing what they want:

#215 Salteóme la serrana	The mountain woman ambushed me
junto a par de la cabaña.	right next to her cabin.

It is hardly surprising that they are so eager for love when they meet a lost traveler, since the sight of a man is a rare thing in the mountains:

#216 Garridica soy en el yermo,
    y, ¿para qué,
    pues que tan mal me empleé?

Charming am I in the lonely
    mountains
and for what?
since so badly I spent myself.

Qu'en el yermo do me veo
mi tiempo muy mal empleo:
si me veo y me deseo
es porque
mi vida tan mal empleé.

For here in the wilderness where
    I am
my time I badly spend:
if I see myself and desire myself
it's because
my life I so badly spent.

This girl is so starved for affection that she is aroused by the sight of herself! She could well be married to one of those hard-hearted shepherds we have yet to meet.

Because the mountain girl is so notoriously direct, she becomes the object of equally direct requests:

#217 La moça que las cabras cría
    de las rodillas arriba dirías:
    —Moça de los calsones,
    ¿si quiere guardar cabrones?

The girl, who raises goats,
from the knees up you might say:
—Girl with breeches,
do you want to keep rams?

Young men find particularly exciting the sight of these unpretentious *serranas* dancing:

#218 ¡Ábalas, ábalas, hala!
    ¡Aba la frol y la gala!

Bring them down, bring them
    down!
Bring down the flower and
    finery.

Allá arriba, arriba,
junto a mi logare,
viera yo serranas
cantar y baxlare,
y entre todas ellas
mi linda zagala;
¡aba la frol y la gala!

There on the heights, on the
    heights,
right next to my town
I saw mountain girls
singing and dancing,
and among them all
my pretty beloved;
Bring down the flower and
    finery!

The singer describes in the gloss this sight of the dancing *serranas*. But what is he saying in the *estribillo*? The command "ábalas" sounds like the rhythmic nonsense syllables of a dance song with no particular meaning until we find the same command in a familiar context:

#219 ¡Ábalos tus ojos
    linda morena,
    ábalos, ábalos,
    que me dan pena!

Lower your eyes,
beautiful dark girl,
lower them, lower them,
for they give me sorrow.

Obviously it is the command of a smitten lover to his beautiful *morena* to *lower* (abájalos) the eyes which smite him. In the song of the dancing *serranas*, the singer also wants relief from the passion their dancing arouses in him. But rather than lowering his own eyes, he wants to see the *serranas* brought down, just as the hunter wants to see the *garza* killed, her desires requited.

After all, the *serranas* really do want to be brought down:

#220 Serranas de Cuenca	Mountain girls from Cuenca
iban al pinar,	were going to the pine grove,
unas por piñones,	some to gather pine nuts,
otras por bailar.	others were going to dance.

When they go to the pine grove, they are asking to be seen by their passionate admirers, as surely as the *galleguitas* who go to the shrine with their mothers, not to pray and burn candles, but to dance and be seen.

Occasionally it happens that the aggressive *serrana* is not worth looking at. This young man's encounter in the mountains with an ugly *serrana* has taught him to stay home when it snows!

#221 Si d'esta escapo	If I escape from this one,
sabré qué contar,	I'll know what to tell,
non partiré dell'aldea	I won't leave my village
mientras viere nevar.	when I see it snow.
Una moçuela de vil semeiar	A little girl with an ugly face
fízome ademán de comigo	gave me to understand
folgar:	she wanted to sport with me:
non partiré dell'aldea	I won't leave my village
mientras viere nevar.	when I see it snow.

In this case he cannot wait to get away from her. Other young men, however, cling to the fickle mountain-girl, and consequently suffer:

#222 En el monte la pastora	In the mountain the *vaquera*
me dejó:	left me:
¿dónde iré sin ella yo?	where will I go without her?

Here we have the same sense of loss that the eyes caused, now associated with the mountain girl. This next poem shows how easily the tradition's poetic elements skip from cluster to cluster. Its second verse is nearly identical to the second verse of #134 "por mi mal los vi." In that poem the object of the seeing was the beloved's black eyes, and the effect of the sight was loss of self-possession: "no fui más de mí." In this poem the object of the verb *ver* is the Sierra Bermeja, the sight of which caused him to lose all the happiness he had:

#223 ¡Ay, Sierra Bermeja,	Ay, Russet mountains,
por mi mal te vi,	to my sorrow I saw you,
que el bien que tenía	for the good that I had
en ti lo perdí!	in you I lost.

The speaker in this poem could be either the *niña* in love with the shepherd, or the *caballero* in love with the *serrana*, for they both, like all the other lovers we have met, feel that the beloved slays or robs them:

#224 D'aquel pastor de la sierra
      dar quiero querella.

Of that mountain shepherd
I wish to complain.

      D'aquel pastor tan garrido,
      que me robó mi sentido,
      dar quiero querella.

Of that charming shepherd
who robbed me of my senses,
I wish to complain.

Again the sense of loss, but what the girl in this poem feels she has lost is her "sentido." In the next, the singer has lost sight of her shepherd, who knows his way through the thick trees, while she is helpless. The mountain is *fuerte*, an adjective which suggests the power which *alto* also connotes. She would agree with the girl who told her mother that the mountains "altas son de subir":

#225 ¡Ay, triste de mi ventura,
      qu'el vaquero
      me huye porque le quiero!

Ay, sad is my fortune,
for the cow-herd
flees me because I love him.

      Triste yo, no le veré,
      qu'está la montaña fuerte;
      lo que siento d'esta muerte,
      que sin velle moriré.
      ¿Dónde iré o qué haré,
      qu'el vaquero
      me huye porque le quiero?

Sad I am, I will not see him,
for this mountain is wild;
what I regret about this death
is that without seeing him I'll die.
Where will I go or what will I do,
for the cow-herd
flees me because I love him.

She blames fate for her situation, like the travelers lost in the mountains. Sometimes the girls we find alone in the mountains are on their way to a pre-arranged meeting with their shepherd-lover, who is new at this game of love.

#226 Llueve menudico
      y hace la noche oscura;
      el pastorcillo es nuevo,
      no iré segura.

Softly it rains
and the night is dark;
the shepherd is young,
I won't go safely.

The shepherd she is going to meet is *new*, that is, he is young and inexperienced, but ardent in matters of love. This next poem which transforms the lovers into birds, not only presents the same situation—the female wanders the mountain searching for her lover—but also offers an explanation for those cries we hear piercing the night from the mountain:

#227 Voces daba la pava,
      y en aquel monte,
      el pavón era nuevo
      y no le responde.

The peahen was calling
there in the mountain,
the peacock was young
and didn't answer.

This poem illustrates particularly well the way the tradition functions: motifs, symbols, all sorts of poetic elements, syntactical units, float around clustering now here, now there. This poem draws together the *gritos-de-la-montaña* motif, and the girl-meeting-innocent-shepherd motif, while suggesting an association with the *garza*, the birds singing at dawn by the spring, and the whole world of mountain fowl.

The image of the "new," inexperienced shepherd who does not answer the "pava's" call in turn breaks loose from the motif of the shepherd who resists love and attaches itself to another motif—the absent-minded shepherd in love.

#228   Si el pastorcico es nuevo   If the good shepherd is young
            y anda enamorado,   and is in love,
            si se descuida y duerme,   if he gets careless and sleeps,
            ¿quién guardará el ganado?   who will watch over the flock?

The syntactical structure of this poem, as well as the lost shepherd / sheep image will lead us in another direction shortly, but now let us see more examples of this motif of the shepherd made irresponsible by love. We have seen it before peripherally related to the dawn poem in which the *vaquera* sleeps while her lambs run loose in the rye. Here it is again:

#229   ¿A dónde tienes las mientes,   Where are your thoughts,
            pastorcillo descuidado,   careless young shepherd,
            que se te pierde el ganado?   for you are losing your flock?

This lack of attentiveness to the flocks causes the singer of this next song to pity them. Now their enamored keeper is a *vaquera*:

#230   Pastora que en el cayado   The *vaquera* who carries a portrait
            trae retratado al pastor,   of the shepherd on her crook,
            herida viene de amor,   comes wounded by love;
            lástima tengo al ganado.   I feel sorry for her flock.

The image of her crook bearing the portrait of her beloved shepherd suggests the same notion of day-dreaming on the job as the question "¿A dónde tienes las mientes...?" Her mind is on her lover's portrait, emblazened on yet another instrument of the same symbolic shape as darts, oars, and thorns.

Sympathy for the abandoned flock reappears in this poem:

#231   Ovejita blanca,   Little white sheep,
            requiere tu piara: summon your herd:
            en hora mala hubiste   bad fortune bestowed on you
            pastora enamorada.   a *vaquera* in love.

            Ovejita prieta,   Little black sheep,
            requiere tu cordero: summon your lamb:
            en hora mala hubiste   bad fortune bestowed on you
            pastor carabero.   a jesting shepherd.

Here we see that it is equally bad to be under the care of a shepherd, as of a *vaquera*, if he, too, is in love.

When the distracted shepherd/ess comes to his/her senses, the realization arises of the danger the flocks are in:

#232 Las ovejas se me van,
        ¿si me aturdirán?

The sheep are leaving me,
will they grow bewildered?

Las ovejas y el ganado
van de collado en collado,
ni las he aballado,
¡A la ho! ¡Que se me van!
¿Si me aturdirán?

The sheep and the flock
roam from hill to hill,
and I have not called them.
Hey! They're leaving me!
Will they grow bewildered?

In this poem we see how the behavior of the sheep reflects the behavior of the shepherd, and both become symbols of the confusion of love, the complete absorption in dreams of the other that "aturden" the mind of the enamored shepherd.

When a shepherd falls in love, he suffers as no other lover, and his isolation which before indicated his reluctance to love, now symbolizes the isolation of suffering. The shepherd who speaks in this poem believed that the loneliness of his profession would protect him from love's pain. But he discovered that even surrounded by his flocks he has been captured and wounded (again the verb *prender*).

#233 No pensé qu'entre pastores
        daba dolor el amor;
        mas a mí, triste pastor,
        herido m'han sus dolores.

I never thought that among shepherds
love caused pain;
but unhappy shepherd that I am,
wounded I've been by its sorrow.

Prendieron m'en el ganado,
quito deste pensamiento,
contento más que contento,
fuera de todo cuydado.
Pensando qu'entre pastores
no tenía fuerça amor,
a mí, cuytado pastor,
herido m'han sus dolores.

It caught me in the flock
devoid of any such thought,
content and more than content,
beyond every such care.
Thinking that among shepherds
love had no such power,
but unhappy shepherd that I am,
wounded I've been by its sorrow.

When urged to abandon his solitary suffering, so that he will not lose his "buen sentido," he shows himself to be as helpless in the clutches of his passion as the girl who sat on the rocks surrounded by the stormy sea:

#234 Dexa ya tu soledad,
        pastor chapado,
        pastor garrido.
        —¿Cómo la podré dexar?
        Qu'estoy llagado,
        qu'estoy herido.

Leave your solitude,
handsome shepherd,
charming shepherd.
—How can I leave it?
For I am hurt,
for I am wounded.

—Dexa tu soledad,
que vives desesperado.
—Antes vivo descansado

—Leave your solitude,
for you live in despair.
—Rather I live in peace

y en ella quexo mi quexa.
—Pues dexa tanto llorar
no pierdas tu buen sentido.
—¿Cómo lo podré dexar?
Qu'estoy llagado,
qu'estoy herido.

and here I complain my complaints.
—Well, stop all your crying,
don't lose your good sense.
—And how will I leave it?
For I am hurt,
for I am wounded.

Through his association with self-imposed isolation, the shepherd is drawn into yet another cluster of poems in which a young girl waits for her lover to visit her during the night, like the woman who waited all night with her door wide open.

#235 Aquel pastorcillo, madre,
pues que no viene,
algo tiene en el campo
que le entretiene.

That young shepherd, mother,
since he doesn't come,
has something out in the fields
that delays him.

The girl in this next song puzzles over her lover's tardiness, too. The syntactical structure and theme of this poem is reminiscent of poem #228. Perhaps the "amigo" in this poem is also "new."

#236 Si la noche haze escura
y tan corto es el camino,
¿cómo no venís, amigo?

If the night is dark
and the road so short,
why don't you come, lover?

Her question is rhetorical. Anyone who falls in love with a shepherd is asking for sorrow:

#237 La que tiene el marido pastor
grave es su dolor.

She who has a shepherd husband,
grave is her sorrow.

La que puso su cuidado
en sujeto de la sierra,
bien es que muera en la guerra
de amor tan mal empleado;
y la que sirve en estado
do el morir sería mejor,
grave es su dolor.

She who placed her care
in a man of the mountains,
it is good that she die
in the battle of such a useless
    love;
and she that serves in a condition
where to die would be better,
grave is her sorrow.

This is a bleak picture of married life in the mountains! Again there occurs a poetic element, here the notion of being "mal empleado," traveling from poem to poem. We met this idea before in the song of the "garridica" who felt herself also to be wasting her life in isolation (#216). If she thought marriage was the answer to her loneliness, one hopes she did not marry a shepherd. If she did, she will end up waiting for his return from the mountain like all the others who are foolish enough to fall in love with a mountain-man:

#238 Mi querido es ydo al monte
y ya tañen la oración:
no se puede tardar, non.

My love is gone to the mountain
and already they're tolling the
    angelus:
he can't delay, no.

"No se puede tardar...," in the context we have just discussed, certainly seems ironic.

Since nocturnal wanderings are so closely related to the mountain setting, another symbol joins this cluster—the moon. Just as the sun provides the energy for the dawn encounter, the moon watches over lovers astray in the mountains at night, providing in some cases the only hope of their ever meeting in its matted "espesura."

#239 ¡Ay, luna que reluzes, toda la noche m'alumbres!

Ay, glistening moon, all night shine on me!

¡Ay, luna tan bella, alúmbresme a la sierra por do vaya y venga! ¡Ay, luna que reluzes toda la noche m'alumbres!

Ay, moon so beautiful, shine for me on the mountain where I wander back and forth! Ay, glistening moon, all night shine on me.

The moon must have done what was asked, for in this next poem the singer regrets what happened after she was guided by its light to her lover:

#240 Púsose el sol; salióme la luna; más me valiera, madre, ver la noche escura.

The sun set; the moon came out; it would have been better, mother, for the night to be dark.

She obviously does not agree with the singer of this last song:

#241 Boca besada no pierde ventura; antes se renueva como la luna.

A kissed mouth doesn't lose fortune; rather it's renewed like the moon.

The moon is an appropriate symbol with which to close this chapter, for her light is simply the reflection of the sun's light. Sometimes she turns her face fully toward the sun, and at others she turns away. She loses and gains. She symbolizes, in short, the constant change of life, of love, and the multitude of attitudes young lovers express in their songs. But as this song assures us, love is not loss, it only appears to be loss, like the waning of the moon appears to be her death. She will wax again under the sun's light, however, and so, too, will the lover be renewed by love's kiss.

The symbols collected under the fire element have very little direct connection with fire *per se*. What we have seen here are the various manifestations of the masculine phase of the sexual-love dynamic. As important as the object symbols are the action symbols in this virile group—verbs, like *prender* and *matar*. The energy of the masculine principle disperses in the tradition and infuses a wide variety of objects and characters with its powerful, invigorating, and, at times, destructive force.

1 *mirar*: este mirar se haze con los ojos poniendolos en el objeto o cosa que miramos: y juntamente la consideracion y advertencia del animo; porque si este no concurre, no se consigue el efeto del mirar. (Covarrubias)

2 Bruce Wardropper points out the poetic identification of eyes and lover in Góngora's *romancillo*, in his article "'La más bella niña'," *Studies in Philology*, 63 (1966), p. 666.

3 There is disagreement among scholars about the second word of the fourth verse of the gloss of this poem. M. F. Alatorre prefers "pino," while Alín and others read it as "vino." Though I believe "pino" makes more sense symbolically, M. Van Antwerp's interpretation of the poem in her article, "*Razón de Amor* and the Popular Tradition," *RPh* 32 (1978-79), pp. 3-4, has convinced me that "vino" is an equally valid reading of the poem.

4 S. G. Armistead and J. T. Monroe, in "*Albas, mammas*, and Code-Switching in the *Kharjas*: A Reply to Keith Whinnom," *La Corónica* 11 (1983), offer a very plausible explanation for these frequent dawn encounters in the Spanish traditional lyric: "Meeting at dawn is the sign of an honorable courtship that is expected to lead to marriage..." (p. 181).

5 *prender*: vale asir, pero comunmente se toma por llevar a la carcel. (Covarrubias)

6 *prenda*: lo que se toma al que es prendado; *prendar*: sacar prenda al que deve alguna cosa o al que ha hecho algun daño. (Covarrubias)

7 The reader should be aware that the word "monte" can mean both "mountain" and "woods." The Royal Academy's *Diccionario de la lengua española*, 19th ed. (Madrid, 1970), lists first "Grande elevación natural de terreno," and second, "Tierra inculta cubierta de árboles, arbustos o matas." (p. 893). Covarrubias gives only "tierra alta."

❧ 4 ❧

Earth

HE TITLE OF THIS final chapter refers not to a large green and blue ball floating in space, nor to the homeland, though as we have seen already, there are poems in which the absent singer longs for the native soil. The earth in the *cancionero tradicional* is quite simply the mother out of whose womb the drama of life arises. She provides the dramatic setting, the background for the action. She is the feminine source of life.

The symbols we have been dealing with are primarily nature symbols. In order to reach the root of each of these symbols, one must observe it as it appears, lives and changes in the natural world. Man observes an element of nature and finds in it a correspondence with the natural world within himself. These outer and inner worlds reflect each other, and the movement and drama of nature are repeated in microcosm in the movement and drama of man's natural inner world. Or we could view it the other way around. Neither world is primary, neither secondary. They are one. Man loses his awareness of this natural unity of the inner and outer as he spends more and more of his conscious life focused on the world outside himself. This world he experiences through the senses and receives as a perception. Sensory perception is aimed at the mind, and the mind then classifies, divides, limits and defines that outer world. At the same time, modern man has lost his ability to perceive his inner world, except insofar as he can perceive it as he perceives the outer world, and can again dissect, define and limit. As soon as man defines himself, he has catapulted himself into a state of isolation, for he no longer feels his essential unity with the whole of creation.

Symbols bridge the inner and outer worlds. Insofar as the eye performs the same function of merging inner and outer, the eye is a symbol of the symbol. But there is no symbol for mother earth, except for the human mother. The eye cannot *see* any symbol in the natural world for the maternal essence. The sun can be seen by the eye, and hence the father essence is the other. But we spring from matter, out of the depths of the earth, and this source from which we spring is not visible in her wholeness to the human eye. The only thing that can symbolize the source of life is the mother who is the source of an individual life. And thus is the earth symbolized in the traditional lyric.

The earth is the mother. She is the feminine principle transformed by the masculine impulse; she has been fertilized by spirit, by wind, by the breath of energy, and has produced. The tale told by the tradition is born from her womb, but it is not the moment of birth which is the topic of the story. The earth's creatures, once born, divide into two camps: male and female. The tension which results from that division ultimately produces the drama which we have been witnessing. The curtain rises on the action just when these children of the earth begin to feel the first stirrings of desire, just when adolescent eyes first open to receive the wounds of love. They are ready to admit the transforming energy of the masculine, they are ready to be fertilized and bear fruit. The fruit they bear will in turn keep the cycle in motion. The drama focuses only on the game being played by the male and the female children in the stormy seas of passion; the eternally repeated drama is condensed into the moment of transformation. Of the entire cycle of life—birth, infancy, youth, maturity, old age—the poetry of the tradition speaks almost exclusively of youth. This is the turning point of the drama, this is the peak of the action. The fruits of last year's drama have reached the age of sexual awakening. They will play out an innocent game of pitch and catch until the tension builds, longing aches within, and union becomes inevitable, irresistible. Once they unite, the story returns to the shadows, and remains beyond the scope of the tradition until the next set of characters, the fruits of this last union, carry on the cycle.

Because this brief moment illuminated by the flame of the tradition is the moment of transition, the moment when innocence enters experience, when youth enters maturity, we find a symbol which corresponds to the old order, and one which corresponds to the new. These two symbols are the mother and the daughter—or more exactly, the mother and the youth, because while not most, a few poems contain a young *man* and his mother. The mother's role in the drama is, necessarily, secondary. The protagonists now are the virgin and her lover. But unlike the father—sun energy—who, when he has done his job, i.e., to set the masculine emissary-symbols in motion, disappears from the action, the mother remains on stage. Her

children, after all, cling to her, seek comfort and support in her. Like
the waters of the mountain stream, they hug the mother earth who
bore them. But a moment comes when the young girl feels the
stirring birth of wings in her heels, and she is ready to rise into the
experience of life. Mother then is left behind.

The mother plays various roles in the tradition, but all in relation
to her daughter (or son, on occasion). By far her main role is that of
confidante and confessor—two words that stem from the same Latin
root *confidere*—to have faith with. The girl entrusts her feelings and
experiences to her mother because she knows her mother can share
them with her; her mother—by being her mother—proves her ability
to comprehend, for it was the love she experienced yesterday that
produced the lovers of today.

An important secondary role played by the mother in the tradition
is that of protectress of her virgin daughter. What we must ask
ourselves is *why* she protects the girl. What are the dangers her
daughter faces without her protection? Normally we think of parents
as social custodians of their children, as the representatives of society
who begin the socializing process in their children. Society has one
end—the perpetuation of itself, and consequently frowns on sexual
relationships outside the sanction of marriage, because its interest is
in the production and socialization of new members. Can we then see
the mother in the traditional lyric as guarding her daughter's virginity
so that she will be marriageable? Impossible! Mothers never talk
about marriage for their daughters. And when marriage is discussed
by anyone in the tradition, it is invariably in a negative light, as we
shall see shortly. The only viable explanation in terms of psychological
reality is that these mothers have experienced love and found it to be
the source of pain and sorrow, and it is this unhappiness they would
like their daughters to avoid. Their protection has very little to do
with society, except perhaps as a negative reaction to socially
sanctioned male-female relationships. Really, the mothers know that
their efforts to restrain the sexual impulse in their daughters are
futile. And not only futile, but as we shall see in certain poems, at
times their restrictions on the girl's freedom cause her to arrange
clandestine trysts with the lover. By damming up the flow of sexual
desire, they only add force to the waters when they break through the
barrier.

The sexual impulse, as has been illustrated in countless poems, is
irresistible. It is a force of nature that cannot be restrained any more
than the maturing of a fruit. This is the theme of the next poem—the
most beautiful of the *guarda* (protectress) poems:

#242 Niña y viña,   Girl and vineyard,
      peral y habar,   pear tree and bean-field,
      malo es de guardar.   hard they are to keep.

Levantéme, oh madre,	I arose, oh mother,
mañanica frida,	one cold fresh morning,
fui a cortar la rosa,	I went to pick the rose,
la rosa florida.	the flowering rose.
Malo es de guardar.	Hard it is to keep.
Levantéme, oh madre,	I arose, oh mother,
mañanica clara,	one clear fresh morning,
fui cortar la rosa,	I went to pick the rose,
la rosa granada.	the red budding rose.
Malo es de guardar.	Hard it is to keep.
Viñadero malo	A naughty grape-keeper
prenda me pedía;	requested of me a token;
dile yo un cordone,	I gave him a cord,
dile yo mi cinta.	I gave him a ribbon.
Malo es de guardar.	Hard it is to keep.
Viñadero malo	A naughty grape-keeper
prenda me demanda,	demanded of me a token;
dile yo un cordone,	I gave him a cord,
dile yo una banda.	I gave him a band.
Malo es de guardar.	Hard it is to keep.

Many symbols merge in this poem, symbols we have met over and over again—the dawn, the rose, the ribbon, the *prenda*, and fruit trees.

The *estribillo* of the poem sounds like (and in fact *is*) a proverbial saying.[1] The girl corresponds to these fruit-bearing plants with which she is included, because like them she has been growing, blossoming, and now she has reached the maturity necessary to bear fruit, as they have. In poem #4, "Aquel árbol que vuelve la foxa," all the different stages of development of the tree were condensed, and the last stage was the bearing of fruit. The singer exhorts the ladies to come out and pick the fruit. If the tree corresponds to the girl, and the fruit represents the reaching of sexual maturity, then the picking of fruit corresponds to loss of virginity, to sexual activity. The fruit is picked, devoured, and its seed falls to the ground to begin the cycle again. But why in that poem would the *ladies* be told to pick the fruit? We must not look for a rational correspondence, but a symbolic one. If the women come to pick the fruit, then they will be under the fruit trees where the young men can pick *their* fruit. So when girls pick fruit, they themselves are asking to be picked. And the same symbolism is associated with the cutting of the rose, another symbol of virginity. If the girl goes out alone to pick roses, she is announcing her readiness for sexual activity.

Before returning to the "niña" who is "mala de guardar," let us take a look at another ancient and lovely song in which three Moorish girls go out to gather olives and apples.

#243 Tres morillas m'enamoran
      en Jaén,
      Axa, Fátima, y Marién.

      Tres morillas tan garridas
      iban a coger olivas,
      y hallábanlas cogidas
      en Jaén.
      Axa y Fátima y Marién.

      Y hallábanlas cogidas,
      y tornaban desmaídas
      y las colores perdidas
      en Jaén.
      Axa y Fátima y Marién.

      Tres moricas tan loçanas,
      tres moricas tan loçanas
      iban a coger mançanas
      a Jaén.
      Axa y Fátima y Marién.

Three little Moorish girls
fill me with love
in Jaen,
Axa, Fatima, and Marien.

Three charming Moorish girls
went to gather olives,
and found them already picked
in Jaen.
Axa, Fatima, and Marien.

And found them already picked,
and they grew faint
and lost their color
in Jaen.
Axa, Fatima, and Marien.

Three sprightly Moorish girls,
three sprightly Moorish girls
went to gather apples
in Jaen.
Axa, Fatima, and Marien.

This is a very mysterious poem until one understands the symbolism of fruit-picking. Again, for one who is not initiated in the language and time of the tradition, it appears that these girls went forth and when they got to the trees discovered that the fruit had already been picked. But we know that the explicit chronology of a poem is deceptive in the tradition. Axa, Fátima, and Marién (and what musical names!) go out to pick olives. While they are engaged in this activity their own fruit *gets* picked. And that is why they faint and lose their color—they drown in a sea of passion, and come out without their virginity.

The girl who met a "viñadero malo" while she was out cutting roses at dawn could no more have been surprised at this encounter than the "velida" who met the wind on the mountain-top at dawn. By going to pick the rose, by going to wash clothes in the mountain spring, the girl is calling, inviting, the masculine energy to meet her. When she calls her lover a "viñadero malo" she is expressing the ambivalent feelings the "velida" expressed by her anger with the wind. Since the poem is a confession to her mother, the epithet could also be a means of camouflaging her true feelings, thereby protecting herself from her mother's possible anger. Or it could just as well be a playfully ironic epithet—he may be "malo," but she loves his "maldad."

Even though it is hard—impossible, really—to "guardar" a young nubile girl, there are many mothers who keep trying. We have already met with three poems in our studies thus far in which the mother plays the role of protectress, although in two of these, as in "Niña y viña," the girl also confides in the protecting mother. In poem #26, the *estribillo* sets the scene when the girl begs her mother not to hit her: "No me firáis, madre/yo os lo diré:/mal d'amores he." She then tells her mother about her lover, "un caballero de casa del rey," who "pidióme la fe." Her response to his petition—"dísela yo, madre,/no lo negaré"—indicates that she has probably already lost what her mother would protect. Consequently her mother resumes the beating and the girl again begs not to be beaten.

In another poem, #87, a "morenica" tells how her mother tied dogs to her bed, which she herself untied in order that her lover might join her there. About her mother, the girl says: "Una madre/que a mí me crió,/mucho me quiso/y mal me guardó." The girl clearly understands that her mother's efforts to guard her are motivated by love, but she is also clearly proud of her own ability to deceive her mother.

Why does the first mother react so violently to her daughter's sexual desires? The answer appeared in poem #96—a *cantiga* which is a dialogue between mother and daughter. The girl speaks first, confessing her love for her "amigo" who has been wounded by her love like a "cervo ferido de monteiro del rei" and who threatens to carry his sorrows to the sea in which he will drown. The girl seems genuinely concerned for his well-being. But her mother responds to her confession by warning her of the possibility of deception:

#96	—E guardade-vos, filha, ca já um atal vi que se fez mui coitado por guaanhar de mi.	Be careful, daughter, for one like that I've seen who looked so smitten my favors for to win.

Here the mother compares her own experience with that of her daughter. Though she does not admit to having fallen for her suitor's line, she must have done so, since she discovered his real motive "por guaanhar de mi." She extrapolates from her experience with love, and advises her daughter not to believe her lover's crocodile tears.

All three of these mothers wish to protect their daughters from the unhappy experiences they suffered. However, the girls *never* submit passively to their mothers' efforts to protect them. About the least rebellious is the girl who asks her mother—rhetorically—if she thinks her lover will dare to speak to her while her mother is present:

#244	Preguntar-vos quer'eu, madre, que mi digades verdade: se ousará meu amigo ante vós falar comigo.	I wish to ask you, mother, and I want you to tell me the truth: will my lover dare speak to me in front of you.

Pois eu migu'ei seu mandado,
querria saber de grado
　se ousará meu amigo
　ante vós falar comigo.

For I have here his message,
I would like to know with pleasure,
　will my lover dare
　speak to me in front of you.

Irei, mia madre, a la fonte
u van os cervos do monte:
　se ousará meu amigo
　ante vós falar comigo.

I will go, my mother, to the spring
where the mountain deer are
found;
　will my lover dare
　speak to me in front of you.

The question she wants to ask her mother, a question thrice repeated in the refrain, is one to which she already knows the answer. She is just trying to get her mother to sympathize, to see her point of view, to stop watching her. Furthermore, her statement in the last stanza indicates that she intends to escape her mother and meet her lover alone at the spring where the deer drink, no matter whether her mother's answer to her non-question is affirmative or negative.

The girl in this next poem, another mother-daughter dialogue of the type that only occurs—and then infrequently—among the *cantigas d'amigo*, has already been to the spring, arriving home later than usual. Her mother's questions about her tardiness turn out to be as rhetorical as the girl's question in the last poem, for after hearing her daughter's reply she reveals that she knew the cause all along:

#245　—Digades, filha, mia filha veli-
　　　da:
　porque tardastes na fontana fria?
　　os amores ei.

—Tell me, daughter, my lovely
　daughter:
why did you tarry at the cold
　spring?
　　I'm in love.

Digades, filha, mia filha louçana:
porque tardastes na fria fontana?
　os amores ei.

Tell me, daughter, my sprightly
daughter:
why did you tarry at the spring so
cold?
　　I'm in love.

　—Tardei, mia madre, na fon-
　　tana fria,
cervos do monte a augua volvian:
　os amores ei.

—I tarried, my mother, at the cold
　spring,
mountain deer stirred the water:
　　I'm in love.

Tardei, mia madre, na fria
fontana,
cervos do monte volvian a augua:
　os amores ei.

I tarried, my mother, at the spring
so cold,
mountain deer the water stirred:
　　I'm in love.

　—Mentir, mia filha, mentir por
　　amigo;

—You lie, my daughter, you lie for
　your lover;

nunca vi cervo que volvess'o rio:	I never saw a deer who stirred the
os amores ei.	river:
	I'm in love.
Mentir, mia filha, mentir por	You lie, my daughter, you lie for
amado;	your beloved;
nunca vi cervo que volvess'o alto:	I never saw a deer who stirred the
os amores ei.	high waters.
	I'm in love.

From the endearing tone she uses to address her daughter, "mia filha velida (louçana)," it is clear that she will not beat the girl, even though she accuses her of lying. When she declares she never saw a stag stir the water, she is at least admitting that she, too, is familiar with the spring-fed waters where lovers meet. This poem contains a complex irony. The girl confesses in symbolic language. On one level it appears that she is purposely deceiving her mother by telling her the truth in symbols she hopes her mother will not understand. Her mother sees through the deception—"mentir por amigo"—because she understands perfectly her daughter's symbolism. Hence her accusation that her daughter is lying is as ironic as the daughter's confession. Consequently, it seems that the mother's reaction is almost playful. One gets the feeling in this poem that there is an unspoken understanding between mother and daughter, an almost conspiratorial relationship, as if the mother knew beforehand what was likely to occur when she sent her daughter to the spring.[2]

This poem is unusual because the symbolism actually becomes an issue in the situation of the poem. The language of poetry, when transferred to the world of reality, makes no sense—rationally. And the mother's accusation is based on reason, albeit ironically.

The girl in this next poem hides nothing from her mother. She informs her that she has arranged to meet her lover at the spring "u os cervos van bever," but now, because her mother will not allow her to go to her rendezvous, she complains bitterly that she will have to lie to him:

#246 A meu amig', a que preito falhei,	To my love, with whom I've made arrangements,
con vosso medo, madre, mentir-l'ei,	for fear of you, mother, I will have to lie,
e se non fôr, assanhar-s'á.	and if I don't go, he'll get angry.
Talhei-lh'eu preito do o ir veer	I made arrangements to go to see him
ena fonte u os cervos van bever,	at the spring where the deer go to drink,
e se non fôr, assanhar-s'á.	and if I don't go, he'll get angry.

E, non ei eu de lhi mentir sabor,
mais mentir-lh-ei con vosso pavor,
    e se non fôr, assanhar-s'á.

De lhi mentir nenhum sabor non ei,
con vosso med' a mentir'lh'averei,
    e se non fôr, assanhar-s'á.

And I don't like to lie to him,
but lie I will for fear of you,
    and if I don't go, he'll get angry.

To lie to him gives me no pleasure,
for fear of you I will have to lie,
    and if I don't go, he'll get angry.

She claims she fears her mother, and that is why she will not disobey her. It is unclear why she will have to lie to her lover, why she cannot tell him that her mother will not allow her to go. Perhaps she is ashamed to admit her mother still treats her like a child. At any rate, she not only fears her mother, but also seems to fear her lover's anger: "e se non fôr, assanhar-s'á." But this could simply be a ploy she uses to convince her mother to let her go. She presents her situation in such a way that she appears to be caught between two equally angry forces, and hopes that her mother will sympathize and relent.

This next song illustrates how this last girl got herself into her dilemma in the first place. Here we have a girl making arrangements to meet her lover, with whom she speaks, at another of the familiar trysting places—the shrine:

#247 Id'oj', ai meu amigo, led'a San Salvador;
    eu vosco irei leda, e, pois eu vosco fôr,
        mui leda irei, amigo,
        e vos ledo comigo.

Pero sõo guardada, todavia quer'-ir
con vosc', ai meu amigo, se mi-a guarda non vir;
        mui leda irei, amigo,
        e vos ledo comigo.

Pero sõo guardada, todavia irei
con vosc', ai meu amigo, se a guarda non ei;
        mui leda irei, amigo,
        e vos ledo comigo.

Go joyful today, ay, my love, to San Salvador;
I will go joyful with you and since with you I go,
    very joyful I will go, love,
    and you joyful with me.

Although I am watched, yet still I wish to go
with you, ay, my love, if my watcher doesn't see;
    very joyful I will go, love,
    and you joyful with me.

Although I am watched, yet still I'll go
with you, ay, my love, if the watcher isn't here;
    very joyful I will go, love,
    and you joyful with me.

She plainly states her problem to her lover: she wants to go, but she is being "guarded." That does not stop her from proceeding with the plans, however, and she consistently speaks in the future indicative, as if harboring a secret design to escape her mother's protective care. She is uncertain what to do, but as her desire grows, her fear of her mother will diminish until she declares:

#248   Seguir el amor me plaze,   To follow love pleases me,
        aunque rabie mi madre.   though my mother be furious.

It is one thing to make such a declaration behind her mother's back, it is another to confront her directly:

#249   No me falaguéis, mi madre,   Don't flatter me, my mother,
        con vuestro dulze dezir,   with your sweet-talk,
        yo con él me tengo de ir.   I must go with him.

This girl defiantly asserts her intention to do as she pleases, though from her perspective it is beyond a question of will or desire. Going with her lover has become a necessity for her, no choice is involved ("con él me tengo de ir"). Therefore the mother's sweet-talk cannot convince her not to go, and hence her command that her mother not waste her breath.

In all these poems we see that, basically, the mother's attempts to protect her daughter from experiencing love are futile. The strength of this inexorable natural urge for union with the lover is beyond her control. The only one who can really protect a girl's virginity is the girl herself:

#250   Madre, la mi madre,   Mother, my mother,
        guardas me ponéis;   you keep watch over me;
        que si yo no me guardo,   but if I don't watch myself
        mal me guardaréis.   you won't be able to watch me.

And this next song demonstrates perfectly the veracity of her defiant assertion:

#251   No me habléis, conde,   Don't speak to me, Count,
        d'amor en la calle;   about love in the street;
        catá que os dirá mal,   watch out, for my mother,
        conde, la mi madre.   Count, will say harsh words
                                          about you.

        Mañana iré, conde,   Tomorrow I will go, Count,
        a lavar al río;   to wash at the river;
        allá me tenéis, conde,   there you will find me, Count,
        a vuestro servicio.   at your service.

        Catá que os dirá mal,   Watch out, Count, for my mother
        conde, la mi madre.   will say harsh words about you.
        No me habléis, conde,   Don't speak to me, Count,
        de amor en la calle.   about love in the street.

Like water, when she finds an obstacle in her path, she simply goes around it.

Earlier we heard the voice of one mother who warned her daughter not to worry so much about her lover's misery, for from her own experience, she suspects that he is simply using his suffering as a means to get his way with her. The mother would like to protect her daughter from the deception of which she herself was once a victim. This is one of the dangers girls face in love—being used and abandoned.

But there is another danger which, judging from the number of poems that deal with it, is the greatest danger of all—marriage.

#252	No querades, fija, marido tomar para sospirar.	Don't wish, daughter, to take a husband in order to sigh.
	Fuése mi marido a la frontera; sola me dexaba en tierr'agena. No querades, fija, marido tomar para sospirar.	Off went my husband to the frontier; he left me alone in a foreign land. Don't wish, daughter, to take a husband in order to sigh.

We have heard the songs of many girls who were deceived by love, and their laments are genuine. However, we also encountered several poems in which the *morena* was considered an object of desire. Perhaps she never finds a husband, but she has no trouble finding a lover after she has been "stained" by love. The plight of the *malcasada*, however, is as bad or even worse, for though she is socially secure, she, too, finds love disillusioning. But since she is married there is no hope for a reversal of her fortune. The *morena* may not have social status, but she still has the pleasures of sex; the *malcasada* has social status but, as we saw in poem #128, she can only gaze longingly at the sea and wait for a wind to blow down from the mountain.

This next poem makes explicit what the *malcasada* lacks—*plazer*.

#253	A la malcasada dele Dios plazer, que la bien casada no lo a menester.	May God grant pleasure to the unhappy bride, for the happy bride has no need of it.

This wife is reduced to bribing her disinterested husband for some of that *plazer*:

#254	Bésame y abrázame, marido mío, y daros h'en la mañana camisón limpio.	Kiss me and hug me, my husband, and I will give you in the morning a clean shirt.

Here we find the shirt, formerly a symbol of sexual involvement between unmarried lovers, being offered ironically to a husband in payment for his sexual attentions.

The situation is so frustrating that this young wife wishes she were dead:

#255 Cuando mi padre me casó,   When my father married me,
      muriera yo.   I should have died.

      Pues que me dio   He gave me
      al mal villano,   to a peasant rogue
      que tarde ni temprano   who early or late
      no sabe, no,   doesn't know, no,
      no puede, no,   isn't able, no,
      ni acierta, no,   doesn't manage, no,
      sino 'n dormir.   to do anything but sleep.
      ¡O qué morir!   Oh what a death!
      Ay, ay, ay,   Ay, ay, ay,
      que muerta so,   for I am dead,
      pues que me dio   since he gave me
      al mal villano.   to a peasant rogue.

The only thing her husband knows how to do, is able to do, and in fact
manages to do, is sleep. She starts out wishing she were dead, and ends
up concluding that, in fact, for all practical purposes, she is.

    This girl's frustration has reached a level of cruel sarcasm:

#256 Mi marido anda cuitado;   My husband goes around afflicted,
      juraré que está castrado.   I could swear he's castrated.

while this one curses her husband and calls him with bitter irony,
"agudo":

#257 Andá noramala, agudo,   Be gone with you, sharp one,
      agudo mío;   my sharp one;
      andá noramala, agudo,   Be gone with you, sharp one,
      que andáis dormido.   for you walk around asleep.

The problem, of course, is that he is not "agudo" at all, and the only
"walking" he does is sleep-walking.

    The husband in this next poem may be "agudo," but in the wrong
place:

#258 Pensó el mal villano   The peasant rogue thought
      que yo que dormía,   I was asleep,
      tomó espada en mano,   he took his sword in hand
      fuese andar por villa.   and went to walk the streets.

His lack of interest in bed is due to the fact that he has outside
interests. He may think he can slip out unnoticed in the middle of the
night, with his sword in hand, but she knows what he is up to. The
sword is another of those dangerous wounding weapons we saw in the
last chapter, and the verb *andar*, with its symbolic connotation, has
appeared in the last three poems.

    The symbolic significance of the eyes lends a special poignancy to
this song. The young wife has to ask her husband to look at her:

#259 Pues que me tienes,   Well, since you have me,
      Miguel, por esposa,   Miguel, as your wife,
      mírame, Miguel,   look at me, Miguel,
      como soy hermosa.   how beautiful I am.

When even such a tactful request falls on deaf ears, the *malcasada* makes one final attempt to get what she needs from her husband:

#260 Marido, ¿si queréis algo?
     que me quiero levantar.

Husband, would you like something?
     for I wish to get up.

But all her petitions are in vain. She has made the decision to "get up" (*levantar*). She can wait for him in his bed no longer. The day dawns, it is time to arise. Consequently neither we nor her husband should be surprised when she says,

#261 No tengáis, marido, a mal
     que de lo que a vos os sobra
     haga bien y buena obra.

Don't take it hard, husband,
that what you have left over
should do some good and charitable work.

¿Para qué gruñís, marido,
si doy al necesitado
lo que vos dejáis sobrado
y queda en casa perdido?

Why do you grumble, husband,
if I give to the needy
what you let go to waste
and leave lost at home?

If her husband wastes what another wants, why not do a good deed and share what he does not appreciate anyway?

This husband apparently was not agreeable to her sharing arrangement:

#262 Y la mi cinta dorada,
     ¿por qué me la tomó
     quien no me la dio?

And my golden ribbon,
why was it taken from me
by one who didn't give it?

La mi cinta de oro fino,
diómela mi lindo amigo;
tomómela mi marido,
¿Por qué me la tomó
quien no me la dio?

My ribbon of finest gold,
my handsome lover gave to me;
my husband took it from me.
Why was it taken from me
by one who didn't give it?

La mi cinta de oro claro,
diómela mi lindo amado;
tomómela mi velado.
¿Por qué me la tomó
quien no me la dio?

My ribbon of shining gold
my handsome loved one gave to me;
my spouse took it from me.
Why was it taken from me
by one who didn't give it?

Once again the symbol of the ribbon appears, and again it is golden. The ribbon symbolizes the twining together of two lovers, and the power of one over the other. In this poem the ribbon is a gift from her "lindo amigo" which her husband takes from her. She feigns ignorance, using the same mystified tone of innocence as the girl who feels the first stirrings of sexuality. But her husband has taken symbolic control when he takes the ribbon. He puts a stop to her twisting and twining with her lover—and she knows it.

In the next poem, the young wife feigns innocence when she asks her question, too:

#263 —Dime, pajarito que estás en el   —Tell me, little bird, there in your
   nido: nest:
   ¿La dama besada pierde marido?   The lady who's been kissed, does
   —No, la mi señora, si fuese en   she lose her husband?
   escondido.   —No, my lady, not if it was in
                                               secret.

The "pajarito" may be a real bird or a handsome young man, but the
girl has plainly been kissed and not by her husband. Her lover assures
her there is no need to worry as long as her husband does not know.
 Yet there is always the danger of his bursting in unexpectedly.

#264 Dixe que te fueras   I told you to go
   y no has querido,   and you didn't want to,
   ¡desdicha de mí   Worse for me,
   si es mi marido!   if it's my husband!

There is no way of knowing whether it is her husband she hears at the
door or not. One is left with the tension of this moment of suspense
and the only way to resolve that tension is by finishing the story
oneself. The beauty of this poetry is that it presents a situation in
which there are opposing energy poles between which tension arises.
The poem expresses that tension, but does not resolve it. The specific
identity of these energy poles can vary infinitely: lover-beloved: virgin-
wind; wind-hair; stag-water; eyes seeing and eyes seen; etc. The
polarity is most often masculine-feminine in essence, but at times it is
mother-daughter. In this poem the tension is of the same basic nature
as the protectress (mother)—protected (daughter) polarity, for the
husband becomes, in a certain group of *malcasada* poems, a replacement
for the mother in her function of *guarda*. There is a striking similarity in
situation between this last poem, in which the lovers are in bed
suspended in a moment of fear as they hear the cuckolded husband at
the door, and this next poem:

#265 Llaman a Teresica y no viene.   They're calling Teresica, and she
   ¡Tan mala noche tiene!   doesn't come.
                                               What a bad night she has!
   Llámala su madre y ella calla;
   juramiento tiene hecho de   Her mother calls her and she re-
    matarla.   mains silent;
   ¡Qué mala noche tiene!   she's sworn to kill her.
                                               What a bad night she has!

Teresica is hiding. It is certain that she hears the calls of her worried
mother because she keeps silent ("calla"). Now there is only one reason
to stay in hiding and keep quiet—she is in the arms of her lover. If she
were alone, why would she hide? She must be shaking with fear—her
mother swears she will kill her! What was planned as a night of
pleasure has turned into a bad night, indeed, due to the unexpected
intrusion of her mother. But her mother is having no less of a bad

night as she worries frantically about her daughter. Note how elegantly the refrain describes the emotional state of both women. The girl is afraid of what her mother will do to her, and the mother is afraid of what the lover will do to her daughter. A triangle is created with the same energy pattern as the triangle formed by the jealous husband, the sexually frustrated young wife, and her lover. These waters, too, will go where they will.

An unfulfilled young wife is as ripe a fruit, as sweet-smelling a blossom waiting to be picked, as is a young virgin. For remember, when a tree stirs its leaves, when it blossoms and bears fruit, it manifests that "algo se le antoxa."

#266	Ya florecen los árboles, Juan;	The trees are flowering, Juan,
	¡mala seré de guardar!	I will be hard to keep!
	Ya florecen los almendros,	The almonds are flowering,
	y los amores con ellos;	and love along with them;
	¡Juan, mala seré de guardar!	Juan, I will be hard to keep!
	Ya florecen los árboles, Juan;	The trees are flowering, Juan,
	¡mala seré de guardar!	I will be hard to keep!

The motif of this poem is the same as that of "Niña y viña." In that poem the young girl told her *mother* that a girl, like a fruit tree, "malo es de guardar." Here the young wife tells her *husband* that the trees are blossoming and "mala seré de guardar." She sees herself as an almond tree, there is no difference between them. Alike they blossom, alike they are so attractive that they are hard to protect—and hard to control.

It seems as though everything in the tradition calls forth its opposite. If we find husbands who jealously try to hoard away what is theirs, we are bound to find husbands who are just as eager to sell what is theirs. This is the theme of the generally satirical "cornudo consentido" poems:

#267	A un honrado marido	An honorable husband
	que callar sabe,	who knows how to keep quiet,
	no ay thesoro en las Indias	there's no treasure in all the Indies
	con que pagalle.	with which to repay him.

In this song the young wife expresses ironic appreciation of a husband who is anything but "honrado." That which makes him so valuable that all the gold in America could not repay him is the fact that he knows how to keep quiet and not complain about her outside activities.

#268	Digan a mi belado	Let them tell my spouse
	que no trabaxe,	not to work,
	bástale por oficio	it's enough of a trade
	que sufra y calle.	to suffer and keep silent.

This wife wants her husband to be advised of what a comfortable life he could have if he just would suffer silently. He has no need to work; she will support him.

#269 Las casadas se venden   Married women sell themselves
      como los libros;   like books;
      con licencia firmada   with the signed permission
      de sus maridos.   of their husbands.

Though this is an effortless way for a husband to live, it has its dangers, not the least of which is that his wife may grow tired of the whole arrangement:

#270 Marido, busca otra renta,   Husband, seek another income,
      que vale cara la cornamenta.   for cuckoldry costs a lot.

After seeing the portrayal of marriage in the tradition, we can understand why this girl says:

#271 Si el marido a de mandarme,   If a husband is going to rule me,
      más vale no casarme.   it's better for me not to marry.

She views marriage as a restriction placed upon her freedom, as does this *serrana*—always an independent type. Neither girl finds any benefit for themselves in this social custom:

#272 Dicen que me case yo;   They tell me I should marry;
      no quiero marido, no.   I don't want a husband, no.

      Más quiero vivir segura   I prefer to live secure,
      nesta sierra a mi soltura,   freely in this mountain,
      que no estar en ventura   rather than have to worry
      si casaré bien o no.   if I will marry well or not.
      Dicen que me case yo;   They tell me I should marry;
      no quiero marido, no.   I don't want a husband, no.

      Madre, no seré casada,   Mother, I won't be married,
      por no ver vida cansada,   for I don't want a tiresome life,
      o quizá mal empleada   or perhaps badly spent
      la gracia que Dios me dió.   the grace which God gave me.
      Dicen que me case yo,   They tell me I should marry;
      no quiero marido, no.   I don't want a husband, no.

      No será ni es nacido   No man is born, nor ever will be,
      tal para ser mi marido;   who's fit to be my husband;
      y pues que tengo sabido   and since I know full well
      que la flor yo me la só,   that the sweetest flower am I,
      dicen que me case yo,   they tell me I should marry,
      no quiero marido, no.   I don't want a husband, no.

She enjoys her "soltura" in the mountains, and does not want to have to worry about whether she is making a good choice of husband or not. Besides, there is not a man alive who is worthy of her, for "la flor yo me la só."

Mothers must not only listen to the confidences of their unmarried daughters, but also the laments of their married daughters:

#273 Madre mía, muriera yo
  y no me casara, no.

  Vida tan desventurada
  yo nunca la vi.
  Para ser tan desdeñada,
  ¿para qué nací?
  ¡Desdichada y sin favor
  qué consuelo de dolor
  es mi dolor!

  Madre mía, muriera yo
  y no me casara, no.

My mother, I wish I had died
and had never married, no.

Such a miserable life
I have never seen.
To be thus disdained,
why was I born?
Cursed and unfavored
what consolation for pain
is my pain!

My mother, I wish I had died,
and had never married, no.

Another young wife wishes she were dead because she is "desdeñada." And it seems that this unhappiness is precisely what the mothers of the tradition hope can be avoided for their daughters. But if these girls are better off not marrying, what are they to do with their lives? Many mothers find the answer in the religious life—they want their daughters to be nuns:

#274 —Meteros quiero monja,
   hija mía de mi corazón.
  —Que no quiero yo ser monja,
   non.

—I want to make you a nun,
  dearest daughter of my heart.
—I don't want to be a nun, no.

The mother's wish that her daughter become a nun is clearly based on deep affection and concern for her well-being: "hija mía de mi corazón." But the girl rebels. Her attitude is expressed in this song:

#275 Casada y arrepentida,
  y no monja metida.

Married and sorry,
and not a hidden-away nun.

From the perspective of a young girl, full of life and desire, marriage, even if she ends up regretting it, is preferable to being stuck away in a convent. After all, these young girls have only recently awakened to the pleasures of sexual love. Having just tasted these pleasures, she has no desire to forsake them, simply because her mother wants to protect her from love's pain.

#276 ¿Agora que sé d'amor me metéis
   monja?
  ¡Ay, Dios, qué grave cosa!

  Agora que sé d'amor de caballero,
  agora me metéis monja en el
   monesterio.
  ¡Ay, Dios, qué grave cosa!

Now that I know about love you
  stick me away as a nun?
Oh God, what a grave thing!

Now that I know the love of a
  gentleman,
now you stick me away as a nun
  in a convent?
Oh God, what a grave thing!

While the thought of becoming a nun after having enjoyed the love of her "caballero" is certainly a "grave cosa," even worse is never to have tasted that joy at all. The girl in this next song is still a "niña en cabello," a virgin:

#277 Agora que soy niña
quiero alegría,
que no se sirve Dios
de mi monjía.

Agora que soy niña,
niña en cabello,
me queréis meter monja
en el monesterio.
Que no se sirve Dios
de mi monjía.

Agora que soy niña
quiero alegría,
que no se sirve Dios
de mi monjía.

Now that I'm a maiden
I want merriment.
As a nun I'm not
pleasing to God.

Now that I'm a maiden,
a girl with flowing hair,
you want to stick me away
as a nun in a convent.
As a nun I'm not
pleasing to God.

Now that I'm a maiden
I want merriment,
as a nun I'm not
pleasing to God.

However, it is not necessarily the case that nuns do not enjoy love games:

#278 Ser quiero, madre,
señora de mí,
no quiero ver
mal gozo de mí.

Dize mi madre
que me meta monja,
que me dará un fraile
cual yo le excoxa,
mas bien entiendo
la su lisonja;
no verá çierto
tal gozo de mí.

Mother, I want to be
my own lady,
I don't want to see
bad use made of me.

My mother says
that I should be a nun,
that she will give me a friar,
any one I choose,
but I'm not fooled
by her flattering talk;
surely none will ever see
such bad use made of me.

This young girl not only wants to be in command of her own life, but she certainly does not want to be stuck in a convent at the beck and call of some friar. She refuses to be deceived by her mother's sweet-talk ("lisonja") any more than the girl who must go with her lover despite her mother's gentle efforts to dissuade her with her "dulce decir."

This girl feels the same way:

#279 Nadie no diga,
que de un fraile e de ser amiga;
no diga nadie
que e de ser amiga de un fraile.

Let no one say
that I'm to be a friar's mistress,
let no one say
that I'm to be the mistress of a
friar.

Yet there are those girls who, recognizing the risk involved in marriage, prefer the religious life:

#280 Monjica en religión   I want to be
      me quiero entrar,   a little cloistered nun,
      por no mal maridar.   so I won't be an unhappy bride.

This girl is ready to enter a convent, but what kind of a nun she will be
is indicated by the diminutive "monjica"—not a very serious one. In
this context the suggestion of the diminutive is not innocence, but
rather that she will be an attractive little nun. Bearing in mind the
suggestion attached to the verb *andar*, we see in this next poem just
exactly what she intends to do when she becomes a nun:

#281 De iglesia en iglesia   From church to church
      me quiero yo andar,   I want to go,
      por no mal maridar.   so I won't be an unhappy bride.

This simple little poem is really quite profound. Most striking is its
tone of bitter yet playful irony. Certainly the singer has a low regard
for marriage. She never considers any alternative to a bad marriage
besides becoming a nun and spending her time in church. She does not
want to end up unhappily married so she chooses a different path in
life—one of only two socially acceptable paths for women in the society
of the tradition, neither of which promises much joy—marriage or the
convent.

But this girl has her own ideas about convent life. She carefully
avoids any mention of actually becoming a nun. The social position she
chooses is merely implied by the place where she performs it—the
church. However, she does not imagine herself in that role as ever
really being *in* church, doing the things that nuns are supposed to do.
She identifies the role not in terms of its socially-imposed image, but in
terms of her own personal image of a nun's life. She envisions herself
walking from church to church, timelessly suspended in between the
actual performance of her role. Perhaps she does not consciously
realize why this image is so appealing to her. She is a young girl full of
sexual energy, and when she imagines her future life as a nun, she just
naturally conjures up the image that is of most interest. The walking
back and forth, the showing off, the seeing and being seen excite her
without her necessarily being conscious of the fact that they suggest
sexual activity.

She could, on the other hand, be perfectly conscious of the
suggestiveness of what she imagines. This may be precisely why she
chooses the role of the nun, because she knows it only *appears* to be
restricting. There are always ways to get around any barrier—mother,
husband, or religious orders. And this notion of overcoming the
obstacles to union is certainly a predominant one in the tradition.

When the obstacle to union is insurmountable—when the lover is
separated from or rejected by the beloved—then the poetry focuses on
the lament. The only way to relieve the tension of desire when union
becomes impossible is to weep bitterly, bemoan one's sorrows in song:

#282 ¡Ay, ay, ay, ay!   Ay, ay, ay, ay!
      ¡qué fuertes penas!   what strong sorrow!
      ¡Ay, ay, ay, ay!,   Ay, ay, ay ay!
      ¡qué fuerte mal!   what strong pain.

The pain is so great that the singer is reduced to moaning, unable to
articulate in words her sorrow. Here we find no indication of the cause
of her suffering, but both her "penas" and "mal" are "fuertes." Twice
before that adjective was employed to describe the mountain, once in
the tale of the young man assaulted "en fuerte lugare" (#213) by an
aggressive *serrana*, and once in the lament of a girl in love with a
"vaquero" who flees from her through "la montaña fuerte" (#225). The
adjective *fuerte* in those poems bore the same semantic import as
alto—the inexorable *power* of the sexual urge. Consequently the
strength of the suffering this girl experiences links her with the
intense suffering of others in the mountain or by the stormy sea. This
pain is always experienced as a feeling of isolation. Not only does the
sufferer feel cut off from the object of desire, but from the entire
world. This sense of isolation was beautifully symbolized by the image
of the girl surrounded by the waves of passion in poem #126. She was
trapped by the stormy sea, severed from the safety of the shore, and
she lacked any means of regaining her contact with the world ("non ei
barqueiro".) Consequently, she felt she would die in her solitude of
passionate longing.

   This next poem closely resembles the inarticulate expression of
suffering we heard in the last poem, with its insistent repetition of
"ay." But now the singer articulates her sense of separation from the
rest of the world.

#283 ¡Ay, que non ay! ¡Ay, que non   Ay, for there's no one! Ay, there
         era!   never was!
      ¡Mas ay, que non ay   But ay, for there's no one
      quien de mi pena se duela!   who takes pity on my pain.

Her "pena" is double: first there is the "pena" of being prevented from
uniting with her lover (is there any other source of "pena" in these
poems?); and second, the "pena" of being alone in her sorrow. Here we
have come across the motivating force of the entire tradition. The
songs of the traditional lyric are expressions of feeling, and feeling is
the climate of the inner world. Insofar as the singer believes her feeling
to be separate and different from the climate of the outer world, she
feels alone. Eyes, we saw, can be a bridge between the self and the
world, they can bind the two into one: "Miraba la mar la mal casada"
(#128). And the breath, too, can be an emissary from the self to the
world, the messenger who communicates one's inner feeling to the
outer world. This was most evident in the song in which a girl
mourned the death of her "amigo" under the olive tree: "Gritos daba la

morenica so el olivar,/que las ramas hace temblar" (#62). Her cries made the branches tremble in sympathy. And in just this way the expressions of sorrow insistently repeated in song after song can be seen as the breath which the singers send into the world with the hope that somewhere, sometime, a branch may stir in sympathy and thus the oppressive isolation of pain may be relieved.

Almost invariably, what these singers really want is to be united with the beloved, with the lover, to be made complete, to return to a state of happiness which was theirs before they experienced love. These children are just awakening to a transforming realization—that they are separate from the world.

Let us trace the process. One is born into the world unconscious. There is no distinction between oneself and the world. There is no desire, there is only need. And when need is expressed—the baby cries—her need is fulfilled by mother. Mother and child are one from the baby's point of view—if the baby had any such thing as a point of view. But that is why there is no consciousness—there is no point from which the baby views the world. It is a supportive, nourishing wholeness, a completion. When there is a void, for example, hunger, the void is filled. Mother consequently symbolizes the happiness of innocence, of unconsciousness. But symbols are only symbols when there is a consciousness to perceive them as symbolic. Hence to the infant the mother does not symbolize wholeness, because there are no symbols—mother just is the wholeness.

But suddenly a need arises in the baby, who has now grown to be a youth, which is not immediately fulfilled—a need for sexual union. That need is both real and symbolic. In adolescence the arousal of sexual desire is as real as hunger in the infant, but not as immediately and spontaneously fulfilled. The void is there, and no one comes along to fill it spontaneously. And hence, consciousness is born from desire. Now there *is* a point of view. An infant is the fruit of a fullness, a completion—the union of male and female; consciousness, on the other hand, is born from an emptiness, a void. But in the lack, in the yearning itself, lies the seed—the need for completion. Completion—the union of opposites, of male and female—will in turn bear fruit. The fruit must always die in order for consciousness to be born—for the seed to germinate and begin its journey once more toward completion. The cycle is endless.

Until the flower blossoms, the tree has been sufficient unto itself with its roots in the mother earth, and its leaves warmed by father sun. But when the blossom appears there is suddenly a need for another tree to provide the pollen necessary for it to produce the fruit that will keep the cycle in motion. Yearning arises, the leaves begin to tremble in a gentle breeze of longing. The blossom yearns for the wind that will carry the pollen she needs in order to be transformed into a seed-bearing fruit. The breath of the wind carries the sighs of the blossom—her longing which is her irresistible aroma. Her song is an expression of her need for completion.

She is incomplete and when her yearning cannot be fulfilled she turns again to her mother, hoping that somehow if she cannot be made whole through union with the man she longs for, she can at least unburden her sorrow onto her mother. For *now*, because she is conscious now, and being conscious *sees* her mother, too, as separate from herself, *now* her mother becomes the *symbol* of lost completion, of innocence, of happiness. Thus we find that the mother is the intended audience of most of the mournful complaints of unrequited love. She is the "other" to whom the "self," the girl, turns in desperation, in her terrible experience of separation, aloneness, solitude. We heard the melancholy complaints of the *morenas* as they longed for a prior state of whiteness. Virginity too, is both really and symbolically wholeness—the wholeness of sexual unconsciousness. And just as virginity is destroyed by penetration of the masculine, consciousness is produced by the penetration of light into the unconscious. The complete darkness of the womb, of childhood, of unconsciousness has been destroyed by the energy of the winds of passion. It was when the breath of God moved over the face of the chaos, the void, that light and darkness were born. The waters were stirred.

When the emptiness of isolation cannot be filled by what is desired, when there seems to be no hope for future completion, then the innocence of the past appears to the consciousness as a golden age of happiness, though at the time neither happiness nor unhappiness were known. The wind had not yet stirred the waters. Light and darkness were not yet born. But precisely because consciousness cannot be unconscious, cannot return to an undifferentiated state of wholeness, it can only *see* its former innocence as desirable, as a release from the very tension of desire inherent in itself. Consciousness longs for its own annihilation, and one way is through a return to lost innocence—but that path has been cut off forever by the penetration of light. This is symbolized in the next poem:

#284   Bonito, pasito,   Fine sir, slowly,
       no me cortéis.   don't cut me.
       ¡Cortado me habéis, cortado! You have cut me, cut me!

Once cut she cannot be made whole. Or the former self has drowned in a sea of passion:

#285   Echa acá la barca hao,   Throw the raft here,
       que en el mar de amor me anego. for I'm drowning in the sea of love.

This is consciousness looking for completion, not by turning away from its knowledge of the other, but by becoming one with the other.

We have already looked at many poems that express the desire for union with the lover-beloved. Let us listen now to the mournful songs of those who look backward at their lost happiness, who bitterly regret the loss of unconscious innocence:

#286 Sem cuidado naci eu,   Free of care I was born,
      ai, amor, e quem mo deu!   Alas, for Love and he who gave
                                          me it.

The verb "nacer" is associated symbolically with the transformation of love. Here unconsciousness is represented as being a state "sem cuidado," into which the singer, the self, is born. But again, there is the lament: "ai..." Someone has introduced "cuidado" into her life. And the culprit? "Amor."

In this Castilian poem, which echoes the last, the state of innocence is represented paradoxically:

#287 Descuidado de cuidado   Careless of care
      estaba yo.   was I,
      ¡Ay, triste!, y ¿quién me lo dio?   Ay, sad me! and who gave me it?

What is this "cuidado" that love brings? Its root lies in the verb *cuidar*[3] which comes from the Latin "cogitare": to *think*! The first verse might then be understood as "unthoughtful of thought," "unmindful of mind," "unconscious of consciousness...," innocent.

And with thought, with consciousness comes that fatal perception of time:

#288 ¡Ay, horas tristes,   Ay, sad hours,
      cuán diferentes sois de lo que   how different you are from what
      fuistes!   you were!

Of course time seems different, for now it exists. Before "cuidado" there are no "horas." That timelessness of innocence was expressed in a few poems before, such as the boy and girl tossing little oranges back and forth, and the *galan* and *galana* who, hand in hand, wash in the spring. Here is another, similar in tone, a celebration of the union of *doncel* and *doncella*.

#289 ¡Oh cuán lindo es el doncel,   Oh, how handsome is the lad,
      y cuán linda es la doncella!   and how handsome is the lassie!
      Lindo es él y linda es ella.   Handsome is he, and handsome is
                                          she.

Doncel and *doncella* refer to the virgin state of the youths they represent, and that is what is being celebrated in this poem—the union of two innocences. There is a perfect balance between the masculine and the feminine, which merge in the third verse. Where there is no tension, there is no time, and no action, no movement toward anything. Just harmony.

#290 La doncella y el garçón   The maiden and the lad
      para en uno son.   are made for each other.

But when there is longing there is an acute perception of time. The present is unsatisfactory. Happiness lies either in the past or the future. The verb *soler* in the imperfect tense becomes pivotal in these nostalgic poems, where the singer compares what used to be with what is:

#291 No es el tiempo que solía,   Times aren't what they used to be,
      madre mía,   my mother,
      no es el tiempo que solía.   times aren't what they used to be.

Again it is the mother, symbol of "el tiempo que solía," to whom the singer turns with her lament. Time, as everyone knows, goes much more slowly when one is conscious of it:

#292 Estas noches atan largas,   These endless nights
      para mí   for me
      no solían ser ansí.   didn't used to be this way.

      Solía que reposaba   It used to be I rested
      las noches con alegría,   at night with joy,
      y el rato que no dormía   and the time I didn't sleep
      en sospiros lo pasaba;   I spent in sighs;
      mas peor estó que'staba;   but I'm worse off than I was;
      para mí   for me
      no solían ser ansí.   they didn't used to be this way.

Longing keeps her awake, just like the girl who is waiting for dawn when she will meet her lover. However in this poem the theme is not the insomnia of excited anticipation, but the insomnia of despair. Insomnia, like the storm of passion in "Sedia-m'eu na ermida" can be caused by either extreme of desire—hope or despair.

#293 Solíades venir, amor;   You used to come, my love;
      agora no venides, non.   but now you don't, no.

When the lover used to come, "en sospiros lo pasaba," she spent her nights in the hot sighs of passion. Now her lover no longer comes and "peor estó que'staba." She is still awake—but alone.

Perhaps what is so exasperating about love is that it is beyond one's control. We have talked a great deal about the relentless power of the wind and water, symbols which correspond to the sexual urge, the urge for union. Just as it arises unexpectedly, mysteriously ("no sé qué me bulle..."), it departs just as suddenly and mysteriously:

#294 Ansí andando,   Just going along this way,
      el amor se me vino a la mano;   love came to me,
      andando ansí   just going along this way,
      se aparta el amor de mí.   love left me.

"Ansí andando / andando ansí." There was no basic difference between what the singer did before and after love's arrival. Just going along unsuspectingly, love suddenly appeared, but then while going along just as unsuspectingly, love leaves. Why did it come? Why did it leave? This is love's mystery. But when it leaves, it does not leave its victim in the same state in which it found her / him:

#295 Los plazeres vuelan y vanse   Pleasures go and fly away,
       y los pesares estanse.   sorrows remain.

Like the wind, pleasure just flies away, leaving sorrow behind in its wake, unmoving, never-ending—"estanse."

#296 Fuí buscando amores   I went searching for love
       para descansar;   in order to find satisfaction;
       harto mejor fuera   much better had it been
       nunca los hallar.   never to have found it.

The singer sought love as a relief from the emptiness of desire, to resolve the tension, to rest. Evidently love was found, for the singer now understands that it would have been better never to have found it, because it does not offer much rest.

The same feeling of love's futility is expressed by this lover who probably is in love with a *casada*. He has lost himself in love, and she is threatened with loss of honor and perhaps even of her husband:

#297 ¿Para qu'és, dama, tanto quere-   What's the point, lady, of loving
       ros?   you so much?
       Para perderme y a vos perderos. To be the undoing of you and of
                           me.

       Más valiera nunca veros,   It would have been better never
       para perderme y a vos perderos.   to have seen you,
                          to be the undoing of you and of
                          me.

What is the point of so much unhappiness, he asks. The blame is placed on the eyes again—"más valiera nunca veros"—since they are the cause of his downfall and hers.

But just as there are songs of sincere regret for having fallen in love, there are songs, too, where the regret is playful. In this *cantiga* the young ex-virgin tells her mother about her activities on the river bank with her "amigo"—activities she claims that she now regrets:

#298   Pela ribeira do rio salido   On the bank of the swollen river,
         trebelhei, madre, con meu amigo: I struggled, mother, with my
           amor ei migo, que non ouve-   lover:
             sse;   I'm in love and wish I weren't;
           fiz por amigo que non feze-   I did for my lover what I wish
             sse!   I hadn't.

Pela ribeira do rio levado	On the bank of the high river
trebelhei, madre, con meu ama-do;	I struggled, mother, with my darl-ing;
amor ei migo que non ouve-sse,	I'm in love and wish I weren't;
fiz por amigo que non feze-sse.	I did for my lover what I wish I hadn't.

The river in the first stanza is swollen, in the second it is high—an adjective derived from the verb *levar*, and related to the sense of power we saw before in the adjective *alto*.

If her regrets are playfully ironic, then she feels confident that she will have plenty of future opportunities for regret. But if her remorse is sincere, then probably her lover turned out to be "falso," like the lover in this song:

#299

Olvidar quiero mis amores;	I want to forget my love;
que yo quiero los olvidar.	I want to forget it.
Mis amores los primeros	My first love
no me salieron verdaderos	didn't turn out true,
sino falsos y lisonjeros;	but rather false and flattering;
que yo quiero los olvidar.	I want to forget it.
Mis amores los de antes	My love of before
no me salieron leales	didn't turn out faithful,
sino falsos y con maldades;	but rather false and evil;
que yo quiero los olvidar.	I want to forget it.

The very fact that she sings this song is evidence that she is not able to forget her "amores primeros," even though she wants to. This, too, seems to be the very nature of love: easy to begin, hard to end.

#300

No puedo apartarme	I can't turn away
de los amores, madre,	from love, mother,
no puedo apartarme.	I can't turn away.
Amor tiene aquesto	Love has something
con su lindo gesto,	with its fine expression
que prende muy presto	that captures one quickly
y suelta muy tarde.	and frees one slowly.
No puedo apartarme.	I can't turn away.

Here the singer expresses this characteristic of love: "amor tiene *aquesto*"—like the mysterious *algo* after which the tree yearns. Whatever it is about love, this is its effect: "prende muy presto/y suelta muy tarde." Even though she may want to forsake love, she cannot. Whichever course she takes, once love has entered, she must change. It *will* transform her.

#301

¿Qué remedio tomaré	What relief is there
para el mal que amor me da?	from the sickness love brings?
Si le dexo, moriré;	If I turn away, I will die,
si le sigo, matar me ha.	if I continue, it will kill me.

But the whole point is that there *is* no remedy to be taken, nothing to be done. The will has nothing to do with love—nor with life. One does not choose to be born or to die, nor to fall in love or for love to end. These things just happen.

#302	¡Ay, quién pudiese hacer,	Ay, who could make it so,
	ay, quién hiciese	Ay, who could make it be
	que en no queriendo amar	that by not wanting to love,
	que no quisiese!	one didn't love.

Not wanting to love, or wanting not to love, is as futile as a mother attempting to make her daughter stop loving:

#303	Dice mi madre que olvide el amor:	My mother says I should forget love:
	¡acábelo ella con el corazón!	let her end it along with my heart.

The only way for the mother to succeed in making her daughter forget love is to destroy her heart. For love burns in the heart beyond the control of the will.

#304	Arded, corazón, arded,	Burn on, heart, burn on,
	que no os puedo yo valer.	for I can do you no good.
	Quebrántanse las peñas	Rocks are broken
	con picos y azadones;	by pick-axes and hoes;
	quebrántase mi corazón	my heart is broken
	con penas y dolores.	by pain and sorrow.

Just as the wind carries the sun's energy, the eyes express the passion of the heart. So when the heart is being beaten by sorrow and pain, the eyes weep.

#305	Lloran mis ojos	My eyes weep
	y mi corazón	and my heart
	con mucha razón.	with a good cause.

But suffering, too, has an end, finally burns itself out:

#306	Secáronme los pesares	Sorrows dried up
	los ojos y el corazón	my eyes and my heart,
	que no pueden llorar, non.	for they can't weep, no.

This singer's love has been dried up by sorrow, the way the *gallega's* love was destroyed by her lover's rejection: "... tolhestes os ramos en que siian"; "... secastes as fontes u se banhavan" (#78). If the spring symbolizes the *gallega's* love, and the heart is the seat of love within, then the heart not only burns like the sun, but also is the source of the water of love, like the mountain spring. And in the poem of the burning heart, the gloss established a correspondence between "peña" and the heart. Both are battered, one by picks, and the other by "pena." Now this phonetic similarity between *peña*[4] and *pena*[5] is obviously not accidental in the poem, though the words are related neither

semantically nor etymologically—they simply sound alike. But the
mere suggestion that the heart is a *peña* conjures up an image of a heart
filled with sorrow, with *pena*. Our next poem depends on that phonetic
suggestiveness:

#307 En aquella peña, en aquélla,   On that rock, that rock,
   que no caben en ella.   they don't fit on it.

This poem and the two *peña* poems which follow, are mystifying. What
is the *peña*, and what does not fit on it? Could the *peña* be the same as
the battered cliff in "Arded, corazón..."? If so, it is the heart, and that
which does not fit—*on* it, if it is a cliff, or *in* it, if it is the heart—are
penas. The heart is bursting with sorrow. There is nothing in the poem
beyond the phonetic suggestiveness of "peña" which would
substantiate this reading.

But then there is nothing in the poem to suggest any other subject
for *caber*. Again we are left to fill in the details. Could the image perhaps
be of two lovers playing together on a steep cliff, and the two do not
fit? This possibility seems unlikely, for then one would expect a tone of
playfulness, and the fact is that the poem's mood is one of sadness and
nostalgia, created through the repetition of "aquélla" and the negative
of the second verse.

The *peña* in this next poem does not demand a symbolic
correspondent in the same way the last poem did. Its literal meaning is
sufficient for an understanding of the poem.

#308 En la peña, sobre la peña,   On the rock, upon the rock,
   duerme la niña y sueña.   the girl sleeps and dreams.

Yet this one, too, raises many questions. The image is clear: a girl
sleeps on a cliff and dreams. Until now, lovers who sleep in the
tradition do so under a tree, or—very occasionally—by the seashore.
Never before have we found anyone asleep in a high place, although
the girl who went alone to the *romería* fell asleep under an "enzina" in
the "montiña." But trees do not grow on *peñas*, and *montiñas* are much
softer, sweeter places—as the diminutive indicates—than are rocky
cliffs. The fact is that *peñas* and *penas* do have more in common than a
phonetic similarity—both are also harsh. Then why would a girl sleep
on a "peña?" The image suggests an unhappy, suffering girl who sleeps
in and on her sorrow, surrounded by it. Perhaps her dreams are a
means of escaping the sorrow in which she is immersed.

In poem #32 we heard the account of one girl who tells her mother
of her experience "en la cumbre," a place semantically suggestive of
peña, since the peak of the mountain is often rocky and barren. She tells
her mother that such a wind blew there that the love she had was
transformed into air. In the context in which we originally discussed
this poem—we were studying the wind—it seemed plausible to

interpret her story as an indication of the contagiousness of sexual passion. But in this new context we could read the poem differently. If the *cumbre*, like the *peña* is a harsh place, exposed to burning winds, perhaps her love was exposed to such cruel sorrow that it blew away like the wind.

As if this combination of symbols were not mystifying enough, there is yet another to add to this cluster. In two of the poems we have already studied we found flowers associated with the *peña*. Here we have a fine example of the functioning of the tradition's symbols. The *peña* is a barren, harsh place where flowers are most unlikely to grow. There's an inherent incongruity between *peña*—massive, hard, eternal, unchanging, invulnerable—and *flor*—small, delicate, ephemeral, and supremely vulnerable to any and all destructive elements:

#40 —Digas, morena garrida,   —Tell me, lovely dark lady,
       ¿cuándo serás mi amiga?   when will you be mine?
     —Cuando esté florida la peña   —When the heights are a-bloom
       d'una flor morena.   with dark flowers.

A young man has been smitten with love of a "morena garrida" and asks when she will be his "amiga" (not wife, just girl friend). Her answer, as we observed before, is a tart "never," for first of all a "flor morena" does not exist, and even if it did, how could it blossom on a rocky cliff? Yet through the symbolism of her image it seems that she is expressing something far more profound than just her disdain for the young man in question. She expresses the paradox of man's existence.

A young man says "Tell me, sprightly dark girl, when will you be my girlfriend?" He finds her attractive—sexually attractive. The adjective "garrida" is mysterious, with an uncertain etymology. Covarrubias suggests that it is associated with "garbo," but he is tentative: "quasi garnido de garbo," i.e., as if adorned with charm. It carries the idea of liveliness, perhaps of flirtatiousness. The point is, the young man does not approach her as if she were a chaste idol to him, but rather he approaches her with a playful directness, indicating the admiration and attraction he feels through the epithet "morena garrida." If we look back over the *morena* poems in Chapter I, we find that when the *morena* laments her condition, she generally refers to herself simply as *morena*. When she is defying the shame that her color implies and asserting her worth in spite of it, she calls herself *morenita*. A fine example of this was poem #36, in which she starts out calling herself "morena," but switches to "morenita" when she declares "yo me lo pasaré." And almost invariably when a young man begs a *morena* for her favors, he uses the diminutive to address her (*morenica, morenita*) or *morena* with an adjective that alludes to her physical charms. The poem which best expresses the attitude with which the *morena* is

usually approached by her admirers is #39. She is a "morena graciosa,"
full of physical charms, with delightful "ojuelos verdes." The greenness
of her eyes may be literal, or it may be symbolic of what she represents
to him. Green is the color, in the tradition, of fresh, lusty sexuality, of
the springtime vigor of the vegetable world:

#309	Verdes sâo as hortas	The gardens are green
	com rosas e flores;	with roses and flowers;
	moças que as regam	the girls who water them
	matam-me d'amores.	are killing me with love.

The greenness of the orchards dotted with roses and flowers
symbolizes the sexual vitality of the virgin "mozas" who water the
flowers. Their activity is proof of their greenness, of their readiness for
love.

#310	Pámpano verde,	Green vine,
	razimo alvar;	white grapes;
	¿Quién vido dueñas	Whoever saw ladies
	a tal ora andar?	out walking at this hour?
	Enzinueco entr'ellas,	Little green oak among them,
	entre las donzellas,	among the virgin ladies.
	Pámpano verde,	Green vine,
	razimo alvar;	white grapes;
	¿Quién vido dueñas	Whoever saw ladies
	a tal ora andar?	out walking at this hour?

In this delightful little poem the green of the "pámpano" and the
whiteness of the "razimo" complement each other at the same time that
they form a contrast. The poem describes a cluster of white grapes
("razimo alvar") which represent the "dueñas-donzellas." The singer
asks in amazement what these virgin girls are doing out at such an hour.
Walking about at night is a very suggestive activity, both really and
symbolically, especially when the walker is a virgin. And among them
walks a "pámpano verde," who is also an "enzinueco." A "pámpano," of
course, sticking out as it does among the white grapes, is not only
suggestive in color, but also in shape. And the "enzinueco" is a miniature
version of the big tree beneath which the pilgrim girl met her lover
(#57.) There is a young man among the ladies, and the green which
symbolizes his own sexual vigor, at the same time, because he has been
allowed to join the ladies, indicates *their* sexual condition, as well. They
may be little white grapes now, but if they are out walking at night with
a young green thing among them, that whiteness will soon be stained.

So we see that when her young admirer notices the green eyes of
the "morena graciosa," he is expressing his perception of what *her* eyes
are expressing. If her eyes are green, she is feeling lusty. He then uses a
string of verbs to describe her effect on him ("mata," "cautiva," y

"prende") and at poem's end the verb which caps the poem and indicates what he is after: "puede." She has the power. When one is a novice at the game of love, the impact, the energy of this new sensation incapacitates, leaves one boiling but helpless ("no puedo andar".) But *morenas* are not new at love's game and the expectation of their admirers is that if they can, they will:

| #311 | Poder tenéis vos, señora, | You have the power, lady, |
| | de matar el amor en un hora. | to extinguish love's flame in an hour. |

"Matar" here means to put out the flames of passion that burn in him, to bring an end to his longing, as it did in poem #189 in which the singer hoped to see the *garza's* restless yearning fulfilled. There is an insistent tone of frustration in these petitions to the *morenica*.

#312	Morenica, dime cuándo	Little dark girl, tell me
	tú serás de mi bando;	when you will be on my side;
	¡ay, dime cuándo, morena,	ay, tell me, dark girl,
	dejarás de darme pena!	when you will cease to cause me pain.

Basically, this singer asks the same question as the young man in the "flor morena" poem. But here his tone is more desperate—he moves from calling her "morenica" to "morena," he is growing impatient. Furthermore, he chooses an image for their relationship which expresses enmity. He asks when she will be on his side, "de mi bando." A "bando" is a group of armed men, and if she is not on *his* side, then she must be on the other side, the enemy. *Bando* also bears a strong phonetic resemblance to *banda* which is semantically related to *cinta*—that ribbon of love which is the tie that binds. If she would be his "amiga," if she would wear his ribbon, if she would just be on his side (join him, unite with him), then she would no longer cause him to suffer. "Pena"—"morena." How often these words are associated! Either the *morena* suffers *pena* or she inflicts it:

#313	Bella pastorcilla	Beautiful little shepherd-girl
	de la tez morena,	of dark complexion,
	no miente quien dize	it's no lie that
	que me dais pena.	you cause me pain.

But when a girl takes pity on a young man's suffering, she is likely to catch it herself. By putting out the flame of his passion she herself gets scorched:

#314	Negra tengo la cara,	Dark is my face,
	negro el coraçon,	dark is my heart,
	como amor es fuego	since love is a fire,
	volvióse en carbón.	it has turned to charcoal.

In Chapter I we heard the explanations of several *morenas* of the cause of their skin color. But this girl goes right to the heart of the matter. The passion burned so intensely that her heart, her love, turned to charcoal. When wood (which, of course, comes from a tree) is burned to a certain point, but is not entirely consumed, it becomes charcoal, blackened but still capable of burning. This blackened heart, then, has been dried out by the flames of passion but not entirely consumed, so that even though no moisture, no love, remains, sorrow and suffering do.

While most *morenitas* can remember better days when they were white, this one feels her sorrow so intensely that it casts a shadow backward through her life so that it feels to her that she has been black since birth.

#315 Parióme mi madre   My mother bore me
      una noche escura;   on a dark night;
      cubrióme de negro;   she covered me with black;
      faltóme ventura.   fortune abandoned me.

Her destiny was written from birth. But she should not despair, because, as this *morenita* discovered, some men are color blind:

#316 Morenica me llaman, madre,   They call me the little dark-girl,
      desde el día en que nací,   since the day that I was born,
      y al galán que me ronda la puerta but to the lad who paces by my
      blanca y rubia le parecí.   door,
                                       white and blonde I seemed.

It is clear what her suitor is after, once one understands the significance of "rondar" and "puerta." It seems she has a spring bubbling by her door like the girl who feared wetting her feet (#83). But this singer does not express the same timid fear because this little "morenica" has already gotten her feet wet, and she is delighted by the fact that her suitor does not know it! She is telling all this to her mother. The *guarda* stage of this mother-daughter relationship is long since over. Have they now joined forces in the battle of love?

Could this next poem, too, be addressed to a mother? The singer delights in the guessing game she provokes:

#317 Morenica m'era yo;   I was a little dark girl;
      dicen que sí; dicen que no.   some say yes, others say no.

      Unos que bien me quieren   Some that love me well
      dicen que sí;   say yes;
      otros que por mí mueren   others who die for me
      dicen que no.   say no.
      Morenica m'era yo;   I was a little dark girl;
      dicen que sí; dicen que no.   some say yes, others say no.

The yes-no structure of the poem resembles the magical "loves me—loves me not" formula that is chanted when a hopeful lover deflowers, petal by petal, a blossom. There is little mystery here, since she plainly states the case in the first verse: "morenica m'era yo"—or is that imperfect indicative supposed to imply that the statement is just hypothetical? Is she keeping us guessing, too? But those who say "yes," she *is* "morenica" are those who "bien me quieren." Is that "bien" serious or not? Does she mean that they are crazy about her, as blindly in love as those who "por mí mueren?" Or are they those who love her *well*, who know her, see her for what she is—a *morena*, and love her still? Or perhaps "bien" is ironic and what she means to say is that "mal me quieren"—they gossip about her.

If the poem is a playful imitation of petal-picking, then both sets of lovers must be equal, must be equally deluded. And the poem can certainly be read that way. But behind the game lies something else—the faintest hint of a cynical defiance of the social code. This is, in fact, at the very heart of the *morena* poems. These are the girls who have escaped the protective restrictions of social conduct and ventured out to the mountain, where they were burned by the wind. And this is why one *morena* we heard in the first chapter said, "si en villa me criara / más bonica fuera" (#42). The heroines of the traditional lyric are country girls, except for the few "damas" who sally into the country to pick fruit or to roam the treacherous mountain in search of the voice that called to them through the night. Things are wilder in the country—nature rules, not man. The elements act out their drama, a powerful, joyful and tragic drama repeated by shepherds, *serranas, caballeros*, virgins and *morenas* as they play their parts in the bosom of nature. And as long as nature rules, every *alva* is going to end up *morena*, every flower will wither and die so that tomorrow's seeds can grow.

But the social order does not follow the natural order. And this, too, is an obstacle that only temporarily dams up the natural flow of the sexual urge. Lovers faced with social condemnation in the world of the tradition all seem to respond with the same attitude, best summed up in this *estribillo*:

#318 Corten espadas afiladas   May sharp swords cut
       lenguas malas.   evil tongues.

But we have strayed far from our "morena garrida" who told her pretender that she will be his when the cliff blossoms with dark flowers. Is this cliff a heart full of sorrow, her own charred and blackened heart, with every drop of moisture scorched from it, like a dried-up spring? How can flowers blossom there?

The impossible happens:

#319	Alta estaba la peña;	The cliff was high,
	nace la malva en ella.	where the mallow grows.

	Alta estaba la peña,	The cliff was high
	riberas del río;	beside the river;
	nace la malva en ella	there grows the mallow
	y el trébol florido.	and the flowering clover.

The cliff is "alta," both high and powerful, towering over the river below. Masculine and feminine symbols of sexual energy appear side by side, united in one image, and their union generates the birth of the "malva." This poem can be seen as part of the girl-picking-flower cluster, since "trébol" like the rose, is the object of many flower-pickers in the tradition, particularly among songs related to the festival of the summer solstice. Seen thus, this may be the song of one who wishes to go pick the mallow and trefoil, or of one who has been picking them already. This poem is very similar, when considered in this way, to the song in which the young girl describes the *sierras* to her mother—"altas son de subir" (#188).

There is another way to understand this poem, however. The mallow is a most common and humble plant, not widely esteemed for its beauty, and most uncommon in the traditional lyric. Its natural habitat is *not* barren cliffs. Consequently, its appearance in this poem is mysterious, if we understand the poem to be about flower-picking. Perhaps the mallow's most distinguishing feature is its color, described by Covarrubias as *morado*, a purplish color unusual in the flower kingdom. The name of this color derives from the same root as *morena*, i.e., *mora*, which in turn comes from the term used to signify the Moslems who invaded and inhabited Spain from 711 to 1492. During seven hundred years of intimate contact with these foreign invaders, they naturally had an enormous impact on the formation of Spain's society and culture. In terms of the traditional lyric, the Moors played two important roles—as marauders who capture and carry off young men and women, leaving a mourning lover behind; and as the historical roots of the *morena* theme. Until now we have consistently discussed the *morena's* color as symbolic. But it is also real. The occupation of Spain by the inhabitants of Mauritania brought many dark-skinned residents to Spain. These were called *moros*. From association with their skin color, adjectives describing colors were formed: *morena*[6]—dark; *morado*[7]—dark purple. Given this association through color with the *morena*, perhaps the *malva* that blooms high over the river is the very "flor morena" that in the other poem was posited as an impossibility (#40).

The color words that come from *moro* in turn led to the naming of the blackish fruit of the bramble: *mora*.[8]

#320	Moricas del moral, madre,	Blackberries on the bush, mother,
	las moras del moral.	blackberries on the bush.

The *moral* is, of course, the bush on which *moras* grow, and is related to another bush we already saw—*zarza* (#171), to which love was compared, "más prende y más mata." In this poem, the *zarza* is blown about by the wind:

#321   ¡Ay, madre, la zarzuela,   Ay mother, the little bramble
       cómo el aire la revolea!   bush,
       ¡Ay, la zarzuela, madre,   how the wind twists it!
       cómo la revolea el aire!   Ay the little bramble bush,
                                   mother,
                                   how twisted it is by the wind.

There is a striking similarity between these two poems. Both are addressed to the mother, both present the naked image of a bush without telling us what the image means to the singer, who in both poems could be either a young man or a girl. The first is probably sung by a man, since it carries a tone of admiration. He is describing a sight which has captured his imagination: the juicy black berries hanging invitingly on the bramble, berries that are little, unripe at first— "moricas"—but the longer his attention remains focused on them, the riper they seem—"moras del moral." Or perhaps he is not describing the berries at all, but rather the young girls he found picking berries there. Remember Axa, Fatima, and Marien—"las tres morillas m'enamoran en Jaen" (#243). And the "tres Maricas de allende" (#112) who wash and wring in such an enticing way, could they have once been *moricas* who got corrupted into Maricas? If the "moricas" he sees in the "moral" are girls and not fruit, then perhaps the air was twisting its branches like the "zarzuela" of the other poem. The swaying of the bramble bush is reminiscent of the swaying poplars in "De los álamos vengo, madre," wherein the singing youth associates the swaying branches with his "linda amiga" (#7). Clearly the air which sways the "zarzuela," entangling its branches full of prickly thorns over the heads of the lovers who imitate its motion, is the same wind of sexual passion that darkens a virgin's skin. Does it blacken the "moras del moral," also?

    The "zarzuela" poem must be sung by a girl, who like the "mora" that grows on the bramble she sees swaying in the wind, got burned by it. Perhaps the "ay" she moans is as remorseful as the "ay" of the girl who fears she is pregnant because "se me hincó una espina" (#162). Or perhaps it is just that her love has been snagged on the bramble and is being tossed about in the wind along with the *moras* that grow on it.

    However one chooses to read these poems, there is no doubt that the *moral/zarzuela*, because of its fruit, comes to be associated with *moricas/moricos* and hence *morenas*. The singer who was pricked by a thorn is either a *mora* or a *morena*, a blackened fruit or a darkened girl. And there is another bush which, because it has thorns like the bramble, is dangerous to get close to—the rosebush.

#322 Aquella mora garrida   That charming little Moorish girl,
      sus amores dan pena a mi vida.   love of her brings sorrow to my
                                           life.

      Mi madre, por me dar plazer,   My mother, for to please me,
      a coger rosas m'envía;   sent me to pick roses;
      moros andan a saltear   Moors are waiting in ambush
      y a mí llévanme cativa.   and take me captive.

      El moro que me prendiera   The Moor who captured me
      allende la mar m'envia;   sent me over the sea;
      lloraba cuando lo supo   when he found out,
      un amigo que yo abya;   my lover wept for me;
      sus amores dan pena a mi vida.   his love brings sorrow to my life.

      Con el gran dolor que siente   With the great pain that he suffers
      estas palabras dezía: these words he spoke:

      Aquella mora garrida.   That charming little Moorish girl,
      Sus amores dan pena a mi vida.   love of her brings sorrow to my
                                           life.

This is a complex little poem which resonates back through our study
of symbols, setting them all to ringing. To begin with it makes the
same sudden switch of speakers between the *estribillo* and the gloss that
we saw in "Las mis penas, madre" (#24). As in that poem, the last verse
of the *estribillo* is woven into the gloss in a different context, which
enriches its suggestiveness in the *estribillo* retrospectively. But in this
poem the voice that sings to us from the present moment of the song
is the voice of the gloss, whereas in "Las mis penas" it was that of the
estribillo. In this poem, the *estribillo* is the lament of the lover she
remembers. For she has been abducted by "moros" who carried her
across the sea, leaving her lover behind to lament. His lament
constitutes the *estribillo*: "Aquella mora garrida / sus amores dan pena a
mi vida." But there is something a little strange about all this,
something that suggests that there is more to this tale than is obvious
at first. It must be the resonance of the other symbols.

Let us begin with the gloss, since this is where the story begins.
Her mother sent her to pick roses—"por me dar plazer." Pleasures, as
we were told before, quickly fly away leaving only "pesares." This time
not only the pleasures have been blown away, but the girl herself, as
well. Once before we found the mother cast in this surprising role of
instigator of love, in this poem:

#93 Enviárame mi madre   My mother sent me
     por agua a la fonte fría: for water to the cold spring:
     vengo del amor ferida.   I come back wounded with love.

Her mother sent her into the mountains where the "fonte frida" is
born, along with the wind and the stag. And like a deer, she returns
wounded, only her wound is from love. In yet another poem we find a
like situation with the addition of some detail:

#323 Envíame mi madre   My mother sends me
      por agua sola;   alone for water;
      ¡mirad a qué hora!   and at such a time!

The girl has been sent out alone, "sola" like the *garza*; and at a time of
day that the girl herself finds surprising: "¡mirad a qué hora!"—like the
"pámpano verde" with his "razimo alvar" who were out walking "a tal
ora." Do these mothers, also, send their daughters out to give them
pleasure? Here we have the opposite pole of the mother-protectress
symbol, a mother who pushes her daughter towards the sexual
experience. And between the mother as protectress and the mother as
instigator lies the dominant force of the mother symbol: the mother
who listens, the confidante. But now, we may fairly ask, how many of
the sexual adventures that have been confessed to the mother did the
mother arrange? If one girl's mother "a coger rosas m'envía," could not
the mother in other poems, like this next one, have sent her daughter
into the arms of experience, also?

#324 A coger amapolas,   Picking poppies,
      madre, me perdí;   mother, I got lost;
      caras amapolas   costly poppies
      fueron para mí.   they were for me.

When these girls go out to pick flowers or fruit, or to draw water, they
always come back changed—lost, wounded, or in this case, with a
different complexion:

#325 Dónde vindes, filha,   From where do you come, daugh-
      branca e colorida?   ter,
                                all white and flushed?

      De lá venho, madre,   I come, mother,
      de ribas de hum rio;   from the banks of a river;
      achei meus amores   I found my lover
      em hum rosal florido;   in a flowering rosebush;
      florido, enha filha,   flowering, in my daughter,
      branca e colorida.   all white and flushed.

      De lá venho, madre,   I come, mother,
      de ribas de hum alto;   from the shores of a stream;
      achei meus amores   I found my lover
      n'hum rosal granado;   in a red rosebush;
      granado, enha filha,   red, in my daughter,
      branca e colorida.   all white and flushed.

Here the mother forms an epithet from her daughter's color—she is
"branca," because she is a virgin, or at least she *was* a virgin when she
left for the "rosal"; and she is "colorida" as a result of her activity there.
The fact that her mother notices her color suggests that her mother
also recognizes what has happened to her. And the girl neither
hesitates to tell her, nor does she cloak her tale in symbols which she

hopes will be misunderstood. She plainly admits that she met her lover in the "rosal florido / granado." Just as the hot passion of the wind is contagious and darkens a girl's skin, the flaming passion of the red rose stains a virgin, leaving her "colorida." At the end of each segment of the girl's account, related in the first four verses of each stanza of the gloss, the mother interjects a comment which sounds like a pensive aside. She repeats the adjective her daughter uses to describe the "rosal," then each time says " . . . enha filha, / branca e colorida." What is this "enha filha"? Her daughter in each stanza has said that by the river she found her lover *in* a rose garden. Her mother takes the adjective the girl uses and transfers it to the description of a rose garden *in her daughter*. Like the rose garden, she is *colorida*—inflamed with passion.

#326 —Colorada estáis, nuestra ama,   —You are flushed, our lady.
      —Vengo del horno y diome la   —I come from the oven where the
          llama.   flames burnt me.

The "horno" from which this lady comes all blushing red is the oven that burns with love's flames. These flames, emanating from the sun, whether carried by the wind or not, have the same power to change the color of a girl's skin:

#327 Cuando el sol se hacía,   When the sun arose
      era yo morenica,   I was a little dark girl,
      y antes que el sol fuera   and before the sun set
      era yo morena.   I was a dark woman.

The sun's energy burns in the rose, the red rose which springs from the black earth.

Now what happened to the girl who began her tale with an account of her rose picking? While she picks roses, "moros" who "andan a saltear" take her captive. One in particular "me prendiera," captures her, and the verb she uses, *prender*, is one which applies equally to the action of the thorny rose and to love. All the lovers who are captured—"prendidos"—by love are transformed. The transformation in this poem, however, differs from others in that not only her condition changes, but her environment as well. She is carried across the sea to a strange land. We have seen a number of poems where the singer is stranded in a distant land and yearns for home, and usually for the lover-beloved left behind there. It seems only natural that this should be a theme in the Spanish traditional lyric, because it was a reality of the historic situation of Spain. Moors did raid coastal towns and take captives. But then many other historical realities were taking place that are not reflected in this poetry. I would like to suggest that the *moro-captivo* theme and the *morena* enter into the tradition, not because they *were* realities, but because they *are* realities with symbolic potential. In like manner, all the absence poems in which a lover stands by the sea longing for a glimpse of the beloved's returning ship, are common in the tradition not only because it was a common occurrence, but because it symbolizes a universal feeling.

In this poem the mother sent the girl to pick flowers. The Moor who captured her then sent her over the sea. She is ostensibly innocent of any wrong-doing. She was just sent here and there, quite passively—she claims. Consequently, she is not to be blamed for the lament of the lover who is left behind and complains. But why does he call her a *mora*? Has she become a *mora* because she has been abducted by *moros*? Or is it that she is *morena* now, stained? Is this lamenting lover related to the one who advised us: "Quien amores ten / ... en dama donzel, / afinque los ben ..." (#20). Did he, too, place his faith in a "dama donzel" who slipped through his fingers? Did someone else pick the fruit while he was waiting for it to ripen? And in fact, who should be held responsible for his sorrow? The *moro*? The girl for going out to pick roses, for pestering her mother with her complaints until her wish was granted—"por me dar plazer?" Or the lover himself for not being in the *rosal*? The fact is, it was his own fault for not recognizing that when the flower blossomed, his beloved would be "mala ... de guardar."

She has been transported "allende la mar," the sea of passion in which lovers drown. Is she on the "other shore"—that symbol of sexual contentment? Or is the last verse of the refrain, when it appears at the end of the second stanza of the gloss, supposed to indicate that her memories of *his* loves, her original *amigo's* love for her, now give her sorrow ("dan pena a mi vida")? Maybe she has found that the other shore is not so wonderful after all. Perhaps she has been disillusioned in the way the *malcasadas* are.

Very simply what I am suggesting here is that *moros* perhaps symbolize the same natural forces, beyond the control of any restriction, as the wind and water; and that the *morena* and the *moros*, because of their darkness, symbolize this natural and uncontrollable flow of sexuality.[9]

Just as the *morena* in her very darkness is immensely attractive— "que morena es la color / que a mí da pena," the *morico* too, is desirable:

#328	Allega, morico, allega, con el barco a la ribera.	Draw near, little Moor, draw near, with your boat to the shore.
	Allega, moro, con tiento, Dios te dé próspero viento, buen viaje a salvamento con que salgas acá fuera.	Draw near, Moor, with care, may God grant you a favorable wind, a good and safe trip, as long as you get off here.

This "morico" can hardly be accused of "anda(ndo) a saltear." If he is about to abduct the singer, she is certainly willing enough. Could the other "mora garrida" have been as eager?

This interpretation of the *moro* symbol gives an interesting twist to the tale of the girl whose laments we already heard in an *estribillo* that was an archetypal expression of the isolation caused by suffering:

#283 ¡Ay que non ay! ¡Ay, que non era!   Ay, for there's no one! Ay, there
       ¡Mas ay, que non ay   never was!
       quien de mi pena se duela!   But ay, for there's no one
                                      who takes pity on my pain.

       Madre, la mi madre,   Mother, my mother,
       el mi lindo amigo   Moors from afar
       moricos de allende   are carrying off captive
       lo llevan cativo;   my handsome lover;
       cadenas de oro,   chains of gold
       candado morisco.   and Moorish lock.

       ¡Ay, que non ay! ¡Ay, que non   Ay, for there 's no one! Ay, there
         era!   never was!
       ¡Mas ay, que non ay   But ay, for there's no one
       quien de mi pena se duela!   who takes pity on my pain.

If "moricos" are dark, uncontrollable forces, her tale turns out to be merely an elaboration of the "algo" which kept "aquel pastorico" (#3) from his waiting *amiga*. In fact this girl's intense suffering is due to her lover's rejection of her—a rejection she cannot accept and which she therefore masks behind an elaborate tale of capture, with golden chains and a Moorish lock. But chains can be symbols—the chains of love. Her lover was not abducted by "moricos," he was captivated by eyes which bound him with golden chains, perhaps by the sight of the same "maricas de allende" who wash and wring so enchantingly.

While these poems about marauding *moros* mean what they say on a literal plane, they mean that and more. People fall in love and people fall out of love, "ansí andando," and when one lover falls out of love and the other does not, there is pain, a feeling of intense aloneness, because the desired object has been stolen, is as far from reach as if he were on the other side of the sea. Whom to blame for this sudden change of affection in the lover? "Moricos de allende" who are triply associated with love's passion: they are darkened by love's fire; they come mysteriously and unexpectedly out of love's sea; and like love, "prenden"—they imprison their victims in golden chains. They are, in short, symbolic personifications of the winds of passion.

The *morena* is so insistently pursued for her favors because her color, like that of the *moros*, represents to the hopeful suitor her experience with love. From desire's point of view, black is the best color. The masculine seeks initiation into the mysterious, dark, feminine world of passion. As the next poem tells us: "Lo moreno, bien mirado / fue la culpa del pecado." Here is the belief that invests the *morena* with such immense symbolic force: She is a creature of darkness. Her darkness, on one level, is regarded as the stain of sin.

And her sin? Having allowed herself to be burned by sexual passion. Yet we have seen that sexual desire is a force beyond the control of reason and will, a natural force in man's inner world which partakes of the same power, is as *alto*, as the wind and sea. Consequently, no one escapes. We are all sinners, fallen, *morenas*. But can we also be flowers? Will the barren cliff blossom with flowers of darkness? Can man be redeemed from his fallen condition? Can the wholeness of childish innocence be regained once love has been experienced? Within the symbolic world of the tradition lies buried, in a handful of poems, a joyful note of affirmation.

It is not surprising that these life-affirming poems should slip easily into both the secular popular lyric and the religious popular lyric traditions. Salvation in the Christian tradition is made possible by the death and resurrection of the sacrificial man-god, Christ. In his person, the fallen condition of sinful man is combined with the divine essence. This same synthesis of opposing conditions appears in the secular tradition as the means of redemption from the suffering state of one who has tasted desire. But in the secular tradition this synthesis of opposites is embodied in woman, the fallen woman—the *morena*. The popular imagination seems uneasy with a masculine symbol of transformation and therefore substitutes, in its lyric expression, the feminine symbol of the virgin mother, both white and black. She is the *morena* who transcends her stained condition by blending it with innocence. She is the dark flower blooming on the cliff, the rose untouched by passion's burning breath.

#329   Yo me soy la morenica,
Yo me soy la modená.

Lo moreno, bien mirado,
fue la culpa del pecado,
que en mí nunca fue hallado
ni jamás se hallará.

Soy la sin espina rosa,
que Salomón canta y glosa,
nigra sum sed formosa,
y por mí se cantará.

Yo soy la mata inflamada
ardiendo sin ser quemada,
ni de aquel fuego tocada
que a los otros tocará.

I am the little dark girl,
I am the dark girl.

Darkness, well considered,
is the fault of sin,
which was never found in me
and never will be found.

I am the thornless rose
about whom Solomon sings and
  writes,
nigra sum sed formosa,
and for my sake it will be sung.

I am the burning bush
in flames but not burnt,
and that fire which burns others
will never burn me.

This poem explores the paradox which we found in the "flor morena" poem, for here again an image is presented which defies apprehension by reason. In the *estribillo* we hear the voice of a girl who is delighted with her darkness, who is delighted with herself. The first three words of each verse point to the "yo" of the singer. Semantically the subject

and object pronouns "yo" and "me" are redundant since without them
the song would still assert that "I am the little dark girl"—"soy la
morenica." But the presence of these pronouns intensifies that
assertion. She calls herself "la morenica," "la morená." The definite
article la plays an important role in her assertion, making the estribillo a
statement of identity rather than a description. Without the article,
"morenica" would be a predicate adjective describing the "yo," the
singer, as in poem #217. If the article were indefinite, "una," she would
be identifying herself with a group of morenas: I am one of them. But
the article is definite: I am the "morena," as though all the many morenas
of the tradition have coalesced into one, an archetypal morena. And she
is absolutely gleeful about this state of affairs. The estribillo, with its
simple rhythm, its very nearly exact repetition, its diminutive, and its
final accented syllable "morená" which lifts the voice, like the spirit,
expresses a childlike innocence: a chant which enchants. She is not a
morena burdened with pena—she longs for nothing, she is content with
herself. And this self-contentment is not dependent on the approval or
recognition of any "other," unlike the morenas who likewise express
acceptance of their condition, but whose acceptance is based on the
fact that their condition does not prevent them from enjoying love. In
those cases the singer first informs us that she is "morenica" and then
proceeds to point out that the consequences we might expect from this
fact do not apply to her:

#330 Aunque soy morenita y prieta   Even though I'm dark and black,
      ¿a mí qué se me da?   what do I care?
      que amor tengo que me servirá.   I have a lover who will serve me.

The songs of these morenas and of those who justify or explain their
darkness—"hadas malas me hicieron negra" (#44)—are based upon a
particular way of viewing the morena. Darkness symbolizes sin.

The gloss of #329 can really only be considered a step-child of the
traditional lyric, being far more conceptual and metaphoric than the
true children of the tradition. But any attempt to weed out those step-
children that have gravitated through association into the tradition
would be as futile as attempting to assert a chronology for these
poems. The glosses which have sprung up and attached themselves to
genuinely traditional estribillos enter the tradition and play their part
in shaping the whole. The distinction I would make between the
natural and step-children of the tradition is this: traditional lyrics
connote, step-lyrics denote—i.e., they limit in some way the semantic
potential of the estribillo. The estribillo in this particular poem is one of
the most purely connotative in the entire tradition, precisely because it
is so skeletal, so barren of detail. The image it evokes is of a charming
dark girl who delightedly asserts her identity. Why? There is not the
remotest hint of a motive for her song and there is nothing which

directs our apprehension of her words toward any one interpretation of her meaning. The *estribillo* stands as a simple celebration of the singer's skin-color, for which we can supply an infinite number of motives. We can fill in the missing detail according to our own individual perception of blackness.

But when we reach the gloss, a radical shift occurs. Whereas the *estribillo* permits a multitude of associations with darkness of skin, the gloss limits those associations, directing our perception of "lo moreno" toward a particular, individual perspective.

She begins her contemplation of darkness conceptually, asking us to consider "lo moreno" as though it were an object, a thing which exists. It is, she asserts, the fault of sin. She reaches this conclusion after having pondered it deeply: "bien mirado"—*bien* being an intensifier here. This qualifier, which indicates how she regarded darkness in order to come up with her interpretation of its meaning, simultaneously implies that there are other ways in which darkness could be regarded. One wonders what conclusion would be reached if "lo moreno" were "*mal* mirado." Since in this first stanza of the gloss she employs a language which is foreign to the tradition ("culpa," "pecado") but pertinent to religion, "bien" carries the further semantic potential of meaning "morally." Viewed from the perspective of moral or religious law, darkness is the consequence of sin. But this is not the only way to view it.

After stating that darkness comes from sin, she proceeds to assert that sin, however, was never found in her. Logically, she must have sinned. It is a simple syllogism: darkness is caused by sin; the girl is dark; hence she has sinned. But she denies this conclusion and pronounces her paradoxical nature. She is dark; darkness comes from sin; but *she* has not sinned. Her very existence, then, refutes the logic of reason. "Bien mirado" takes on an added shade of meaning: "viewed logically." And the "bien" has become retrospectively ironic by the end of the first stanza, because as deeply as darkness is pondered, as logically as it is considered, the wrong conclusion is reached. Darkness is not always caused by sin, because this *morena* never has sinned and never will (a pretty bold statement!). But what is sin, anyway? Deviation from the path of moral rectitude, according to Covarrubias. We once saw a "velida" who deviated, or rather was "desviada" by the wind on the mountain. The "mora garrida," too, was deviated from her path by marauding "moros." We have seen a lot of deviation occurring in these poems, but was it from the path of moral rectitude? The simple fact is that nature does not recognize rectitude of any type, for rectitude is straightness and there is nothing straight about nature. In order for there to be straightness there must be two points, a beginning and an end. But in nature, there is no beginning and no end.

Which comes first, which is the beginning? The seed or the tree? This is nature's law:

#331	Al cabo de años mil,	After a thousand years
	vuelven las aguas por do solían ir.	the waters return to where they used to flow.

If the waters moved along a straight path they could never double back over territory already travelled.

Darkness, then, can only have resulted from a deviation from the path established by reason, for reason is the result of division. Reason perceives the "other," and once there is a split in the wholeness, once there are two—the self and the other—then there are two points between which a straightness exists. But if the world is not viewed through reason, if it is "mal mirado" rather than "bien mirado," then "pecado" ceases to exist. Sin and reason arise simultaneously—in the act of eating the apple which permits the distinction between good and evil.

In the first stanza, then, our "morenica" in essence asks us to enter with her into another way of viewing darkness. She has shown us that reason will not work in this case, it leads to wrong conclusions. In each of the next stanzas she presents us with examples—paradoxes that are simultaneously scriptural and natural. She makes explicit reference to Solomon's *Song of Songs* and implicit reference to Moses' encounter on the mountain top with the burning but unconsumed bush from which he heard the voice of God. Both paradoxical images she relates to a third image: that of the rosebush. She is a rose without thorns, a *morena* without sin. She is both the flower and the bush—a bush like Moses', in flames but unburnt. Sin is the thorn that pricks and the fire that consumes, and these are both symbols of passionate sexual desire, a desire that never touches our "morenica."

We saw the unburnt rose once before in a poem that tells of the birth of the rose under the cliff:

#29	Debajo de la peña nace	Beneath the cliff is born
	la rosa que no quema el aire.	a rose the wind won't burn.

When we first met this poem, I said that it is a celebration of the birth of the Virgin Mary—which is only a partial truth (like all truth!). The symbols of this poem permit its association with the Virgin, to be sure, but do not limit it to that particular association. In the same way, "Yo me soy la morenica," poem #329, can be understood to refer to the virgin mother of God, especially the gloss. The *estribillo* of that poem alone, however, connotes an infinity of possible associations, while the gloss, of later ilk, directs the meaning of the *estribillo* toward the Virgin Mary. In other words, the *estribillo* is sung by a *morenica* who could be any *morenica*, while the symbols of the gloss point toward a particular *morena*: Mary. However, if the singer of that gloss can *only* be the Virgin, then the poem ceases to be traditional, and becomes strictly religious. Can the poem no longer be the song of any *morena*? Viewed from within a particular religious perspective there can only be one referrant for this miraculous rose, since only one woman has transcended the blackness of sin. But if we understand that this religious symbolism arose in response to a basic human need, the need to transcend the apparent duality of life, then our *morenica* can be both the Virgin and every other woman burned by passion's flames. And just as the Virgin gains in associative potential by sharing the condition of the *morena*, the *morena*, likewise, gains symbolic force from her association with the Virgin. What is the miracle of the virginal birth of the man-god? It is the merging of the duality; in the case of Christ, the merging of the divine and the human. He is conceived by spirit in matter. He is the ultimate paradox of the Christian tradition, just as the *morena* is of the Spanish traditional lyric. And through the Virgin Mary a bridge is created between the two traditions.

But we are studying the symbols of the tradition as they function within that tradition, and not the directions in which those symbols have spun off into other realms of literature. Insofar as the *morenica* and the rose of poems #329 and #29 function as symbols, their associative potential radiates in other directions besides the religious. They are, at root, symbols of a unified reality behind the apparent dialectic of the cosmos. Mary and Christ symbolize this, as well, but in our tradition they are necessarily secondary symbols. In a Christian poetic tradition they would be the primary symbols of this transcendence, at the very center from which semantic potential radiates. In our study they are not primary, but rather single rays emanating from two primary symbols of the traditional lyric, the rose and the *morena*.

#332 Del rosal sale la rosa,
¡Oh, qué hermosa!

From the rosebush comes the rose.
Oh, how beautiful!

Del rosal sale la rosa
¡Oh, qué hermosa!
¡Qué color saca tan fino!
Aunque nace del espino
nac'entera y olorosa.

From the rosebush comes the rose.
Oh, how beautiful!
What a fine color it has!
Even though born of the thorn,
it is whole and fragrant.

Nace de nuevo primor
esta flor.
Huele tanto desdel suelo
que penetra hasta el cielo
su fuerça maravillosa.

It is born with a fine new beauty,
this flower.
So fragrant here on earth
that its marvelous aroma
reaches the heavens.

The rosebush connotes, first of all, an amorous encounter, since lovers meet there when the girl goes out to pick flowers, sometimes like the *mora garrida* of poem #322 at her mother's behest. From this encounter love emerges, like the rose that emerges ("sale") from the rosebush. Pointy objects, including the thorn of the rosebush, symbolize the intrusion of masculine energy into the feminine consciousness, awakening it to an awareness of time, space, and consequently suffering. The thorn pierces the wholeness of innocence, dividing, fragmenting, creating the illusion of separateness between self and other. This is the same effect the wind has on innocence, but the wind, rather than cutting, burns and blackens. The exclamation of the *estribillo*, "¡Oh, qué hermosa!" implies that this rose, like the one born in the shelter of the cliff, "no quema el aire." The gloss makes this explicit, describing the color of the rose as "fino," delicate, rare, exquisite—an adjective which suggests vulnerability. The miracle is this: though she is born from the thorn, conceived in sin, the offspring of pain and division, she is intact and fragrant in her innocence.

While the first stanza of the gloss centers around the thorn, the second focuses on the air. She is born out of "nuevo primor," and *primor*, according to Covarrubias, is "excelencia en el aire." The wind which engenders this rose is not a scorching wind, but one which is delicate and rare, *fino* like her color. Not only does this air not harm the fragile rose, it actually functions in her service. The normal relationship between wind and rose is inverted, the movement of the wind is reversed. Now it does not carry the masculine energy from the creative source to the feminine, but rather bears the fragrance of innocence to the heavens. And this fragrance *penetrates* heaven with its "fuerza maravillosa." The rose, the feminine, vulnerable, passive, weak, has taken on masculine qualities—it pierces and it is powerful. Each logical expectation which these symbols suggest is defied.

While the logic-defying miracle of the *morenica* in poem #329 involved phenomena beyond the natural order, the miracle in this poem is part of nature's drama. Perfect, beautiful, fragrant flowers do indeed spring forth from thorny rosebushes. The paradigm for redemption from suffering exists within nature. We know from other poems that the meeting of male and female by the rosebush normally gives rise to the painful yearning of desire. But here the potential for transcendence also lies buried in the rosebush from which a love, a blossom can emerge, unstained by pain. And nature provides yet another model for this transcendence:

#333	Aunque soi morena	Though I'm dark,
	blanca io nací,	I was born white,
	que la tierra negra	for the black earth
	pan blanco suele dar.	produces white bread.

This poem begins like others in which the *morena* asserts the fact that she is dark but once was white. In this instance, however, the motivating idea is not to explain, as others did, how she acquired her dark color, but rather to offer a new perspective on darkness. She reminds us that the earth, the maternal womb from which life springs, is also black. And out of that blackness grow the seeds which will provide nourishment, bread, the staff of life. Paradoxically, the bread which began in blackness, comes out white. Really this paradox is no less miraculous than the thornless rose, the flower immune to the burning wind and the cliff covered with dark blossoms. But unlike those miracles, this one is a natural, common occurrence, part of the everyday reality of a peasant girl. Consequently, how much greater the consolation it offers to one who has been conditioned to view her darkness as shameful. She calls on us to observe the natural cycle of change and transformation, and to recognize with her the essential role which darkness plays in that cycle. Without the black earth there could be no white bread. By describing herself as dark now, but as having been white at birth, she identifies her own essence not with any one phase of this miraculous natural cycle, but with the entire process of transformation. At birth, she was white, whiteness emerging out of darkness. All mothers were *morenas* before they became mothers, and all *morenas* were white before the wind darkens them. Our singer is, at the moment of her song, caught in the phase of transition, the *morena* phase, no longer virgin white, not yet the fertile source of life. Yet there is no cause for despair, no need to justify or explain, for she has seen beyond the appearance, she has looked past the momentary condition and has observed the whole. She understands that it would be as meaningless to identify with her darkness as it is to identify with her lost whiteness.

Herein lies the key to salvation, to the transcendence of the suffering which seems to be the inevitable outcome of love. In poem after poem we heard the mournful voices of lovers who not only are immersed in love's pain, but whose suffering is aggravated by the contrast which memory provides with happier times in the past. Those past times are only considered happier, however, because change has taken place. When sorrowful singers were happier they did not know it, for there was nothing to compare it with. The real suffering arises not from change, but from the inability to recognize that change is not linear, it is cyclical. Water, the symbol of female-libido, eventually returns to where it began after traveling the circuitous route of experience. But the particular limitation of consciousness is that it can perceive the past but not the future. It can compare its present suffering with what it now regards as its past happiness, but not with any future condition, unless it recognizes in the cycles of nature the symbolic paradigm for its own existence. The symbols of the tradition remind us of our bondage to the same natural laws of transformation as the rest of the natural world. But in that bondage lies freedom. As long as the *morena* fights her darkness, rejects or regrets it, she remains trapped in despair. When she at last realizes her intimate connection with the natural process of change, then she knows that her present condition is as ephemeral as her prior whiteness, and furthermore that it, too, is transitory, an inevitable stage in the grand cycle of life. Consciousness must descend into the black depths in order to be reborn in an innocence that cannot be lost, an innocence that now regains the wholeness of pre-consciousness by understanding that the fragmentation of conscious perception is merely a transitional phase and not its ultimate essence.

This *morena* has gained that awareness. She is capable of seeing the entire process of existence as a unified whole, a never-ending cycle. She knows what she is, *morena*, and what she has been, *blanca*, but identifies with neither state. She is not deceived by time. Unlike the *morenas* who identify with their suffering and cannot see beyond it, and hence wallow in despair, this *morena* senses her essential connection with the miraculous cycle of transformation evident in the vegetable world. Like a grain of wheat, she must be harvested and returned to the black depths of the earth in order to emerge again unsullied. Once this understanding arises in human consciousness, despair ceases.

I spoke before of life-affirming poems, those which celebrate rather than lament the stain of love. We have discussed songs which in their perfect balance of tension between the masculine and feminine, represent the innocence of unconsciousness prior to the invasion of desire. But those poems celebrate innocence, not life-experience, and they are typified by a noticeable absence of any disturbing element which might represent the invasion of their pristine harmony. The other group which celebrates experience rather than innocence, is typified by the inclusion and transcendence of the disturbing aspect of love. The perspective of these poems is synthetic, drawing together logically disparate elements into a miraculously paradoxical image in defiance of reason. There is a humble dark flower blossoming on a barren cliff; a thornless rose; a burning but unconsumed bush; a thorny rosebush that produces an undefiled rose with an aroma that bridges heaven and earth; muddied waters that will again be crystal clear; black earth producing white bread. In each case, the disturbing element is present, be it blackness, the thorn, the wind, fire, but its expected effect is either negated or transcended.

And all the symbols of transcendence are feminine symbols. The subject of this poetry is transformation, with the masculine-energy symbols functioning as transformers, and the feminine-energy symbols receiving the effects of this masculine energy and undergoing transformation as a result. This does not imply that only women are transformed by love. A man transformed by love partakes of the feminine essence insofar as he, too, is the passive recipient of the active male principle. This was amply demonstrated by the poems that express the wounding quality of the sight of the beloved, whose beauty emits an energy which pierces the heart through the eye. The male and female *personae* in the lyric tradition do not necessarily represent masculine and feminine energy on an archetypal level. A young woman can embody the aggressive disturbing energy which muddies the crystal innocence of a male youth as readily as a young man can stir the nascent waters of the feminine libido. Whosoever experiences the birth of desire has first felt the effects of the wind, suffers through a sense of isolation, and ultimately either remains trapped in suffering or arrives at a transcendent vision of the cycles of change. But men are seldom portrayed in this role. Virgin maidens, unhappy brides and *morenas* are the principal representatives of the feminine energy pole. The virgin represents the movement from unconsciousness to consciousness. The disappointed bride corresponds to the pain and disillusionment of consciousness. And the *morena*, whose color indicates that she has already experienced the suffering of consciousness, represents the potential for ultimate liberation from suffering through a synthetic vision of the ceaseless cycle of change. When she can see beyond the illusion of time and space engendered by the penetration of reason, when she ceases to identify with any part of the whole cycle and recognizes that she *is* the entire process, virgin-*morena*-mother, then she can celebrate the mystery of her being.

The same integrated vision is evident in this song:

#334 Turbias van las aguas, madre,   The waters flow muddy, mother,
     turbias van,   they flow muddy,
     mas ellas se aclararán.   but they will become clear.

Water, symbol of feminine libido, has been muddied by the stag, but there is no struggle, no regret, for this singer like the last, has reached a level of awareness that sees beyond the temporary condition. Experience has taught her that this phase, too, will pass, and the muddied waters will be pure again.

All the symbols in the traditional lyric function like energy vectors, moving between two poles that appear to be in opposition. Wind simultaneously divides and connects; water drowns and bestows new life; eyes wound and are wounded; the rose seduces with its beauty and aroma, but hides within its seductive exterior the piercing thorn of pain. Each symbol changes meaning as perspective shifts. Nothing is static, though nascent reason, dawning in the dark unconsciousness of innocence, produces the illusion of fixed identities, of separateness.

That illusion creates the suffering which is the dominant theme of this poetry. Since the first step in the cycle of change, the movement from innocence to experience, brings pain, those who suffer long to regress to the prior state of innocence which appears from the perspective of experience to have been happy. But happiness is merely the opposite pole of sadness and neither exists in a state of innocence. By rejecting pain, by struggling against it, the possibility for happiness becomes obscured. Like quicksand, the more one struggles to disengage oneself from pain, the more hopelessly enmeshed in it one becomes. The subtle tone of irony which saturates most of these poems springs precisely from this phenomenon. The conscious experiencer struggles in vain against the natural urges that mysteriously arise from the dark mystery of the unconscious, urges to which he/she must ultimately succumb, willfully or not.

The virgin arises at dawn to wash clothes on the mountain top where she encounters the wind. When the wind disturbs the harmony of her existence, when it interferes with her activity, she grows angry, perceiving it as a force separate from and harmful to herself, for it brings change. What she is unable to understand is that the wind that stimulates change is a force from within herself. Victim and victimizer, white and black, male and female arise simultaneously with the birth of consciousness, symbolized in that poem by dawn. In the poems of longing for past innocence we saw that purity is not perceived until it has been lost. We never hear virgins celebrate their innocence, for they cannot know it as a condition until it has been transformed by experience. In a sense the mother is the symbolic objectification of the dual impulse of the libido. As protectress she represents the libido's regressive tendencies, and as instigator (when she sends her daughter alone to the spring) she represents the inexorable pull of libidinal experience. The tension which arises from these apparently opposing tendencies produces the movement, the song and dance of life. At the very beginning of our study this movement was represented by the restless activity that was indicative of love, the pacing to and fro of those smitten by desire.

The *morena*, as nexus between virgin and mother, becomes the prototype of transformation within the tradition. She represents womankind, earth, matter, the world of appearance in constant flux. She is the feminine manifestation of being, and as such can symbolize the feminine within individual male beings as well as beings manifestly female. The *morena* is all that endures transformation.

Truly, darkness is the single motif which distinguishes the Spanish tradition from the symbols of the folk traditions of other cultures. Spain's peculiar socio-historical reality provided the seed which sprouted within the popular lyric into the symbol group which centers around the *morena*. But ceasing to be an element of social reality, the *morena* becomes the primary symbol of transformation. In her most exalted manifestation, she symbolizes a transformation of consciousness which transcends duality and hence represents wholeness. But it can never be a return to the wholeness of innocence, unconscious wholeness. The synthesis this *morena* represents is conscious wholeness—in Christian terms, salvation. This is the highest good man can envision, and the ultimate desire which underlies all other desire.

#335 Viva contenta y segura   May she who has beauty
      de cuanto pueda dar pena   mixed with darkness
      la que tiene hermosura   live content and safe
      mezclada con ser morena.   from all that can cause pain.

This benediction captures the essence of the synthetic vision. *Hermosura*, like the *rosa hermosa*, implies purity and innocence. When beauty and darkness merge ("nigra sum sed formosa"), pain is vanquished, joy and certainty reign.

---

[1] Compare M. F. Alatorre's article, "Refranes cantados y cantares proverbializados," *NRFH* 15 (1961), 155-68.

[2] Again, S. G. Armistead and J. T. Monroe's suggestion that dawn meetings are part of a socially-sanctioned process of courtship, (see note 4, Chapter III), supports my reading of the poem. A. Deyermond, in his article, "Pero Meogo's Stags and Fountains: Symbol and Anecdote in the Traditional Lyric," *RPh* 33 (1979), views the mother in this poem as a comic and tragic character who "shows herself incapable of understanding her daughter's experience," p. 280.

[3] *cuidar*: pensar, advertir. (Covarrubias)

[4] *peña*: piedra grande viva y levantada en forma aguda. (Covarrubias)

[5] *pena*: el castigo que se da en razón de culpa. Pena vale algunas vezes cuydado y congoxa. (Covarrubias)

[6] *morena*: color, la que no es del todo negra, como la de los moros, de donde tomó nombre, o de mora. (Covarrubias)

[7] *morado*: color de mora. (Covarrubias)

[8] *mora*: la fruta del moral. (Covarrubias)

[9] For a different reading of the significance of the *morena* in the *cancionero tradicional*, see B. Wardropper's article, "The Color Problem in Spanish Traditional Poetry," *MLN*, 75 (1960), 415-421. Wardropper believes that the *morena* is essentially an unfortunate, ugly girl in a society that values blonde hair and fair skin.

Appendix

The following is a list of the sources of the poems discussed in this book. Many of these poems are contained in all the anthologies mentioned in this list, as well as in other anthologies mentioned in the bibliography. I refer the reader to these anthologies for additional information on the source, chronology, etc. of each poem.

Alín: Alín, José María, *El cancionero español de tipo tradicional*.

Alonso y Blecua: Alonso, Dámaso y Blecua, José María, *Antología de la poesía española. Poesía de tipo tradicional*.

Beltrán: Beltrán, Vicente, *La canción tradicional*.

Cummins: Cummins, J. G., *The Spanish Traditional Lyric*.

Nunes: Nunes, J. J., *Cantigas d'amigo dos trovadores gallego-portugueses*.

Sánchez Romeralo: Sánchez Romeralo, A., *El villancico*.

1. Sánchez Romeralo, #98
2. Alín, p. 259
3. Alín, #124
4. Alonso y Blecua, #332
5. Sánchez Romeralo, #286
6. Sánchez Romeralo, #300
7. Sánchez Romeralo, #105
8. Alín, #573
9. Alín, #702
10. Alín, #630
11. Alín, #673
12. Alín, #161
13. Alín, #587
14. Alín, #547
15. Sánchez Romeralo, #115
16. Alín, #593
17. Alín, #536
18. Alín, #292
19. Beltrán, #111
20. Alín, #269
21. Alín, #714
22. Alín, #271
23. Sánchez Romeralo, #194
24. Alín, #75
25. Alín, #37
26. Sánchez Romeralo, #141
27. Sánchez Romeralo, #255
28. Alín, #121
29. Sánchez Romeralo, #191
30. Alín, #742
31. Sánchez Romeralo, #325
32. Sánchez Romeralo, #285
33. Sánchez Romeralo, #354
34. Alín, #804
35. Alín, #804 note
36. Sánchez Romeralo, #274
37. Alín, #513
38. Beltrán, #116
39. Alín, #853
40. Sánchez Romeralo, #158
41. Sánchez Romeralo, #326
42. Sánchez Romeralo, #222
43. Sánchez Romeralo, #325
44. Alín, #12
45. Sánchez Romeralo, #465
46. Sánchez Romeralo, #331
47. Alín, #274
48. Sánchez Romeralo, #43
49. Sánchez Romeralo, #145
50. Sánchez Romeralo, #342
51. Sánchez Romeralo, #355
52. Alín, #771
53. Alín, #511
54. Sánchez Romeralo, #260
55. Alín, #923
56. Sánchez Romeralo, #302
57. Alín, #72
58. Alín, #807
59. Alín, #920
60. Alín, #925
61. Alín, #740
62. Sánchez Romeralo, #160
63. Alín, #822
64. Alín, #346
65. Alín, #768
66. Alín, #758
67. Alín, p. 58
68. Alín, #876

69. Alín, #739
70. Alín, #864 note
71. Alín, #908 note
72. Nunes, XX
73. Alín, #64
74. Sánchez Romeralo, #196
75. Nunes, CCCCXV
76. Nunes, CCCCXVI
77. Alín, #288
78. Nunes, LXXV
79. Nunes, DVI
80. Alín, #674
81. Nunes, CCCCXIV
82. Alín, #205 note
83. Sánchez Romeralo, #215
84. Alín, #624
85. Alín, #830
86. Sánchez Romeralo, #360
87. Sánchez Romeralo, #212
88. Sánchez Romeralo, #138
89. Alín, #57
90. Sánchez Romeralo, #148
91. Alín, #78
92. Alín, #764
93. Sánchez Romeralo, #177
94. Sánchez Romeralo, #109
95. Alín, #877
96. Nunes, CCCCXIII
97. Sánchez Romeralo, #186
98. Alín, #679
99. Alín, #691
100. Alín, #482
101. Alín, #551
102. Alín, p. 286
103. Alín, #175
104. Alín, #845
105. Alín, #128
106. Alín, #113
107. Sánchez Romeralo, #211
108. Alín, #785
109. Sánchez Romeralo, #240
110. Nunes, LXXIX
111. Sánchez Romeralo, #266
112. Sánchez Romeralo, #365
113. Alín, #99
114. Sánchez Romeralo, #133
115. Alín, #162
116. Alín, #919
117. Alín, #579
118. Alín, #689
119. Cummins, p. 87
120. Alín, #611
121. Alín, #576
122. Alín, #600

123. Alín, #850
124. Alín, #584
125. Alín, #775
126. Nunes, CCLII
127. Nunes, CLXIX
128. Beltrán, #153
129. Beltrán, #27
130. Alín, #721
131. Alín, #568
132. Sánchez Romeralo, #112
133. Alín, #333
134. Alín, #275
135. Alín, #30
136. Sánchez Romeralo, #217
137. Alín, #529
138. Alín, #385
139. Sánchez Romeralo, #100
140. Alín, #704
141. Alín, #672
142. Sánchez Romeralo, #87
143. Sánchez Romeralo, #207
144. Beltrán, #139
145. Alín, #56
146. Sánchez Romeralo, #144
147. Alín, #826
148. Sánchez Romeralo, #150
149. Sánchez Romeralo, #259
150. Alín, #395
151. Sánchez Romeralo, #253
152. Alín, #677
153. Alín, #107
154. Alonso y Blecua, #56
155. Alín, #688
156. Sánchez Romeralo, #74
157. Alín, #95
158. Alín, #105 note
159. Alín, #929
160. Alín, #125
161. Sánchez Romeralo, #116
162. Alín, #571
163. Alín, #134
164. Alín, #197
165. Alín, #797
166. Sánchez Romeralo, #319
167. Sánchez Romeralo, #284
168. Alín, #305
169. Sánchez Romeralo, #171
170. Alín, #653
171. Alín, #735
172. Sánchez Romeralo, #214
173. Alín, #745
174. Sánchez Romeralo, #154
175. Sánchez Romeralo, #146
176. Sánchez Romeralo, #101

177. Alín, #255
178. Alín, #61
179. Alín, #225
180. Alín, #89
181. Sánchez Romeralo, #414
182. Alín, #866
183. Alín, #229
184. Sánchez Romeralo, #188
185. Alín, #521
186. Alín, #869 note
187. Alín, #436
188. Alín, #27
189. Alín, #273
190. Sánchez Romeralo, #108
191. Alín, #167
192. Alín, #54
193. Alín, #862
194. Alín, #690
195. Alín, #70
196. Sánchez Romeralo, #140
197. Alín, #834
198. Alín, #320
199. Alín, #610
200. Sánchez Romomeralo, #281
201. Alín, #916
202. Alín, #122
203. Sánchez Romeralo, #159
204. Sánchez Romeralo, #269
205. Alín, #31 note
206. Alín, #92
207. Sánchez Romeralo, #152
208. Sánchez Romeralo, #155
209. Alín, #893
210. Alín, #34
211. Sánchez Romeralo, #232
212. Sánchez Romeralo, #251
213. Alín, #3
214. Alín, #324 note
215. Sánchez Romeralo, #224
216. Alín, #80
217. Alín, #43
218. Sánchez Romeralo, #233
219. Alín, #465
220. Alín, #917
221. Alín, #16
222. Alín, #827
223. Alín, #55
224. Sánchez Romeralo, #147
225. Alín, #94
226. Alín, #142
227. Sánchez Romeralo, #377
228. Sánchez Romeralo, #125
229. Alín, #118

230. Alín, #353
231. Beltrán, #276
232. Alín, #338
233. Alín, #66
234. Alín, #446
235. Alín, #124 note
236. Alín, #58
237. Alín, #631
238. Alín, #852
239. Alín, #420
240. Sánchez Romeralo, #280
241. Sánchez Romeralo, #378
242. Alín, #47
243. Alín, #73
244. Nunes, CCCCXVII
245. Nunes, CCCCXIX
246. Nunes, CCCCXI
247. Nunes, CCCCLIX
248. Alín, #711
249. Alín, #597
250. Sánchez Romeralo, #328
251. Sánchez Romeralo, #99
252. Alín, #112
253. Alín, #799
254. Sánchez Romeralo, #236
255. Alín, #620
256. Sánchez Romeralo, #190
257. Sánchez Romeralo, #322
258. Alín, #651
259. Alín, #345
260. Alín, #541
261. Alín, #802
262. Sánchez Romeralo, #93
263. Beltrán, #37
264. Alín, #886
265. Sánchez Romeralo, #246
266. Sánchez Romeralo, #130
267. Alín, p. 686
268. Alín, p. 686
269. Alín, p. 686
270. Sánchez Romeralo, #338
271. Alín, #796
272. Alín, #186
273. Alín, #93
274. Sánchez Romeralo, #163
275. Alín, #414
276. Sánchez Romeralo, #119
277. Sánchez Romeralo, #129
278. Alín, #583
279. Alín, #539
280. Sánchez Romeralo, #173
281. Sánchez Romeralo, #181
282. Alín, #24

283. Alín, #117
284. Alín, #731
285. Alín, #727
286. Alín, #699
287. Alín, #344
288. Sánchez Romeralo, #358
289. Alín, #932
290. Alín, #650
291. Alín, #627
292. Alín, #141
293. Sánchez Romeralo, #12
294. Alín, #209
295. Alín, #703
296. Alín, #634
297. Alín, #381
298. Nunes, CCCLXXXIX
299. Sánchez Romeralo, #209
300. Alín, #131
301. Alín, #635
302. Alín, #660
303. Alín, #713
304. Alín, #40
305. Alín, #829
306. Alín, #110
307. Sánchez Romeralo, #226
308. Alín, #361
309. Alín, #678

310. Alín, #68
311. Sánchez Romeralo, #206
312. Alín, #468
313. Alín, #752
314. Alín, #757
315. Sánchez Romeralo, #262
316. Sánchez Romeralo, #197
317. Sánchez Romeralo, #118
318. Sánchez Romeralo, #97
319. Sánchez Romeralo, #237
320. Alín, #566
321. Cummins, p. 34
322. Alín, #114
323. Sánchez Romeralo, #310
324. Sánchez Romeralo, #324
325. Alín, #249
326. Sánchez Romeralo, #391
327. Alín, p.256
328. Alín, #574
329. Alín, #430
330. Sánchez Romeralo, #170
331. Sánchez Romeralo, #298
332. Alín, #447
333. Alín, #355 note
334. Alín, #720
335. Alín, #255

Bibliography

Aguirre, J. M. "Moraima y el prisionero: Ensayo de interpretación," *Studies of the Spanish and Portuguese Ballad*, ed. by N. D. Shergold. London: Tamesis, 1972, pp. 5?-72.

Alatorre, Margit Frenk. *Estudios sobre lírica antigua*. Madrid: Castalia, 1977.

————. *Las jarchas mozárabes y los comienzos de la lírica románica*. México: El Colegio de México, 1975.

————. *Lírica española de tipo popular*. Madrid: Cátedra 1977.

————. "Permanencia folklórica del villancico glosado," *NRFH* 29 (1980), pp. 404-11.

————. "Refranes cantados y cantares proverbializados," *NRFH* 15 (1961), pp. 155-68.

Alberti, Rafael. "La poesía popular en la lírica española contemporanea," *Prosas encontradas*. Madrid: 1970, pp. 87-103.

Alín, José María. *El cancionero español de tipo tradicional*. Madrid: Taurus, 1968.

Alonso, Amado. *Materia y forma en poesía*, 3rd. ed. Madrid: Gredos, 1965.

Alonso, Dámaso. *Poesía de la edad media y poesía de tipo tradicional*. Buenos Aires: Losada, 1942.

Alonso, Dámaso, and Blecua, José Manuel. *Antología de la poesía española. Poesía de tipo tradicional*, 2nd ed. Madrid: Gredos, 1969.

Alvar López, Manuel. *Cantos de boda judeo-españoles*. Madrid: C.S.J.C., 1971.

Armistead, Samuel G., and Monroe, James T. "*Albas, mammas*, and Code-Switching in the *Kharjas*: A Reply to Keith Whinnom," *La Corónica* 11 (1983), pp. 174-207.

Armistead, Samuel G., and Silverman, Joseph H. *Judeo-Spanish Ballad Chapbooks of Yacob Abrahan Yoná*. Berkeley: University of California Press, 1971.

Asensio, Eugenio. *Poética y realidad en el cancionero peninsular de la edad media*, 2nd ed. Madrid: Gredos, 1970.

Atkinson, Dorothy M. "Parallelism in the Medieval Portuguese Lyric," *MLR* 50:3 (1955), pp. 281-87.

Bachelard, Gaston. *L'Air et les songes*. Paris: Librarie José Corti, 1943.

Beltrán, Vicente. *La canción tradicional*. Tarragona: Tarraco, 1976.

Blouin, Egla Morales. *El ciervo y la fuente*. Studia Humanitatis. Madrid: Porrúa Turanzas, 1981.

Bousoño, Carlos. *Teoría de la expresión poética*, 3rd. ed. Madrid: Gredos, 1962.

Bowra, C. M. *Primitive Song*. New York: Mentor Book, 1963.

Campbell, Joseph. *The Masks of God: Primitive Mythology*. New York: Penguin, 1969.

Cassirer, Ernst. *Language and Myth*, trans. Suzanne Langer. New York: Dover, 1946.

Cejador y Frauca, Julio. *La verdadera poesía castellana: Floresta de la antigua lírica popular*. 9 vols. Madrid: Imprenta RABM Gráficas Nacional, 1921-30.

Cirlot, J. E. *A Dictionary of Symbols*. New York: Philosophical Library, 1962.

Corominas, Juan. *Diccionario crítico etimológico de la lengua castellana*. 4 vols. Madrid: Gredos, 1954-57.

Correas, Maestro Gonzalo. *Vocabulario de refranes y frases proverbiales*. Institut D'Etudes Ibériques et Ibéro-Americaines de L'Université de Bordeaux, 1967.

Covarrubias, Sebastián de. *Tesoro de la lengua castellana o española*. Barcelona: Editorial M. de Riquer, 1943.

Cummins, J. G. *The Spanish Traditional Lyric*. New York: Pergamon Press, 1977.

Deyermond, Alan. "Pero Meogo's Stags and Fountains: Symbol and Anecdote in the Traditional Lyric," *Romance Philology* 33 (1979), pp. 265-83.

Empaytaz de Croome, Dionisia. *Albor: Medieval and Renaissance Dawn-Songs in the Iberian Peninsula*. University Microfilms International: 1980.

Empaytaz, Dionisia. *Antología de albas, alboradas*. Madrid: Colección Nova Scholar, 1976.

Entwistle, William J. "From 'Cantigas de amigo' to 'Cantigas de amor'," *Revue de Littérature Comparée* 69(1938), pp. 137-52.

Henríquez Ureña, Pedro. *Estudios de versificación española*. Buenos Aires: Universidad de Buenos Aires, 1961.

Jackson, W. T., ed. *Interpretation of Medieval Lyric Poetry*. New York: Columbia University Press, 1980.

Jung, Carl G. *The Archetypes and the Collective Unconscious*. New York: Bollingen, 1959.

———. *Symbols of Transformation*. New York: Bollingen, 1956.

Langer, Suzanne K. *Feeling and Form: A theory of art*. New York: Charles Scribner's Sons, 1953.

Le Gentil, Pierre. *Poesie lyrique espagnole et portugaise à la fin du moyen âge*. 2 vols. Rennes: Plihon, 1949.

Magis, Carlos H. *La lírica popular contemporánea*. México: El Colegio de México, 1969.

Méndez Ferrín, X. L., ed. *O cancioneiro de Pero Meogo*. Vigo: Editorial Galaxia, 1966.

Menéndez Pidal, Ramón. *De primitiva lírica española y antigua épica*. Madrid: Austral, 1968.

Musurillo, Herbert, S. J. *Symbol and Myth in Ancient Poetry*. New York: Fordham University Press, 1961.

Navarro Tomás, Tomás. *Métrica española*. Madrid: Ediciones Guadarrama, 1974.

Neumann, Erich. *The Great Mother*. Princeton: Princeton University Press, 1974.

Nunes, J. J. *Cantigas d'amigo dos trovadores gallego-portugueses*. 3 vols. Coimbra: 1926-28.

Onians, Richard B. *The Origins of European Thought*. Cambridge; Cambridge University Press, 1954.

Pellegrini, Silvio, and Marroni, Giovanna. *Nuovo repertorio bibliográfico della prima lirica galego-portoghese*. L'Aquila, Japadre Editore, 1981.

Plénat, Marc. "Relectura de una *Cantiga d'amigo* de Martín Codax," *NRFH* 28 (1979), pp. 327-34.

Rajneesh, Bhagwan Shree. *The Hidden Harmony.* India: The Rajneesh Foundation, 1976.

Reckert, Stephen. *Gil Vicente: espíritu y letra.* Madrid: Gredos,

—————. *Lyra Minima. Structure and Symbol in Iberian Traditional Verse.* London: 1970.

Reckert, Stephen, and Macedo, Helder. *Do cancioneiro de amigo.* Documenta Poética III. Lisbon; Assírio e Alvim, 1976.

Rogers, Edith Randam. *The Perilous Hunt.* Lexington: University of Kentucky Press, 1980.

Romeu Figueras, José. *La música en la corte de los Reyes Católicos: Cancionero musical de Palacio.* 2 vols. Barcelona: 1965.

Sánchez Romeralo, Antonio. *El villancico.* Madrid: Gredos, 1969.

Sponsler, Lucy A. *Women in the Medieval Spanish Epic and Lyric Traditions.* Lexington: University Press of Kentucky, 1975.

Torner, Eduardo M. *Lírica hispánica. Relaciones entre lo popular y lo culto.* Madrid: Castalia, 1966.

Van Antwerp, Margaret. "Razón de Amor and the Popular Tradition," *Romance Philology* 32 (1978-79), pp. 1-17.

Walker, Roger. "Possible comic elements in the *Cantigas de Amigo.*" *Medieval, Renaissance and Folklore Studies in Honor of John Esten Keller,* ed. by Joseph R. Jones. Newark: Juan de la Cuesta, 1980, pp. 77-88.

Wardropper, Bruce W. "'La más bella niña'," *Studies in Philology* 63 (1966), pp. 661-76.

—————. "On the Supposed Repetitiousness of the *Cantigas d'amigo,*" *RHM* 38 (1974-75), pp. 1-6.

—————. "The Color Problem in Spanish Traditional Poetry," *MLN* 75 (1960), pp. 415-421.

Wheelwright, Philip. *The Burning Fountain.* Bloomington: Indiana University Press, 1954.

Zimmer, Heinrich. *Myths and Symbols in Indian Art and Civilization.* New York: Harper and Row, 1962.

Index of First Lines

Index